CHINA
SHALL RISE AGAIN

Generalissimo Chiang Kai-shek, Madame Chiang Kai-shek
and General Joseph Stilwell

CHINA
SHALL RISE AGAIN

By

May-ling Soong Chiang

(Madame Chiang Kai-shek)

Including Ten Official Statements
of China's Present Progress

HARPER & BROTHERS PUBLISHERS
New York and London

CONTENTS

Preface, by Generalissimo Chiang Kai-shek   vii

Foreword   xiii

Part I

I SHALL RISE AGAIN

 I. The Spirit That Is China   3

 II. Know Thyself   8

 III. The Road to Passionate Patriotism   13

 IV. Educational Centers of Resistance   18

 V. The Education of the Masses   23

 VI. The Cornerstone for Founding a Regenerated China 29

 VII. Seven Deadly Sins   37

 VIII. Seven Deadly Sins (continued)   44

 IX. Women and the Family   53

 X. The Need of Spirituality   62

Part II

THE CONDUCT OF THE COUNTRY IN WARTIME,
BY TEN OFFICIALS IN CHARGE OF GOVERNMENT
DEPARTMENTS

 XI. Holding China's Financial Front   73

 XII. China's Strategy in the War   102

[v]

XIII. China's Foreign Relations During the Sino-Japanese Hostilities, 1937-1940 — 118

XIV. Industrialization of Western China — 141

XV. Free China's Reconstruction Work in the Field of Communications, July, 1937 to June, 1940 — 153

XVI. Chinese Culture and Education During Three Years of War — 165

XVII. The Chinese National Health Administration During the Sino-Japanese Hostilities — 198

XVIII. The Chinese Army Medical Service — 218

XIX. The Chinese Red Cross Medical Relief Corps in Three Years of War — 229

XX. The Chinese Industrial Co-operatives — 261

Part III

TOWARD A NEW CHINA

XXI. New Life — 287

XXII. Women's Work — 306

XXIII. Chinese Thought on Democratic Policy — 339

FOR the rebirth of a people certain factors are necessary. Of these one is that the people should go through a period of trials and tribulations.

The most important, however, is that the people must have full confidence in their national destiny. The possession of such confidence makes them aware of their responsibility and gives them strength to carry out their historic mission.

The Chinese have a culture and a history of more than five thousand years. They are now being threatened with extinction by the ruthless aggression of Japan. In this unprecedented crisis, their national spirit has risen to the occasion: the longer they fight, the more determined becomes their will to survive and conquer.

The ancients have a saying: "Great difficulties make a nation." How true this is! Out of her tribulations and suffering, China will surely emerge a stronger nation. This is the conviction in the heart of every true son of China, as it is also the belief of everybody the world over.

"Any medicine," runs an old proverb in China,

"which does not make a man dizzy will not help him to recover." This is one of my favorite sayings, which I often quote to encourage our soldiers and fellow countrymen.

What this means is that strong doses of medicine are necessary to cure any deep-rooted and chronic ailments. Such medicine may cause a violent reaction in the patient, but only by going through such a drastic treatment will he completely regain his health. The reason for this is plain: in everyone of us there is a store of vital potential energy, and medicine which we take during illness helps to release this energy to fight against the disease germs, and thus restore us to health. Indeed, how often have we seen men become stronger and more healthy after a dangerous illness! It is even so with a people.

Only by going through a life-and-death struggle will an old nation be reinvigorated. As with individuals, so with nations: without pain there can be no pleasure; and without suffering, no happiness.

In writing this volume, the author has striven, as her religion and her patriotism have dictated to her, to point out the many shortcomings of her people which must be remedied, if China is to be regenerated. The temptation is ever present with her to whitewash and conceal the weaknesses of her fellow countrymen, but her conscience does not allow her to do so.

There are a few remarks I wish to make to those of our people who will read this book. First of all, I should

[viii]

like readers not to read it in a casual and cursory manner. They should be as earnest in reading it as the author has been sincere in writing it.

As is the fashion of youth, some young readers may derive satisfaction from the author's criticisms of our people. But her motive in pointing out the shortcomings of our people as a whole is to induce each individual to examine his own heart and see if he has not sinned in the same way as his fellow countrymen.

Each reader should ask himself: "Those qualities which I detest — callousness, selfishness, indolence, untruthfulness, hypocrisy and perfunctoriness — are they not present in me? I call myself a patriot, but am I sincere; and mixed up with my patriotism, are there not ulterior motives? Have I sufficient strength to stick to my convictions? In making sacrifices for my country, do I do so with a clean heart? Can I go through suffering for the sake of my fellow countrymen? Can I resist and not yield to the temptations of glory, power and material interests? Have I counted the cost and not found myself wanting?"

If a person can stand up to these questions; wash his heart clean of past faults of character; turn his face to the future with determination to carry on the good fight, then only will he deserve the name of warrior in China's struggle for regeneration.

The second point I wish to make is this: In order to be able to contribute his share in the work of national regeneration, a man must have absolute faith in the bright future of his country.

He must feel it in his bones that his people are fundamentally sound, and their present confusion and weaknesses only temporary.

China is like a mirror which becomes blurred because dust has been allowed to accumulate upon it; but it requires only a little polishing to make it bright again.

In this connection we have to take to heart what our leader, Dr. Sun Yat-sen, has taught us. He exhorts us to restore our traditional morality and spirit.

Anyone who looks down upon the traditional morality of our people as inadequate and valueless denies the *raison d'être* of the Chinese nation. If one denies that, then all talk of national regeneration is vain.

We, sons and daughters of China, in order to make ourselves worthy of inheriting the glorious heritage of our ancestors, ought to wipe out our present humiliations and keep our country abreast of the times.

With our feet firmly planted in the best that is in our heritage, we should look forward to the future with hope.

If this is not done, there will be no rebirth of a new and stronger China.

Lastly, all those who desire to participate in the gigantic task of national regeneration must set themselves to practice what they believe.

To know what is good and not to have the will to

PREFACE

carry it out has been the besetting sin of our forefathers.

To this defect must be ascribed the backwardness and degeneration of our people in times past.

The youth of China today ought to do better. They have before them the teachings of their leader, Dr. Sun Yat-sen, who has propounded this profound truth: To act is easy; to know is difficult.

Speech without action is despicable; following the line of least resistance is the way of a coward; blaming others instead of oneself is only another form of selfishness and disloyalty to one's country. The revolutionary youth of our country ought to be made of sterner mettle.

The road before us is thick with thorns and brambles. It is only by pushing our way forward with perseverance and courage that we shall be able to bring a new China into existence which shall be a blessing not only to herself, but also to the world at large.

Chungking, Szechuan
China
June 4, 1940

FOREWORD

THE first section of this book originally appeared in Chinese in the *Central Daily News*, a Chungking paper. The first chapter was written to inaugurate the weekly Woman's Page sponsored by the New Life Movement. Its reception was such that it led me to hope that a series of pieces under the title "Resurgam" — "I Shall Rise Again" — might help to stimulate true patriotism and serve as a plumb line in the laying of an unshakable foundation for a strong and invigorated China.

The exposure of certain of our national weaknesses and foibles was not overwhelmingly enjoyed by some of my compatriots. They could see no advantage in my public airing of vices. The fact that I branded as characteristically Chinese those vices not peculiar to us celestials, but common to humankind, seemed to them a further folly. To make matters worse, the Generalissimo took pains to have certain parts clipped and sent to various quarters where he thought they would have a salutary effect.

Part I was written purely for home consumption. That it was scribbled in odd moments between conferences, lectures, during air raids, or even on inspection tours with the Generalissimo to the front, is perhaps noticeable from the uneven composition. I have decided, however, to leave it untouched, for the uncouthness is symbolic of the rough-and-ready character of much of our material reconstruction during these distressing days.

The task of each nation should be to face existing conditions with courage and candor; to remove with resolution and sincerity those obstacles which retard the progress of an enlightened and more humane world order.

For this reason the Chinese people should not be afraid to acknowledge where, in the past, China has fallen short of fulfilling her duties as a member of the family of nations.

History has shown that in the long run integrity is true wisdom. The present calamity that has come upon the world is due mostly to the breakdown of good faith in international dealings. Civilization can only be saved when it is recognized that observance of integrity must be the guiding principle of life.

From the annals of Chinese history is drawn the following story. Two thousand five hundred years ago, during the Warring Period, the Duke of Chi battled with the Duke of Lu. Thrice was Lu defeated. In suing for peace, the Duke of Lu agreed to cede a portion of his kingdom to Chi. Chi accepted.

Forthwith the Duke of Chi proceeded to the place of covenant where blood sacrifices were being prepared to seal the pact. During the ceremony Tsao Muh, a general of the Lu army, approached the dais on which sat the

Duke of Chi. Unsheathing his short sword he pointed the naked blade toward the Duke, saying:

"Chi is a powerful kingdom; Lu a weak one. Thrice has Chi invaded Lu, burnt her cities, ravaged her people. Is not that enough? And now you come to wrest from us our land! Reconsider."

In fear, the Duke of Chi promised to waive his claim. Thereupon Tsao Muh, without changing color, sheathed his sword, returned to his seat, and resumed converse with his companions.

Later, in anger, the Duke of Chi repented of his promise. He thought of putting Tsao Muh to death. But his Premier, Kwan Chung, stayed his hand, saying:

"When you were threatened with death, you made a promise. Now with the threat removed, you would break faith. What will this profit you? A passing gain. What will this cost you? You would lose the trust of the feudal lords and thereby the support of all the people under heaven. You cannot."

The Duke of Chi thereupon returned the region ceded to him. The feudal lords hearing of this rallied round him, and proclaimed him their leader.

M. S. C.

Chungking, Szechuan,
China.
August, 1940.

Part 1

I SHALL RISE AGAIN

I

THE SPIRIT THAT IS CHINA

ABOVE the southern portal of St. Paul's Cathedral, London, is an odd stone upon which is graven the one word *Resurgam*. The story of it is that when the great dome was about to be built the architect, Sir Christopher Wren, asked for a stone to mark the center as a guide for the workmen. From a rubbish heap was brought a piece of old tombstone which bore that one Latin word. Its significance — "I shall rise again" — so impressed the architect that he decided to give the stone a permanent place in the structure. There it has remained ever since, a source of stimulating optimism for all who see it. And to us who witness our people being slain and maimed and our country desolated, the word should possess special inspiration and cause us to brand it upon our hearts and emblazon it upon our banners.

If we look at a map of China we can easily realize how the enemy, by virtue of his superior military and naval armament and air force, has been able to penetrate into many eastern provinces and wrest from us, for the time being, the peaceful use of most of our railways, highways

[3]

and waterways. In addition to that the barbarous invaders have murdered multitudes and have uprooted from their homes, their businesses, and their farms millions of our people who have been forced to travel far afield in search of sustenance and safety from bombardment and assault.

Those eastern provinces which have suffered so grievously from enemy attacks were our richest possessions in agricultural production and cultural development.

The provinces of the west were, until quite recently, remote and inaccessible except by the expenditure of much time in travel; and the endurance, in most cases, of great hardship. These provinces were regarded by most of the dwellers in the east as the fascinating home of valuable medicinal herbs, beautiful and rare flowers, giant pandas and other animals, as well as precious metals. There it was known lived strange tribesmen who inhabited majestic mountains which were the source of our principal great rivers, but all far too difficult of access ever to be reached by eastern inhabitants.

Up to the time of the fall of Nanking our people as a whole paid little attention to the far-flung provinces of the west. Now, however, tens of thousands of our people — among whom are leaders of industries and institutions of learning, with their staffs and students — have moved in, coming on steamers, motorcars, trucks, or on foot. As a result of this mass migration the development of Szechuan and other western provinces, which has so long been delayed, will be accelerated until there will be done in a year what would, in normal times, have taken perhaps five decades to accomplish.

Here our country will make up for more than it has lost, for we shall build faster and surer upon the foundations already laid, and erect the edifice of a rejuvenated nation — a new, strong and robust China.

The pioneers of America were attracted to their west by the lure of gold and land, and they went into a virgin region. In our west, remote as it is, and difficult of access as it used to be, there has long been established a civilization and a great population. The people were, however, unable to develop the natural resources because of lack of skilled labor and because of baffling distances and staggering mountains, over which toiled the coolies and ponies and donkeys, the only means of transportation except the steamers and junks which touched at points along the Yangtze River and its tributaries.

Now the great migration has given artisans to the west, and the lot of all has been alleviated by the creation of air services and motor highways which connect all provinces and run to the outer world through Yunnan to Burma, and through Sinkiang to Europe. Our new railways will, in time, connect the southwestern provinces with the lines of neighboring western countries.

There are many — especially the enemy that has invaded our country — who think that the end has come to the independence and the individuality of our nation. There are those who think that it is but a matter of time when the yoke of subjugation will be placed upon our necks.

These people — be they pessimistic or hopeful — overlook one important and outstanding revelation of history. That is, we Chinese, as a race and a nation, have survived centuries of natural calamity and domestic upheaval solely because of the possession of remarkable powers of recuperation.

That power is undiminished. It is still with us, as all contemporaries know, just as it ever has been with us in our agelong struggle to safeguard the heritage that has been handed down to us from remote times. And we intend to foster that power and use it, for we shall never permit this or the coming generation to bear the shame and the dishonor of sacrificing our ancient birthright.

Our people will continue to fight, as well as to live and thrive and multiply, even through adversity in the regions where the enemy erroneously imagines he is supreme, but where, in reality, he has but a precarious hold. And that tenuous grip will, with the flight of time, become ever more uncertain until it will finally relax under the pressure exerted by our heroic manhood and womanhood.

In the west, with the courage and the heroism and the powers of endurance which are inherent in us, we will create a new China — a nation tempered in the fires of

[6]

war, and emerging wise (I hope), progressive, indomitable, and unafraid.

Our friends whose sympathy we have, and the barbaric enemy who is ravaging our land — if they possess the imagination to sum up the significance of the past months of unflinching resistance — can surely see the metaphorical writing on the wall. It is illuminating the walls of our west, aye, our Great Wall and our seaboard, too. On them all, as in challenging radiance — vibrant with the spirit of the blood that has flowed from our people and the fires that have burned our earth — can be seen, through the eye of the mind, endurable and prophetic letters marking our destiny. They are *resurgam*. . . . "I shall rise again" — and they embody the spirit that is China.

II

KNOW THYSELF

W<small>HEN</small> the Greek philosopher Socrates impressed upon his students the injunction "Know Thyself," he undoubtedly meant that they should make an impersonal, cool, objective self-analysis as a method and means of self-improvement.

To build a new, strong, unified China it behooves us all to engage in intensive introspection, to be scrupulously honest in our estimate of our past shortcomings, and to acknowledge frankly our past mistakes with a view to correcting them in the future.

We are the product of our own performances. Slackness which was permitted in the past has, in the flight of years, developed into a strangling national habit. If our nation seems to have been internationally circumscribed we have no one to blame for it but ourselves.

If a new China is to arise out of the blood and the ashes of the old one, those who accept positions of responsibility must awaken to the understanding that they have automatically undertaken positions of trust and the definite obligation to devote all their energy, their thought, and their care to the interests of the people and the State. Those who are unable to do this should resign.

[8]

KNOW THYSELF

To save China from the consequences of this war character is essential. There must be intellectual honesty, general integrity, and, above all, sober common sense; there must be, indeed, actual wisdom.

As personal conduct is the matrix in which character is cast we have it in our own hands to develop our moral excellence by reforming our lives, revitalizing our attitude of mind toward our individual and collective duties, and so develop an efficiency which will contribute to the effective resurgence of our entire nation. If we cannot carve our way to salvation we are not worthy of our heritage.

Any man who is in a position of authority, even if he is able to do but a little good, should be inspired and be glad and eager to do that little, if only to escape the charge of being incompetent or of deliberately neglecting at a time of crisis the welfare of his country and his people.

On the one hand strict accountability for actions judged to be contrary to the popular good should be imposed upon all who accept office and payment for services on the pretense of being able to fulfill important national duties.

On the other hand penalization should be expected by all who hold any position or who draw money of any kind from the National Treasury if they are guilty of dereliction of duty.

Approbation should be the minimum reward for all who acquit themselves competently and honestly.

It is the duty of each of us to clear our national records of the old stigma of dishonesty and corruption. Close upon the heels of Corruption is always Cowardice, the handmaiden. And we must never forget that it was the evil combination of corruption and cowardice that was solely responsible for the disgrace and humiliation and territorial losses which were inflicted upon us in 1894.

We have the chance now to wipe that ignoble stain from the pages of our history. The gallant soldiers at the front who are giving up their lives that we shall be safe are already obliterating it.

Only a traitor to whose cheeks could not come a blush of shame would betray the trust of those brave men by using his safety to divert to his own pockets directly or indirectly, funds intended for national purposes or for the pursuance of our resistance.

All of us who are in the rear should leave no stone unturned to see to it that all money as well as all effort are applied to the full to the cause for which our civilians are suffering and our soldiers are dying.

We must do that not only because the fate of our whole nation is at stake, infinitely more so than it was in 1894, but because we want it inscribed in history that we are honorable and that we are courageous.

What we have suffered in the past was expressed by Edmund Burke when long ago he wrote that "corruption loads us with more than millions of debt; takes away vigor from our arms, wisdom from our councils, and every shadow of authority and credit from the most venerable parts of our constitution." Is there any one of us who wants a repetition of the bitter lesson we have had? Echo surely answers "No." Then it is more than ever imperative that every official should be compelled to keep ever before him the important fact that the monies he handles, or the monies he accepts from the National Treasury, belong to the State, and come, one way or another, from the people.

No one accepting office should forget, or be permitted to forget, that since he is paid from funds coming from the people he is the servant of the people. All his actions should be guided by that knowledge; should be stimulated by the promptings of unimpeachable integrity and should be directed to the immediate as well as to the ultimate service of the people.

Into the depths of oblivion must be cast the corroding assumption of olden days that the officials are the masters of the people.

Out of the flame of freedom must come the acknowledgment that the people who pay the taxes are deserving of good and honest government, and must at all costs be accorded that to which they are entitled.

If good and honest government is accorded the people, the people will be prosperous. If the people are prosperous the State will be rich. If the State is rich the State will be peaceful and strong.

[11]

CHINA SHALL RISE AGAIN

If the State becomes rich, and peaceful, and strong, then a new China will have emerged, like her fabled phoenix, from the embers of the fires that have burned her, and will, in all truth, have achieved the destiny embodied in the prophetic word *resurgam*.

III

THE ROAD TO PASSIONATE
PATRIOTISM

How can we, the so-called intellectuals, contribute to the great task of preparing our people to give their full assistance to the work of national resistance and rehabilitation?

No matter how efficient and honest our government officials may be in the performance of their duties, we cannot build up a strong and virile China if our people themselves continue to remain without understanding of, and cold to, the ideals of freedom.

Here is an avenue for the application of the talents and the energy of the educated. Where ignorance exists among the great masses of the population it must be dissipated. Where articulation is possible it must be marshaled in the interests of good, and enlightened, and honest government.

The adage that people have the kind of government they deserve contains much truth. Dr. Sun Yat-sen, when he advocated a period of political tutelage, had the sagacity to foresee that the proper training to enable our people to shoulder political and social responsibilities would be necessary if they were to learn how to apply effectively the practical working principles of a modern democracy.

Along this line we have progressed some distance, but, I may ask, what are we doing to disentangle ourselves finally from the bewildering labyrinth of complicated political theories and isms which now menace the world, so that we may focus our entire attention upon those simple fundamentals so vital to the successful governing of ourselves and the State? There are lessons to be learned on all sides; lessons from the world around us, lessons from our own experiences and from our national past.

During the Manchu regime the shadow of the executioner's sword hung ominously over the heads of all who dared openly to express critical political opinions, or showed undue curiosity with regard to the conduct of national affairs. It had the effect of preserving administrative functions as the prerogatives of the so-called "official class," while the interests of the people became confined within the circumscribed scope of family life.

The effects of such devastating restrictions upon thought and action strangled public opinion and stifled patriotism. They are, too, strikingly reflected in the dry and pedantic nature of the writings produced during the Ching Dynasty. With rare exceptions, barrenness of thought and conventionality of treatment of political and social topics characterized the output of the literati of that period.

The masses of the people, in these circumstances, be-

[14]

came not only ignorant but also inarticulate. Indifference and apathy to all matters of public concern resulted and continued until the overthrow of the decadent regime responsible for this deplorable condition.

A new era having been fortunately initiated by the Revolution, we have come into the priceless possessions of freedom of thought and action. The tragic shadow of the executioner's sword has been replaced by the transcendent power of the pen and the press; and the possibilities have come to us to develop public opinion upon a basis beneficial to our own State and helpful to the world at large. Here is where we intellectuals can make our great and lasting contribution to the resurgence of our country.

The rich harvests of knowledge garnered from the fields of accumulated wisdom and experience of ages past, sustained by the scientific and cultural fertility of our own times, are ours for the taking and the expression.

Because of these blessings it is incumbent upon us to help cast off whatever shackles of subservient silence may still remain upon us, and, with our liberated breaths sound a clarion call to create enlightened public opinion for the purpose of assisting in the promotion of national freedom.

To crystallize the voice of the people, and to make it effective, emphasis must be laid upon its wise uses in the interests of the body politic. If criticism is necessary at any time it should be constructive criticism. Freedom of expression of opinion, whether collective or individual, must always be connected with order; be characterized by self-restraint, and be used for the greatest good of the greatest number

There is a warning for us in the words of George Washington which we should not overlook, that "in a free and republican government you cannot restrain the voice of the multitude. Every man will speak as he thinks, or, more properly, without thinking, and consequently will judge of effects without attending to their causes."

This may or may not be true, but if we have concrete aims to develop enlightened public opinion, one, at least, should be to make a national maxim of our old classical proverb — Heaven sees as the People see; Heaven hears as the People hear — which finds its parallel in the more concise Latin dictum, *vox populi, vox Dei* — "The voice of the people is the voice of God."

We have nothing to gain and everything to lose if we permit the popular voice to become mere sound without sense.

Personal recriminations and destructive criticisms, jealousies and vindictiveness should, on the one hand, be discouraged whenever and wherever they may be heard so that license and abuse may not assume the importance of — and be mistaken for — liberty.

On the other hand we must strive to shape public opinion so that its articulation may inspire men in public office or in private life, consciously and conscientiously,

[16]

to develop and apply to all affairs the influence of the best traits of their character.

That would mark a first step on the road to the establishment of commendable passionate patriotism, and to the permanency of those ideals of honesty, service, and co-operation without which no nation can prosper or long endure. That, too, would assure the materialization of the courageous determination necessary to fulfill for China the prophecy signified by the word *resurgam*.

IV

EDUCATIONAL CENTERS OF
RESISTANCE

THERE are two outstanding reasons why enlightened public opinion is essential. One is the necessity of making resistance a primary national purpose in which all the people must participate. The other is the immediate need and advisability of beginning the gigantic task of national rehabilitation.

To develop public opinion among the masses of the people and effectively to direct their energies into national productive channels, talent and energy, such as are possessed by the intellectuals, are required.

There are two major approaches to the solution of the problem involved. One is through personal contact with the people by the students in schools and universities, and the other is through systems of mass adult education. There are numerous minor methods which might be developed and adopted, but these can be postponed for later consideration.

Just now I wish to confine attention to the unique opportunities for national service which are open to the universities, the colleges, and the schools. These halls of learning have the first access to the receptive minds of the rising generations, which very fact imposes upon the professors and the teachers a grave responsibility. For good or for evil they have it in their power to determine, by the fundamental instruction and form of learning that they impart to the students, and by their own conduct, the stature of our future citizens and the status and the character of our nation.

The teachers should always bear in mind that to shape the future of our race for the good of the nation the plastic minds of the young must be fired with a proper understanding of the patriotic purposes of life. They must be inspired with a comprehensive idea of service; and they must be stimulated to manliness by the knowledge that their education is primarily to be employed for the betterment of their fellow countrymen. If this is effectively done, the universities will find it easy to guide the growing intellects along channels which will spontaneously generate in the mature graduates an insatiable urge for national service. That, at least, should be their aim.

Success in producing worth-while citizens with the ability to pass on to the people their learning, and the principles instilled into them, can be achieved if a determined effort is made to educate the students to think and to act along constructive lines beneficial to the nation. The spirit of usefulness can be fostered during school sessions by providing actual experience in practical systematic service to the people living near the campuses. During va-

[19]

cations, this work may be extended to the neighborhoods of the students' homes. Early in their lives young men and women will thus be able by personal contact to taste to the full of the joys derivable from actual service to their less fortunate fellow countrymen. In addition, they should be able to experience the exhilaration that should come from the knowledge of returning in a practical way to the people some of the benefits secured through education in institutions founded and conducted at public expense.

This active participation in service to the people was demonstrated as practicable by the students of the School for the Sons of the Revolution at Nanking. Middle school boys devoted their afternoons, after class hours, to teaching the children of farmers in schools which the students themselves founded. They gave their week ends to helping personally in the surrounding villages — teaching hygiene, patriotism, better methods of agriculture, and other subjects which they had learned in their classes. Clinics were held for the benefit of the peasants; and instructive programs were given for their entertainment. Now most of these boys are at work helping to win the war. Many are in the battle areas actively assisting the soldiers, while others are doing practical work behind the lines. What those boys did then, the students now at school can do.

There is immense scope for patriotic effort everywhere — among the villagers and among the refugees. In every town there are calls for assistance to guide the people along ways to help in the winning of a great victory, as well as in developing the knowledge and judgment necessary for them to assist in rehabilitating and reforming our country.

The faculties of universities should never forget that their institutions are instruments, or vessels, from which ultimate blessings are expected to flow direct to the people. Were it otherwise there would be no justification for spending on their maintenance public funds which are so sorely needed for purposes of resistance. It would also be shameful for those connected with such institutions to try, in such times of national stress as these, to preserve them as a means of personal subsistence.

The Japanese, in an effort to justify their bombing of universities, claim that our schools and universities are centers of resistance. That argument now justifies all educational institutions in living up to the charge. They should be centers of resistance; so much so in fact that they should be empty because the students were away on the battle lines fighting for their country. That would be the case with the great universities in other lands. I know of universities in Great Britain, for instance, which emptied themselves of every student fit for service when war was declared in 1914. Those heroic students had no doubt about where their sphere of activity should be, or what they owed to their country. Without hesitation they laid down their books, picked up rifles, and went forth to war to pay the debt, which most of them did with their lives. Since, however, our armies are sufficiently large at present not to need recruitment from our schools, our students should requite their obligation to their country in other ways.

Why, may I ask, is Oxford University today endeavoring to replace many of the valuable books in our university libraries which were destroyed by the Japanese? Not for the sake of the universities, themselves, but, it is certain, for the sake, directly or indirectly, of awakening the intelligence of our people and ameliorating the conditions of their lives. That, too, should be the specific aim of our own universities.

As centers of enlightenment, education, and service, the universities have their definite duties in times of crises even more than in time of peace. They have a moral responsibility placed upon them to direct all their efforts toward one goal — the attainment of victory, and the rehabilitation of the country. If they can help to achieve that, as they should do — and that is what the country is watching and expecting them to do — then they will be entitled to be proud of contributing in great measure to the fulfillment of the determination of their bludgeoned country to survive and progress.

V

THE EDUCATION OF THE MASSES

THE education of the masses may appear to be a stupendous problem, since eighty per cent of our population is illiterate. Yet consideration will show that the difficulties are more apparent than real. If each of us who has something to contribute to the solution would cheerfully and diligently apply himself to the bearing of his share of the burden, the task would be by no means hopeless, especially if methods are adopted which would make the transition from illiteracy to competency in citizenship as progressive and simple as possible.

The education of our fellow men must have as its object the ultimate conversion of these hitherto undeveloped western provinces into an intellectual, an industrial, and an economic base for national resistance and reconstruction. The potential hidden wealth must be won for the material purposes of national survival, while the richness of the popular mind must be cultivated so that intelligent citizenship might contribute not only to victory but to the future intellectual grandeur of our race.

As a foundation for all this we have our ancient culture; as a goal we have free constitutional government, upon

[23]

the threshold of which we now, fortunately, have our feet firmly set. But to fulfill our destiny, we must win the complete loyalty of the people, for as Dr. Sun Yat-sen has already pointed out, "The hearts of the people are the basis on which to establish a nation."

An incentive to the intellectuals, if one is needed, to implement the verity pronounced by Dr. Sun Yat-sen, should be the recognition of the unstinted assistance which we owe to our compatriots to help them to realize their responsibilities as citizens, to understand national issues, and to attain competency to exercise the franchise which, we hope, all will enjoy in time. To proceed successfully we must systematize so that there shall be no waste of effort through overlapping or useless duplication. The organization for work which must be done can be effected by the intellectuals themselves, or they can save time and trouble by working under the aegis of the New Life Movement which is already functioning and which has for its sole object the betterment of the lot of the masses. This movement is prepared to offer its services and experience as a channel through which this work might be done. It already has under way some of the projects which I shall mention below. But thousands of volunteer workers are necessary to carry out this comprehensive program both behind the fighting lines and in these western provinces. It does not matter, however, under what auspices work is carried on since our object is only to teach and train the people quickly and satisfactorily to become modern citizens.

The aims of the intellectuals should, therefore, be to teach the people to read and write and to train them to think; to help them to better their living conditions; to increase their ways of earning a livelihood; to improve their crops and their animal husbandry; to produce more raw materials; to develop village industries and co-operatives, and to manufacture their needs from what they produce.

The means to that end may be by direct teaching — by object lessons; by charts, pictures, pamphlets, posters; by news sheets in simple vernacular; by illustrated lectures; by radio broadcasts. Work could be begun without any costly equipment. All those who are interested could gather groups of their less favored neighbors at their homes, or at any available place, for reading and writing, as well as for brief talks on citizenship, on patriotism and its obligations, on sanitation, on household remedies for simple ailments, and on the improvement of their environment. Always it is a stinging disgrace to see our beautiful countryside littered with dirt and filth which is aesthetically repulsive and physically nauseating.

Funds to purchase essential equipment to carry on the work could be secured, in all probability, from the general public, or from philanthropists. Each village could be induced, or be helped, to buy a simple, inexpensive radio.

Towns could buy two or more to be installed at certain places where the public could assemble to hear the programs of instruction and entertainment.

This form of education and entertainment has long met with much success in India and Russia. Such radios could be procured cheaply by being designed to receive only the special programs broadcasted from the central station. Programs could be prepared covering farm and handicraft information, national news, interpretation of world news and developments, and, always, encouragement of mutual service and patriotic endeavor.

For lantern lectures small, cheap stereopticon sets could be obtained in any number (the New Life Movement already has one hundred of them with suitable programs). These are usually an unfailing source of entertainment and interest. Through the medium of storytellers the heroic tales of ancient and modern times could be recounted, while theatrical entertainments would prove valuable in instructing and enlivening the usually dreary lives of the people.

Mass education, it must be mentioned, has been carried on in limited areas of our country by various organizations. That, however, is not sufficient, since to make it effective — and immediately so — the work must be carried on by all intellectuals on a voluntary basis, and not merely by a few patriotic citizens and paid staffs.

The gentry everywhere could be mobilized to help, and

intelligent people with a will to work for the good of their country should be able to arrange innumerable ways of carrying forward the great national work that is involved in preparing the people to assume the patriotic responsibilities for which they should now begin to fit themselves. The intellectuals must not forget that the existing cultural institutions, useful in themselves, are not enough. They were created for the educated, but nothing similar exists for the illiterate masses.

The devising and the setting in operation of the means to instruct and awaken the masses should prove of tremendous interest to all those intellectuals who have the patriotic impulses which, when mobilized and unleashed, could do much to inspire others to strive and labor for national emancipation, prosperity, and greatness.

Failure on the part of the intellectuals to recognize their responsibilities and to respond wholeheartedly to the urgent crying need of educating our illiterate masses cannot be too vigorously censured, and will undoubtedly bring upon their heads the denunciation of succeeding generations, as well as the withering contempt of the outside world.

The material that the patriotic and enterprising will have to work upon — their industrious fellow men — is the finest ever given to the hands of human beings to shape. "If we work marble, it will perish," wrote Daniel Webster, "if we work upon brass, time will efface it; if we rear temples, they will crumble into dust; but if we work upon immortal minds and instill into them just principles, we are then engraving that upon tablets which no time will efface, but will brighten and brighten to all eternity." Thus will the intellectuals — as guardians of the State, and moulders of true enlightened public opinion — have an unequalled opportunity nobly to discharge a momentous national duty, and make their ineradicable contribution to the determination of China to translate into deeds, *resurgam* — "I shall rise again."

VI

THE CORNERSTONE FOR FOUNDING
A REGENERATED CHINA

IF ONE task is more outstandingly important than any
other in connection with the reform and rehabilitation of
our country it must be the eradication of the criminal stagnation that has for so many generations stifled the natural
development of our economic life and stood upon our
horizon like a grim specter of predestined ruin. It began
far back in the history of the Manchus, extended like creep-
ing paralysis through their reign, was inherited by the
Republic in 1911, and has become the chief handicap in
our present war of resistance against Japanese aggression.

To discover the means to combat its sinister influences
and exercise them, we must first discover its causes. To
do that we must not be content with superficial examination. We cannot airily declare that it has been due to
some obvious political, official, or social system that has
proved inadequate, and dismiss it. The cause goes far
deeper than that.

Ideologies have had little to do with the origin or the
perpetuation of this ominous clog upon our national progress. Not only has it, through the long years, prevented
our country from attaining the international eminence

[29]

and prosperity which is rightly ours — and for which we are peculiarly fitted by our culture, by the vastness of our natural resources, and by our great industrious population — but it now menaces our very existence because we have become almost completely dependent upon outside countries for the supplies which would mean life or death to us, if we did not have space and time, and flesh and blood, fighting on our side in comradeship with right and justice.

The causes are deeper, are more profound, than any that can be produced by relatively ephemeral systems. They are, indeed, psychological rather than political. In my opinion they were due to two primary and complementary evil personal qualities — self-seeking and stupidity. These, in combination, unquestionably formed the basis of our industrial backwardness and apparent economic apathy. Out of them arose, in course of time, all manner of iniquities which have kept our country — at least up to the time of the awakening caused by this war — in an undeveloped state, and the masses of our people in poverty.

Manchu officials who were cursed with the feverish immoral urge to fatten upon projects which should have been part of the normal expansion of our economic life soon became stupid with insensate greed, and forgetful of national needs. They were the originators of the obstructive tactics which drove away in disgust many expert planners and many potential investors of capital, thus drastically delaying by generations our emergence from the agricultural phase of our existence.

Unfortunately the atavistic influences of this unrestrained dishonesty are being felt to the present day.

Self-seeking led to the establishment of the belief, in the minds of avaricious officials, that industrial schemes were specially devised for their enrichment. Resultant stupidity became responsible for the heedless wrecking of innumerable projects — which could have been operated to the advantage of the State — because the responsible officials failed to secure what in gangster terminology is known as their "rake-off."

Most high officials who pretended to superiority, but who yearned for the unsavory commission, had underlings to transact the questionable business for them. The underlings, in their turn, developed their own technique, and, if they failed to secure their price, they contrived means to cause the collapse of the negotiations and the shelving of the project.

Thus this Republic has much to live down, many lingering bad habits, evil notions and distorted conceptions to extirpate. Our past and present diplomatic and industrial highways have been strewn with the corpses of lost causes and the bleaching bones of strangled industries, while innumerable schemes of potential value have been stillborn and have long choked the pigeonholes and archives of various ministries.

[31]

Follies have, in general, retarded the effective development of our natural resources, hampered our national prosperity, and lowered our standing in the eyes of progressive peoples. That is a disgrace we should be quick to eradicate. Now, if never before, should come the recognition that the power and the wealth which are enjoyed by all great nations have been wrung from the earth, and that out of our failure to open our earth has come our great physical and financial weakness, it is a weakness that is scandalous in this age of advanced scientific and mechanical perfection; that has involved us not only in incalculable material sacrifices but also in loss of respect and prestige.

There is no legitimate excuse to account for the absence in our country of up-to-date, well-conducted flourishing and expanding industries, producing much of our needs for peace or for war from our raw materials, and building up for us strength, independence, and self-reliance.

If we are worthy of our heritage we will boldly face the facts, unpalatable though they be, and with genuine intellectual honesty admit the faults that are ours. Only by doing that can we know where to place our feet in the steep ascent from the Avernus of apparent incompetency in which lack of official loyalty, wisdom and integrity have for so long kept us immured.

We have, of course, made much comparative progress in the few past years, but there is a deep and yawning abyss between that and the monumental advancement there should have been, and might have been, had our mineral wealth and manufacturing opportunities been opened up, and the production of better and increased raw materials been encouraged, as they should have been. New avenues of employment would have been provided for the masses, and prosperity would have replaced the heartbreaking low standard of living which they still have to endure.

I have briefly traced the causes of our stagnation, with perhaps brutal frankness, with the object and the hope of begetting honesty in all departments of our political and social life. We must have that to survive and to effect our resurgence. If we could learn quickly from the lessons of our past how to achieve national impeccability and pluck salvation from the crucible of war we would just as quickly become powerful and prosperous (as we should be) and would have nothing, or no one, to fear in the future.

The doors of reform are now fortunately wide open to us, and former dishonest officials have inadvertently left guideposts which should keep us from falling into the putrid sloughs of ignominy which beset their paths. We have to accept those glaring warnings or fail in safeguarding our heritage. If we do fail, then posterity will hold us strictly accountable, if the rising generation does not do so.

While we have been staggered by the very nature and

complexity of our inheritance from the Manchus that is no reason why we should falter in shouldering it, or why we who know what should be done should sit too long by the wayside wiping our brows, or catching our breaths, or grieving.

Grave civil wars and various types of political upheavals have admittedly extended through the major years of the Republic to hamper constructive and progressive reforms. And it was our tragic misfortune that no sooner had we achieved national unity than we were pounced upon by one of the best-armed, and, it has been proved, most ruthless and merciless military nations in the world. But to our great and lasting credit, be it said, we discounted our unpreparedness and our weakness and gave battle to the invader of our country. We are still giving battle. We have been shocked out of our old-time apathy to be galvanized into unwonted warrior-like activity.

While we are exhausting every nerve in defending ourselves, we are hearing the cries of survivors coming from every corner of our country urging us to fight on. We are fighting on — fighting so that we may flourish. To flourish we must build as we withdraw from the crushing blows of our enemy, and build well.

The cornerstone of the foundations for a regenerated China must be the materialization and administration of wise, honest and competent laws and measures for the free and secure opening up of our natural resources; for the establishment of modern industries; for the encouragement, benefit and protection of workers, as well as investors. There should be no experimentation, because there is neither necessity nor time for it. Doubtful and unproved panaceas should be given no consideration. There are tried roads for present-day officialdom to follow in using the opportunity which has now come to them to remove the stigma placed upon our name by their predecessors of the past. Time will prove how they have acquitted themselves at this eventful period in the history of their country, and acclaim or blame will be their reward.

Departure from a stern policy which will correct industrial and general economic stagnation and give protection and relief to the masses of the people should not be tolerated. If it is, it will surely cause anything that we may allow to be jerry-built to tumble about our ears, or about the ears of posterity, and impose the silence of ruin and inaction where there should be the resounding echoes of progress and prosperity.

When we refresh our minds with the recollection that it was the very administrative and economic futility of the Manchus which hastened the Revolution we will surely realize the nature and the gravity of the responsibilities imposed upon us by their overthrow. To us has come the duty of cherishing and enhancing the possessions and potentialities of our race; and that duty can be faithfully fulfilled if each and every one of us dedicates every shred of honor and integrity we possess, and every ounce of strength that is in us, to sustaining unsullied the will to survive that is voiced in the word *resurgam*.

VII

SEVEN DEADLY SINS

IN surveying the history of so ancient a nation as China, one should take a comprehensive view of the determined factors of our development from the simple life of a primitive people to the complex culture evolved during the last 5,000 years. In seeking, however, a realistic evaluation of the present with the object of hastening our victory so that we may emerge from the present war with a sound basis for national reconstruction, we must make a microscopic study of those evils which are hindering our progress toward the attainment of our goal. Thus the deadwood which has cluttered about us to our national detriment may be pruned and cleared away.

This war has shown in high relief many of our shortcomings. Now is the logical and psychological moment for us to correct them. All other nations of the world have found it necessary and politic to institute immediate reorganization and reforms when the shadow of war has approached; responsible officials are galvanized into action to estimate the possible consequences of incompetency in hostilities and to prepare the necessary housecleaning measures to meet all emergencies. Now that war is upon her, China should do likewise. She must be swift and lavish in action, slow and miserly in talk, in order to avoid laying herself open to charges of laxity or indifference.

I have mentioned that our national economic life has become stagnant by the stupidities of self-seekers. Self-seeking, in my opinion, is the most vicious of several evils, which may, for brevity's sake, be catalogued as the "Seven Deadly Sins." They are: (1) Self-seeking, (2) "Face," (3) Cliquism, (4) Defeatism (Mu-yu-fa-tze), (5) Inaccuracy (Tsa-pu-tu), (6) Lack of self-discipline, (7) Evasion of responsibility. Long ago they combined to retard our emergence as a first-class world power, and they now delay our victory in this war. Especially is this true in cases where people have taken advantage of their positions to hide their iniquities under the voluminous cloak of patriotism in order to enrich themselves even at the risk of the continued impoverishment of the people. Profiteering is another form of self-seeking, or "squeeze," and is a speciality which has characterized all wars in every part of the world. That fact, however, does not make the offense less heinous, and it should be rigorously condemned.

In the upbuilding of China we have to remember that the success of any undertaking, great or small, depends primarily upon the ability of the participants to abandon thought of personal interests or prejudices, and to view the whole from the objective standpoint of the common good. Until we willingly abide by such a policy, everyone trying to do anything will be pulling in different directions. The result will be that although much activity may be seen, the movement will not be in a forward direction, but will head toward a profitless, meaningless, sideway tug of war which will not only dissipate the energy of all concerned, but will be a permanent pernicious drag upon national progress.

Closely allied with self-seeking is "face." This is a curse which affects most of us from the cradle to the grave. More incompetency and ruin have been engendered by "face" in social, official, political, and national phases of our life than one could conceive or care to admit. As an illustration: Lest he loses "face," many a misguided man confronted with a problem, even of national consequence, will not "demean" himself to consult his subordinate, although the latter may be an expert and have the solution at his finger tips. The superior, to assert his position, and hence save his "face," will thus, in his ignorance, oftentimes make the most monumental and fatuous decisions. On his part the subordinate, who may fully realize the consequences of the error, customarily says nothing, thereby saving his superior's "face," as well as his own job. But the country loses. Even when later developments expose the stupidity of the decisions to other circles, no one else, either within or without the department, would dare call attention to the mistake in case criticism should cause the loss of the "face" of the one responsible. Instead, a conspiracy of excuse making and camouflage automatically begins to operate to protect the superior. Investigation to correct the error is baffled and defeated, and the damage and loss to the country become more insidious and far-reaching.

Apart from the millions upon millions of dollars which the country loses by such scandalous procedure; apart from the criminal waste of precious time, and apart from the resultant sacrifice of national prestige, welfare and interests, time has proved that this slavish devotion to the preservation of "face" as a cult has direful reactions in other directions. For one thing, it discourages ardent patriotism in young people. It frustrates their idealism, wears down their morale and changes them into spiritless automatons able only to perform their tasks mechanically; it transforms creative ability — which, under favorable auspices, might have made constructive contributions to the revitalization of our national life in all its phases — into destructive resentment, bitterness, and discontent. Stagnation results; but worse than that hotbeds of disaffection are created, and it is usually from such that rebellion gets its impetus and chief support.

To have seeds of discord such as these sown at any time is bad enough, but to have them germinate now while the nation is engaged in a life-and-death struggle is pregnant with grave danger, because they are demoralizing to society in general, damaging to the fighting spirit, and disastrous to the character and the future of the disappointed individuals themselves.

In analyzing the reasons for apparent national lethargy in general it is soon realized that "face" is one of the most baneful factors contributing to our tardy progress. Among other things it operates against the full and intelligent utilization of the knowledge and experience of foreign technical and other experts who have, from time to time, been engaged at great expense from many countries, and been employed in many spheres, by our government. In this respect the old regime permitted the initiation of a system of fanatical face-saving which even now, if not suppressed, will impede the aims of our government, discourage and render idle the experts, rob the country of wealth and power, and irreparably retard industrial expansion. Experience has revealed only too poignantly that some so-called responsible government officials, as well as students, still feel that loss of "face" is involved in accepting or seeking expert advice. Even worse, they aggravate the situation by wasting time in an effort to disparage the worth of the advice proffered, and to prove the possession by them of knowledge and ability far superior to that of the experts. I know whereof I speak.

The Generalissimo has been called upon time and again to rebuke the ignoramus, and to emphasize to his students the profound importance of following the advice of technical experts in order that the best shall be got out of the modern equipment that has been purchased both for purposes of peace and war.

I have personally had many an occasion to feel ashamed, and to grieve, for my country, but particularly so when I have heard foreign technical advisers ruefully say: "Well, it seems that I am paid to listen to how and why these people know more about the job than I do." People of this type of mind who are, perhaps unwittingly, jeopardizing both the good repute and the progress of our country, and who cannot see either the light of reason or the shadow of impending catastrophe which their actions create, should ask themselves what is to be done with them; what is to be done about such a condition of affairs? There is an answer which they themselves can supply, and action that they themselves can take. If they fail to do something of their own volition, then the authorities should do it for them. But I may well ask: Are we to lose a nation to save someone's "face"? I hear the answer, "No!" echoing around the confines of our land.

An echo should be warning enough to the wise in this significant mutable year of grace. The war we are fighting has done more than unify the nation under the banner of resistance. It has shocked the suffering patriotic people into a realization of the nature of some of our national problems, and it must be understood that the causes and the cure of some of them are not likely to escape the

Argus-eyed among the distressed. Neither is there likely to be much further tolerance of the degenerating consequences of "squeeze" and "face," because apart from the immoral stigma that attaches to them they are being more clearly recognized as among the chief obstacles to progress. They are now being put in their right category. They are no longer being regarded as proper perquisites of position and power, but as distinct national dangers. During recent years our advancement in all directions has been notable; but, freed from these and other correctable evils, it is clearly realized that this country of ours could progress by leaps and bounds, and quickly be able in unison, sincerity, and determination to shout, from the ashes of our burned homes and from the tops of our mountains, the word *resurgam*.

VIII

SEVEN DEADLY SINS (cont.)

WHEN our country really gets down to the business of setting its house in order it will not be long before we shall see our faces reflected in the polished surfaces of its furniture. It is the ambition to see these surfaces shine that has encouraged me to apply some elbow grease to the wholesome swabbing out of the dirt, and to the exposure of the dark corners to the cold white light of publicity. It is not, of course, a savory business, and many would naturally prefer to do without the airing and the cleansing — but in the interests of honesty and progress and organization it must be done.

We must have organization, and we can get it as soon as we have rid ourselves of some of the morally offensive cobwebs and garbage which have blinded our eyes and obstructed our social and official feet.

Already I have appealed for the cleansing away of several pernicious customs, for the eradication of outstanding noxious evils, and for the extirpation of deleterious habits which assume in their effects, the nature of sins. I have said that there were seven deadly ones. There are more, in reality. I have dealt at some length with two of them, and there remain others for brief arraignment and condemnation.

Cliquism is one of them. Cliques seem to hold sway in many places. They are like dry rot in the administration. They stifle enterprise and initiative. They operate to oust honesty and efficiency by preventing a patriotic "outsider," or a stranger to the clique, from gaining a position, no matter how capable he may be. And they eject, or try to, anyone of any independence of character or mind who may happen to be near them but not of them. Every clique is a refuge for incompetents. It fosters corruption and disloyalty, it begets cowardice, and consequently is a burden upon and a drawback to the progress of the country. Its instincts and actions are those of the pack.

Lack of Self-Discipline, another of the sins, contributes to exactly similar conditions. Its origin may be in the failure of schools and colleges to teach mental discipline, or it may be the lack of standards in officialdom. Whatever the origin it is a crippling weakness. The student who has not been taught how to think succumbs easily in his adolescence or maturity to the influences of evil environment. Indolence and inefficiency, indifference to the interests of the State, or disregard of the incidence upon national life of misguided actions, place a distinguishing mark upon those who never knew, or who have forgotten, how to control their actions. When lack of self-discipline is displayed by high officials it demoralizes all beneath them, even down to the coolie who keeps the door, and, like acid, it corrodes the very fiber of nationhood.

Evasion of Responsibility — still another sin — is a contemptible evil in anyone. In officials it is comparable to crime. It is equivalent to, in the colloquialism of the day, "passing the buck." It used to be almost a national pastime in the old days of the Mandarins. High officials then dodged responsibility with a degree of mental and physical nimbleness that is only equaled by the "no b'long my pidgin" of the house servants — a song that is very familiar to the ears of foreigners resident in China, and, at the same time, aggravatingly incomprehensible to them. It may be due, in some cases, to "face," but mostly it is the product of ignorance, incompetency and lack of character, or the manifestation of a will for downright obstruction. Its effects are far-reaching in their injuriousness. It has produced stagnation of all kinds in all directions — particularly economic.

Dodging of responsibility in the past has delayed beyond reckoning the development of natural resources — especially minerals. It prevented the materialization of industrial and transportation schemes, and caused the shelving of scores of advantageous cultural and other proposals for the improvement of the moral, mental and material conditions of the people. Where there has been confusion it has made it worse confounded. The shirkers

[46]

of responsibility are, in reality, those upon whom will rightly fall most of the blame for China's backwardness which posterity will surely apportion when it writes the history of our current times. That would be a measure of retributive justice; but the pity of it would be that such punishment would be merely historical and not retroactive.

Those who avoid responsibility are the ones who have cluttered our official life with deadwood — human, unproductive deadwood which encumbers the pay roll of almost every department of public service. Those who so casually abandon their duties to their country have created a strata of prideless persons that might well be called the Grand Army of the Paid Unemployable. The rank and file of this army are too incompetent to work — and their superiors were too spineless or too conscienceless to dismiss them — but they are not too proud to collect their unearned pay. Millions of dollars of the taxpayers' money are thus continuously flooding down the drains of absolute waste. It is all money that could well be used to employ competent persons in a thousand places where technical and other knowledge would make for our advancement.

Then there is the sin of Defeatism, as expressed in that lugubrious phrase "Mu-yu-fa-tze." What does it mean? It is any excuse that will permit the irresponsible, the indifferent, the lazy, the incompetent and the cowardly to escape the trouble or the accountability which would be involved in doing something new or something important. It is the word that Napoleon declared was not in his dictionary. It is the lever the Manchu officials used whenever they wanted to oust from their sight progressive and enterprising people with ideas, the acceptance of which would encroach too closely upon their cushioned ease or erupt them out of it. It means "impossible," "there are no means," or, in the pidgin English of the scullery, "no can do." Its echo was wont to reverberate through all the yamens of former periods. It has come — to our shame — ringing with undiminished resonance down the corridors of time to these parlous days — days that I hope the near future will see being used for our emancipation from crowds of stifling inexcusable evils, and so shield us from those potent and damaging "slings and arrows of outrageous fortune," which are the bogies of the unknown days ahead. The man with the glib "Mu-yu-fa-tze" is, in short, a living menace to our land; the personification of indecision and do-nothingness.

Close upon his heels comes another curse — "Cha-pü-tu." It also has been inherited by us. Ever it is on the lips of the casual-minded, the slipshod, and the lazy. It spells inaccuracy — another sin. "That will do"; "Oh, well, it is almost right"; "That's good enough"; "Never mind," will define it. It is the most used phrase in the vocabulary of the inefficient. It is foremost in the phraseology of the timeserver and the sloven. It signals danger in the machine shop where accuracy is almost an art in modern machine making; it sounds the knell of reliability wherever it is tolerated. Its effects are seen, among other things, in the loss of our silk and tea trades, where samples were not lived up to, where care of crops and cargoes were neglected. Can you not hear the silk reeler say: "There are some diseased cocoons here"; hear "Cha-pü-tu" come from the lips of the one responsible; and, from the far, far distance of a foreign land, hear "This silk is streaky and inferior, we must not buy any more"? That's what "Cha-pü-tu" does to us — and it does it with sickening thuds in a variety of directions.

On top of this list of sins there are others. There are envy, and jealousy, and intolerance — common enough, be it said, the world around — but which operate constantly, through the medium of inefficiency, to our national detriment. There is penny-wise-and-pound-foolishness; there is mental and moral obliquity in some in selecting purchases for national needs, and there is that iniquitous folly — forgetfulness of orders, or slackness in carrying them out. Worse, probably, is the failure of those who issue orders to find out if they have been obeyed, and their laxity in not levying penalties upon delinquents. The way of the transgressor is proverbially hard, but in our country it seems to be softened with the carpets of connivance.

Where foreign relations are concerned — and jeopardized — there are two important failings. One is the stupidity of appointing a layman to negotiate a technical contract, and the other is the folly of using persons deficient in languages and knowledge as translators or interpreters. Very little imagination is necessary to picture the type of irreparable misunderstanding and costly failure which arise from faulty acquaintance with words and their meanings, and from unfamiliarity with the nuances of speech. Incredibly fatuous and grave errors have been committed to my own knowledge, and I have heard strings of stories of unbelievable stupidity on the part of supposedly qualified interpreters which would have been grotesquely comic had they not been gravely tragic.

If the causes of past breakdowns and unfriendliness in negotiations with foreign interests on economic projects could be traced, I am convinced that they would be found to have been due mostly to gross and inexcusable ignorance on the part of translators of foreign languages. This fruitful source of difficulty and totally unnecessary estrangements is one that merits serious consideration whenever important negotiations are to be entered upon.

Only persons fully acquainted with technical terminology should be entrusted with the task of interpretation or translation when financial, economic, or industrial projects are being discussed or negotiated. What we have hitherto lost by reason of inaccurate interpretation or translation is impossible to compute, but there is no reason why

[50]

we should lose anything more or allow further unpleasantness or misunderstanding to be engendered in the
course of negotiations connected with projects or problems
from the successful outcome of which the country is expected to benefit. Those responsible for such negotiations
should possess the highest of qualifications, the most flexible of intelligences, the best of characters, the most understanding of hearts, and the soundest of imaginations.
Their instructions, before entering upon negotiations,
should be designed to secure the successful conclusion of
mutually satisfactory agreements — I underline mutually
— and, if failure results, require the production of sound
and legitimate reasons for inability to arrive at a satisfactory conclusion. Punishment of some kind should follow
inability to show reasonable cause for failure of negotiations. Hitherto efforts to arrive at agreements have col-
lapsed because the negotiators sought commissions in
vain. That is a stigma we should be quick to remove and
eager to prevent in the future.

If the variety of sins and bad habits and customs which
I have been exposing are to be absolved, cured, or changed,
then the decision to inaugurate a civil service which the
People's Political Council so recently agreed upon must be
translated from ideas into deeds as quickly as possible. In
the meantime all those guilty of evasion of responsibility,
of subordination of national affairs to personal interests,
or of neglect of duty should be branded "traitor" so that

all who see them may know them for just what they are.

The shortcomings I have mentioned combine to cause the stagnation in which we have so long been floundering and from which we now see, I hope, the means of escape, and from which, with resolute courage we can and must escape. These evils can be cured because we know what we have to cure; and we will cure them in time because patriotism and pride will, inevitably, impel even the weak and the negligent to respond to the spiritual and material stimulation embodied in the word *resurgam*.

IX

WOMEN AND THE FAMILY

PICTURESQUE pages have been contributed to our ancient history by women, and, correspondingly, modern women are destined to provide colorful passages for the chronicles of this current epoch. They will do so because they are developing; because they are becoming nationally conscious; because brains, education, foresight, enterprise, and courage are not the monopoly of men. All these are shared by women, who also have the good fortune to be endowed with the additional qualities of motherliness and gentleness which single them out for special service in the great work now confronting our whole race in the safeguarding of our heritage and particularly in the rebuilding of our nation. It is not even the sole prerogative of men to be soldiers, to strut in the glamour of uniform, or to hear the diapason of the cannonade. Women have already proved the valor that is in them; have shown that they can endure the hardships of battle zones; can stand the shock and crash of war's wrath. Girls have been trained, and have marched off to the fronts, in their thousands, shaming — if any shame is in them — the hordes of young men who boisterously pretend that they want to help their country, but who shelter somewhere in safety, or cling to the cover of distant places far removed from those front lines where gallant deeds are done.

The constructive part women must play in the winning of the war and the resurgence of their country is becoming increasingly important. Many men now declare that half of the responsibility for the fulfillment of these great national tasks should fall upon women because they constitute half of the population. If that argument is to be carried to its logical conclusion should the women also enjoy half of the power and half of the glory? They are not thinking in such terms, however. They are thinking of sustaining resistance, fully realizing that national victory should be the primary concern of every citizen in the country. It would not harm the men, however, to remember what is due to the women. They are individuals and citizens as well as women, even though they have only recently asserted themselves and demonstrated their value in realms other than that connected with the home.

It is not, of course, the fault of the women of China that hitherto their lives have been circumscribed; that they have been cribbed, cabined, and confined; shut off from participation, in the solution of national problems; converted into household chattels, or, if they possessed what is now known as "glamour," kept as pampered adornments of boudoirs like animated pieces of delicate porcelain.

Women are now fast breaking down the barriers which

have for aeons excluded them from taking part in public affairs. They are escaping from the cloistered confinement that prevented them from contributing the leaven of their intelligence and their ability that is so essential to the success of social and political reforms and national progress, and they will supply the energy and incentive which are needed for successful and progressive improvements.

Women must do their best to see to it that the piles of patriotism and probity are driven deeply into our despoiled soil to form the foundations for a resurgent China. They must try to ensure that honor and integrity and fair dealing shall characterize the national superstructure. They must labor unceasingly to create the atmosphere of loyalty, tolerance and justice to permeate for all time the halls of State and the confines of the home. Given competent organization and adequate opportunity they can do all this, and they can improve personal attitudes of mind and relationships, which will be to the abiding good of humankind.

There are women in our past for us to honor and to emulate; there are some to avoid but to study as a warning. There were women of literary brilliance such as Pan Chao, of the Han dynasty, she of the Nu Chieh, or the Precepts for Women. There were Lady Wei, Lady Li, Lady Kwuan, and others. There were, too, heroic figures such as Hua Mu-lan, Liang Hung-yu, and Ching Liang-yu. These women were of those who dedicated their brains and their energies to the upbuilding and improvement of the nation. On the reverse side were what are regarded as self-seeking women such as Tan Tsi, Pao Chi, Wu Tsei-tien, and Yang Kuei-fei. Perhaps they were guilty of harmful intrigue, or perhaps they wielded a baneful influence which reduced the rulers of those times to degenerates. Perhaps they did both, and nothing of good for the country. Whatever they did they have been anathematized by historians — who, however, happened to be men — and consequently by later generations. At any rate, they are not for us to vie with. One exception was Chiu Ching, a woman educator revolutionist who was decapitated because of her uncompromising stand against the corrupt Manchu regime. Her tomb at Hangchow is the invariable scene of displays of respect and reverence. She is known to have died for the good of her country.

Pan Chao cannot well be passed over with mere perfunctory mention. She was the younger sister of the former Han dynasty historian Pan Ku, and she carried on his work after his death. That was six centuries before Christ. She became the tutoress of the Empress, although she did not succeed to the title of Court Historian. She laid down the pattern for women's education in her famous "Three Obediences and Four Virtues." She advocated obedience to the father during girlhood, obedience to the husband after marriage, and obedience to the son after the husband's death. The "Four Virtues" included

[56]

chastity, gentleness in speech, modesty and simplicity in appearance, and moderate proficiency in house-wifery. The exemplary woman should not strive to excel, it would seem. What she taught, if measured by the ideas of today, hindered the development of women, but was undoubtedly suitable for her period and her environment.

Nowadays, however, there are commentators who read into Pan Chao's writings treachery to womanhood; betrayal of womanly status. She is blamed for fortifying the men in their desire to keep the women immured in the home, and for preventing their entrance into public life and society for so long a time. She is charged by critics with the sufferings and difficulties from which Chinese womanhood is only now escaping. To my mind she was right according to her lights and her time — but fortunately times change and we change with them. What was right then would not fit in at all with the emancipated ideas of the women of today, or with the Sam Browne campaigning belts of the girls.

All things in life are relative, yet there is one unquestioned basic principle which Pan Chao laid down, and which time will never shake. It is that "virtue is more important than learning." To my mind, if one has to choose between virtue and learning, virtue is the more to be cherished. There is, however, no reason why a woman should not be both virtuous and learned.

This is a truth that must be indelibly stamped upon

the minds of the young so that it may become the most durable part of their characters, so that it will withstand the rough and tumble of adolescence, the familiarities of coeducation, and the lures of modernized life in general.

While the cloistering of our womenkind in the past was injuriously restrictive, the liberty afforded today is probably injuriously ungoverned. Only resolute characters will withstand the dangers of the unaccustomed independence and the untoward relinquishment of parental control. Looseness and license often seem to be mistaken for liberty. It is a pity, but the responsibility, in large measure, belongs to the parents. Perhaps the repressions of the old family system were overthrown with two much suddenness, and the stampede of youth was too precipitate to permit parents to make the necessary mental readjustments and erect essential safeguards to meet the new time. Youth escaped, and it is difficult to effect a successful roundup. The only thing to do is for the educators to put youth upon its honor, and with wisdom and patience direct the energy and vitality which must effervesce, along channels contributive to national well-being.

As for the parents, they must themselves recapture at least the guidance of their grown-up children more by example than by precept. Youth is irked by pious exhortation, especially if the lives of the parents are inconsistent with the "preaching." To bring up the younger generation in the way that it should go, the woman, if she is to make definite personal contributions to national advancement, must be a good wife, a good mother, and a good citizen. If she cannot be a good citizen, she cannot be a good mother or a good wife, and if she cannot be either then she cannot be a good citizen. Nor can her children bring credit to her name or to their country.

The duty of the mother of today is no different from that of the mothers of old, except for its enhanced importance. The ancient mothers conceived it to be their obligation to bring up their children so that they might devote their lives to the welfare of the nation. That principle and that practice are needed now more than ever, for we have a ruthless invader stalking our land who must be exterminated, just as all his evil influences must be eradicated.

The present generation, and those to come, have the heroic task imposed upon them of resurrecting their nation, as well as of avenging the crimes of ruin, rape, and rapine which have been inflicted upon our country and our people. Consequently the mothers of today, and of tomorrow, have a national duty confronting them infinitely more onerous and more sublime, than any ever fulfilled by the mothers of our time-honored and revered heroes and scholars. All of their children must reach manhood with inbred intelligent resolve as the outstanding feature of high, purposeful, and patriotic character. Only by example can such children be reared, so with mothers and fathers reform of character and outlook must begin at once. Physical and mental apathy must be discarded. It must be replaced by the will to work ceaselessly for national resistance and national survival. There is room for intelligent effort in a thousand directions. The well-educated women who have, since their marriages, had their brains in cold storage must voluntarily take up their share of the national burden, or be compelled to do so.

This is no time for slackness in either sex, and it must be understood that slackers will be pilloried in history, if not before this war is over, and will have to drink up the lees and the dregs of popular contempt; for slackness is despicable and akin to treachery. Those who have growing sons must train them and dedicate them to the salvation of their country; those who have sons already grown should encourage them to take up arms to defend the heritage handed down by their ancestors and to drive into the sea the despicable violators of our womanhood and the desolators of our homes.

Victory having been won there will be still more to do. There is a new China to shape and to build up on the ruins of the old one. The mothers must mold the minds of the sons and the daughters in preparation for that great emprise. Introspection will quickly reveal to the conscientious where changes are needed. Action based upon those revelations will soon fit everyone for serious and productive national service, and the good which will come of it will be nationwide. In "The Great Learning" it is recorded that Confucius said:

After the heart is cultivated then the body will become regulated; after the body becomes regulated there will be order in the family; after the family becomes orderly the country will become governed; after the country becomes governed there will be peace under the heavens.

Here, surely, is the inspiration at this time of national need for all of us to fling our energies, our enthusiasm and our abilities into the common pool of effort, and with all our patriotism, and with our whole hearts, help our stricken and struggling country to defy its remorseless enemy and be able, with exaltation, to cry aloud and unafraid: *resurgam*.

X

THE NEED OF SPIRITUALITY

It is a commonplace of modern life that if a person is ill he should be cured. To be cured the cause of the illness must be diagnosed. If an operation is deemed necessary the surgeon's knife is invariably applied without hesitation. If neglectful living has caused the internal economy to fail in its functions drastic action is taken to restore normality.

As it is with man so it should be with his country and its administrative organs; so it is with those countries capably organized and wisely governed; so it must be with China.

To the end that this country of ours should adopt the quickest means to renew its vigor — which it can do by wise application of proved modern scientific advice and treatment — I have been exposing the cankerous growths which have debilitated our body politic so seriously during recent generations. I may have been too brutally frank in laying bare some of the ills to which our flesh is heir; but I have knowingly been so, feeling that it is imperative that we should know the worst in order effectively to achieve the best.

THE NEED OF SPIRITUALITY

It has been my hope to inspire all delinquents possessed of a sense of shame to reform or resign. I have hoped to inspire all patriotic people blessed with integrity, with forthrightness, with the will and the capacity to detect and overcome national shortcomings, to unite and align their honesty of purpose and their zeal on the side of energetic reform and reorganization.

I have hoped, by challenging all sections of our society, to sow the seeds of a nationwide movement in which all our intellectuals would co-operate to work for the abandonment of worn-out, costly, and inefficient methods — as well as bad customs and habits — in all spheres of administrative and economic activity. And I hope with equal earnestness for the intelligent speedy adoption of tested new methods to wisely, honestly, and forcefully develop all our innate powers and resources so that early victory may come to our resistance of Japanese aggression, and so that a new China may be forged in the fires of the war which is now consuming so many of our people, so much of our material wealth.

I have been stressing mostly the necessity for care of the material side of national reorganization and reconstruction. Now I want to speak of the supreme need and importance of national spiritual development.

In this respect the National Defense Council anticipated a suggestion of action by launching, on March 11, 1939, a program for National Spiritual Mobilization.

[63]

That scheme seizes hold of the essential need for the blotting out of evils I have already exposed to public scorn, and moves to marshal for national requirements the best of national character. Its objective is:

"To concentrate the spirit of the entire people under one simple and common aim so that the citizens may each adhere to the ethics of national salvation and possess a common belief in national reconstruction with the object that each citizen may struggle and sacrifice for the very ethics and beliefs he upholds."

In this nutshell has been embodied the principles I have been urging for adoption. A committee under the chairmanship of the Generalissimo has been appointed to elucidate and enforce them, and in the latter task is the opening for all true citizens to become active and to exert themselves to secure the kind of national life and develop the type of patriotic citizen which are necessary for a rejuvenated and rehabilitated China.

Here is the long-awaited opportunity knocking at the door of all who possess the qualifications or knowledge requisite for the institution of radical reforms. Those who fail to take advantage of it are unworthy of their citizenship; those who do so will have the lasting satisfaction of knowing that they are contributing materially to the triumph and the regeneration of their country.

The important bearing that spiritual stimulation will or will not have upon a people may be gauged by but a moment's consideration of the character of the Japanese, as revealed for all the world to see, during their unjust and remorseless aggression in our country. Hitherto the Japanese have prided themselves upon two transcendant qualities: One, their chivalric spirit as embodied in the teachings of their Samurai and their Bushido; and, two, their material progress as evidenced by their industrial development and their accumulation of modernized military strength.

Before the military leaders of Japan had decided to proceed with their plans for expansion upon the continent at the sacrifice of China, the world at large accepted the Japanese upon their own valuation as being civilized, cultured, and chivalrous. And the world also accepted them unconditionally as an invincible military race upon an exactly similar premise.

Japan went to war, unjust as was the excuse, with the world convinced of her swift and merciful victory; but perhaps the most remarkable revulsion of opinion in history took place within a few months. Horror piled upon horror, and the Christian world stood aghast when Japanese officers and soldiers, in their exasperation at the quality of the courage shown by the Chinese troops, and the high spirit of resistance displayed and maintained by the Chinese people, defiantly dropped the mask of civilization and the chivalric pose, and conducted themselves as unrighteous and unprincipled beings who would stop at no

[65]

illegality, injustice, untruth, inhumanity or bestiality to attain their ends.

The world was shocked, and it wondered, but the Japanese continued month after month to outrage humanity and stood in time completely stripped of the veneer of spurious spirituality by which they had won the good graces of the world. They became more and more exposed as the ungovernable product of unadulterated brutal materialism and as the ruthless vindicators of the fallacy that might is right; the self-acclaimed descendants of gods to whom all people who do not serve their purpose are regarded as being no better than scum upon the surface of the earth.

History will show just how much all their unspiritual materialism will profit them; but what is already revealed to us should be an immediate profitable lesson to all of our people. And what we see is that Japan's fall is approaching fast, and will be due to her devotion of sixty years of intense effort to the development of material and martial grandeur while utterly neglecting to inculcate in her people spiritual qualities which, in any case, are inherent in humanity.

With this warning burned by the Japanese into our very national and personal souls we must see to it that we cling to and absorb into our lives those old virtues of our forbears which have enabled us to survive not only through the centuries but also through the most inhuman calamities of warfare that have ever been inflicted by superior calculated might upon a vast industrious, unarmed population.

The way for us to elevate and enrich ourselves is to march along the spiritual path opened to us by the plans just promulgated by the government. We must follow them constructively, confidently, and unfailingly. We must enlarge upon them, and we must use, too, whatever other spiritual support we can find that is satisfying and salutary.

More than ever it behooves us to see to it that our nation is rebuilt upon a spiritual foundation, to foster our valued cultural heritage, and to build soundly and well whatever we do build. With our people spiritually mobilized for the good that can be done for our nation we can save our birthright and our race; we need never fear for ourselves or be afraid of anyone, and we can find inspiration as well as infinite solace and pride in the unqualified acceptance of the stimulating watchword *resurgam* — "I shall rise again" — which we will implement to the full.

Part II

THE CONDUCT OF THE COUNTRY
IN WARTIME

THE critical delineation of character which is the burden
of Part I must not be regarded by foreign readers as evidence of individual mental or moral bankruptcy in China,
or as a confession of national incompetence.

The subject was developed because the era upon which
we are now entering requires complete severance from the
attitude of mind toward administrative affairs which
characterized our people in the past. This has to be if we
are to make good in the development work which had
already been started before we found ourselves plunged into the vortex of a devastating war. Substantial foundations were being laid for the new China which we are
destined to erect upon the ashes of the old one now being
destroyed so industriously by the Japanese. That, in fact,
is the reason Japan set out to destroy us.

In an endeavor to make clear to foreigners the cause of
the apparent apathy of the Chinese toward affairs of gov-

ernment, I have, on several occasions in the past, pointed out that our people were, before the establishment of the existing Republic some twenty-nine years ago, always discouraged from participating in any way in those affairs of their country which should deeply concern them. When it is remembered that official life was the monopoly of the so-called "official class," and that the executioner's sword was freely used upon those who had the temerity to complain or plan to effect changes, it will be easy to understand why our people failed to be public spirited or nationally conscious.

It is only since the foundation of the Republic that the people of China have been able to raise a voice, as citizens, with regard to the conduct of the nation's business.

The popular ignorance of government, and the attitude of mind of the officials with regard to their responsibilities toward citizens, takes a long time to correct. But there have been great improvements. The leaven of reform has been effectively introduced, but, to my mind, the change was not moving fast enough in times that are so parlous as these. Therefore, I have been endeavoring to inspire both officials and citizens to meet the conditions that are now arising throughout the world and to take advantage of the great opportunities that now exist to effect complete transformation in our own country.

Lest foreign readers should misinterpret the situation in China, I think it advisable to say something of the progress that has been made, particularly during the past three years of resistance against Japanese aggression.

The fact that we have been able to sustain ourselves so long and so well in battle against a believed "invincible" military power of the first rank is a test of the qualities inherent in our race. Those qualities are capable of great development, and that is what I work and hope for by the forthright exposure of weaknesses that have become, in the past, accepted as national characteristics.

To illustrate the progress that has been effected in various directions, I have asked certain responsible officials to prepare special up-to-date statements showing how reforms are being inaugurated, and how various departments of the government have been able to meet the national calamity which has overtaken us, and which has now spread with such terrible consequences to Europe. These statements constitute Part II of this book and deal with national reconstruction in its several phases.

XI

HOLDING CHINA'S FINANCIAL FRONT*

THERE are two fronts in modern warfare; one is military and the other financial. Although armies, navies and air forces figure conspicuously in the public eye, yet the less spectacular weapons of warfare in the financial field are of equal importance in the conflict of modern nations. Especially in the case of a long-drawn-out conflict — which is a contest in the power of endurance — the prospects for ultimate victory depend on a nation's financial staying power as much as on its military prowess.

At the outbreak of the present hostilities in the Far East, Japan's military chieftains boldly predicted that China could be "beaten to her knees" within three months, while its financial strategists wishfully foretold that China's war finance would collapse within a year. Even some neutral observers entertained serious doubts as to the financial power of China's resistance for any length of time.

WARTIME PROBLEMS AND DIFFICULTIES

Admittedly, the problems and difficulties confronting

* By Dr. H. H. Kung, Vice President of the Executive Yuan and concurrently Minister of Finance.

[73]

China's wartime finance are as enormous as they are numerous. Immediate ways and means have to be found for meeting a war budget several times larger than peacetime expenditures. Heavy outlays are required for war-relief purposes arising from the enormous destruction of life and property both in the front and in the rear. Still greater funds have to be provided for accelerating various reconstruction projects essential to national defense and rehabilitation. Strenuous efforts have to be made for mobilizing and co-ordinating the nation's financial and economic resources and for overcoming the wartime difficulties hampering the normal development of trade, industry, mining, agriculture and communications. Sound measures have to be adopted for maintaining the stability of the nation's currency and credit structure, especially in face of the enemy's sinister plots to undermine it.

At the same time, China's public finances have suffered severely from the seizure and destruction of its revenue sources by the invading forces. New taxation could not be expected to replace these losses at once; not only because Japan has occupied so many important cities but also because China has not yet developed a relatively productive system of direct taxation. Elasticity of tax yield is difficult to obtain even under normal conditions, and especially when indirect taxes form the main source of revenue. Besides, due to China's low per capita wealth, the people's taxpaying capacity could not be increased

[74]

overnight to meet the country's urgent great needs. Finally, lack of full jurisdiction over foreigners both throughout the country and in the foreign concessions and settlements has added to China's difficulties in enforcing rigid measures of financial control such as adopted by other countries at war.

China's Surprising Achievement

Without doubt, defense of China's financial front against Japan's aggression has been no simple or easy task. The fact is all the more gratifying therefore that the government has so conducted its financial administration that today, after three full years of strenuous operations on all fronts, China is still holding its own financially as well as militarily, while facts indicate that its continued ability to endure the strains of a protracted war is greater than its enemy has estimated. Such an accomplishment, indeed, has been a surprise to China's foes and friends alike. But it cannot have been an accident. Rather it is due to the strong foundation of China's financial front laid before the war, as well as the strengthening of that important structure since hostilities began.

Building the Financial Front

Under the old Manchu dynasty, China had no modern fiscal system to speak of. The successive Peking regimes that followed the establishment of the Chinese Republic in 1911 were ineffective and were unable even to finance the minimum services of the State. Following its inauguration at Nanking in 1928, the National Government had to face various internal problems, and though a good start was made, financial progress was not as fast as hoped. During the four years immediately preceding the outbreak of the Sino-Japanese hostilities in July, 1937, however, China underwent a financial and economic transformation with few parallels in history.

When I was called upon to assume charge of China's financial administration in the fall of 1933, I immediately saw the necessity of developing an adequate fiscal system in order to provide the essential services of the State and to ameliorate the economic life of the people. It was obvious that to improve the revenue receipts of the government, it was necessary first of all to increase the people's productive power and to modernize the system of financial administration. To attain this object, the government must remove the hindrances to trade and industry, rehabilitate rural economy, simplify the machinery of revenue collection and provide the country with an adequate banking and currency system. But development of revenue sources must be accompanied by the rational adjustment of State expenditures so as to attain the desirable state of budgetary equilibrium. Moreover, to attract capital for various reconstruction projects, the credit structure of the country must be rehabilitated and strengthened both at home and abroad. To these basic tasks I set myself resolutely.

REFORM OF TAXATION

Space permits only a passing reference to the reform of the taxation system before the war, such as adjustments made in the administration of the customs, salt, consolidated taxes and other internal taxes, and the institution of the income tax as an experiment in direct taxation. Suffice it to say that important measures were enforced with the view to the adjustment of tax rates, simplification of tax procedure, opening up of revenue sources, increase of administrative efficiency and centralization of fiscal control.

ABOLITION OF MISCELLANEOUS LOCAL LEVIES

Illustrative of the financial authorities' anxiety to remove the past hindrances to trade and industry was the abolition of miscellaneous, exorbitant local taxes. In the summer of 1934, a National Financial Conference was called for the adjustment of local finances. As the result of measures adopted, more than 7,100 items of such harmful levies, representing an annual revenue of nearly 70 million dollars were abolished; while abolition and reduction of more than 300 items of local farm surtaxes amounted to nearly 39 million dollars a year. The enforcement of these local tax reforms was made possible

[77]

through the Central Government granting subsidies to the local governments.

DEVELOPMENT OF REVENUE SOURCES

As a result of the persistent efforts of the Ministry of Finance in opening up revenue sources and reorganizing taxes, receipts from the customs, salt and consolidated taxes improved considerably. Compared with 369 million dollars in 1929, the total of these three taxes increased to 763 million dollars in the twenty-fifth fiscal year (1936-37); in other words, more than doubled in the space of seven years. The following table illustrates the recent growth of revenues (figures in millions of dollars):

Year ending June 30	Customs	Salt	Consolidated Taxes	Other Taxes	Total Tax Receipts	Total Revenue	Increase over preceding year
1933	325	158	80	23	586	614	—
1934	352	177	105	25	659	706	92
1935	353	167	105	24	649	780	74
1936	272	184	135	32	623	808	28
1937	401	203	159	33	796	889	81

ADJUSTMENT OF PUBLIC EXPENDITURES

While seeking to develop revenue sources, the financial authorities paid equal attention to the rational adjustment of public expenditures by curtailing the unnecessary ex-

[78]

penses and increasing the essential outlays. Between the fiscal years ended June, 1933 and 1937, expenditures of the National Treasury steadily mounted from 705 million dollars to 1,180 million. Nevertheless, despite unusual difficulties the government devoted substantially increased funds for the promotion of education and culture, economic reconstruction, and subsidies to local governments for various constructive purposes. Whereas the total expenditures of these three items amounted to only 97 million dollars in the year ended June, 1934, it was increased to 201 million, 270 million and 238 million respectively in the three fiscal years that followed. In the budget for the fiscal year 1937-38, special attention was paid to the acceleration of reconstruction projects by setting aside a special fund of 400 million dollars for launching a five-year economic development program. That was a significant part of China's financial policy and was closely related to the future of the nation's finance. Moreover, although deficits obtained during all the years, the government was able to keep them within manageable limits and to avoid impairing the long-run prospects of China's finances. In fact, in the year 1936-37, substantial budgetary equilibrium was attained.

ENFORCEMENT OF BUDGETARY CONTROL

Indicative of the progress made in recent years toward effective fiscal control was the institution of the Comptroller-General's Office which operates the budgetary system. All budgetary estimates of the various grades of government have to be submitted to the Comptroller-General's Office for examination before they are referred to the Legislative Yuan for adoption. The accountants of the various government offices are directly appointed by the Comptroller-General's Office, while the function of auditing government accounts is vested in the hands of the Ministry of Audits. In this manner government appropriations and disbursements are regularized and controlled so as to conform to the general financial policy of the government. The institution of the budgetary system represents a distinct improvement in the conduct of China's financial affairs and testifies to the painstaking and progressive efforts made during recent years toward unifying and systematizing the methods of government accounting throughout the country.

CONSOLIDATION OF INTERNAL DEBT STRUCTURE

An important cornerstone of China's war finance which was laid before the war is the consolidation of its internal debt structure. During the years under review, loans were issued only on adequate securities while debt services were meticulously met. In February, 1936, a scheme of loan consolidation was placed in effect, whereby five series of consolidated bonds totaling 1,460 million dollars were substituted in place of 33 former issues with the period of principal payments considerably extended. The operation of this scheme reduced the internal debt charges by about 85 million dollars yearly. Undoubtedly, the solid basis of the internal debt structure and the confidence it has inspired among the people is largely responsible for the singular success with which the government has floated enormous amounts of internal loans to replenish the war chest during the past three years.

REHABILITATION OF NATIONAL CREDIT

No better evidence of the National Government's honorable record could be furnished than its conscientious and courageous efforts in recent years to settle the mess of defaulted debts inherited from the former Peking regime. When I took over the financial reins of the country in 1933, I made it a primary object to settle these debts in arrears so as to rehabilitate China's credit. After unsuccessful efforts at a general settlement with all creditors, a program of piecemeal negotiations was undertaken. By mid-1937 the National Government had negotiated the settlement of a total of about 850 million dollars, or roughly two thirds of claims arising from loans, including notably the Tientsin-Pukow, Lunghai, Hukuang, Honan, Peiping-Hankow, Canton-Kowloon, Nanchang-Kiukiang, and Peiping-Suiyuan Railway loans, the Vickers-Marconi loans, the Chicago Bank loan and the Pacific Development Corporation loan.

These settlements, in conjunction with the other financial policies of the National Government, strengthened confidence in China's credit so much that, during my visit to Europe and America in the spring and summer of 1937, I was able to conclude a number of new credit arrangements abroad, some of which concluded even after the outbreak of hostilities. These and the more recent credits extended to China by various countries bear eloquent testimony to confidence abroad in China's financial integrity and stability.

STRENGTHENING OF BANKING STRUCTURE

Greatly contributing to the solidifying of China's financial front was the strengthening of China's banking structure during the years immediately preceding the hostilities. In my concurrent position as the Governor of the Central Bank of China, it has been my object to make this institution a veritable tower of strength to the national economy. In 1934 the bank's capital, appropriated by the government, was increased from 20 million dollars to 100 million. In the summer of 1937, the government was about to place into effect a plan for reorganizing the Central Bank as the Central Reserve Bank, so as to put it on a more independent basis and make it more truly a bank of banks, when unfortunately hostilities broke out.

In 1935, as a further measure of strengthening the banks, the government subscribed additional funds to the capital of the Bank of China and the Bank of Communications, substantially increasing the capital of both banks. Also, measures were adopted to improve the system of provincial and local banks and to strengthen government supervision over the commercial, savings and other private banks. For the specific purpose of assisting the rehabilitation of rural economy, the government appropriated substantial funds for creating the Farmers' Bank of China and the Agricultural Credit Bureau. Meanwhile, the development of modern-styled banks, particularly at Shanghai, displayed remarkable progress. As a fruit of this banking progress, confidence in the strength of the banking structure was greatly enhanced; bank deposits increased rapidly, enabling the banks to extend loans to needy industry and agriculture at lower rates of interest.

Without doubt, the foundation thus laid in organizing support through the strengthening and co-operation of banks has proved to be an invaluable wartime asset in enabling the government to further consolidate and co-ordinate the resources and facilities of the nation's banking structure, so as to cope with the monetary vicissitudes and needs of the present hostilities.

REFORM OF CURRENCY

The development of a sound and uniform currency system was long the objective of China's monetary policy. In 1929 the Kemmerer Commission of Financial Experts candidly reported that "China has unquestionably the worst currency to be found in any important country of the world." The abolition in 1933 of the *tael* as a standard of value established the standard dollar system throughout the greater part of China. But there remained to be solved the highly difficult problem of the silver standard.

Unquestionably, the most important foundation of China's financial front is the adoption of a managed currency by the Currency Decree of November, 1935. The reform provided for the adoption of an exchange standard which might indeed be called "credit" standard. Exchange was stabilized at about the level then existing, to be maintained by means of exchange operations of the government banks. Silver was nationalized and a fiduciary currency substituted, making notes of the government banks full legal tender. Bank-note issue was unified and currency reserves centralized under the control of a Currency Reserve Board. The Central Bank of China was to be reorganized as the Central Reserve Bank, and the commercial banking system was to be strengthened. Meanwhile, a decimal system of subsidiary coins was introduced, supplanting the old heterogeneous coins.

The helpful action of both the American and British Governments in facilitating this monetary reform should be recalled with appreciation. The British Government issued an Order-in-Council prohibiting British subjects in

China from making payments in silver. Particularly helpful was the purchase by the American Treasury of a substantial amount of Chinese silver. This and subsequent purchases have been a great aid to China in carrying out the scheme and in maintaining the exchange value of its currency both before and during the hostilities.

FAR-REACHING SIGNIFICANCE OF NEW MONETARY POLICY

Thus, in a brief time, as if by a miracle, China acquired the essential elements of a modern currency system, to the great benefit of Chinese and foreign businessmen alike. The new monetary policy produced a marked improvement in China's financial and economic situation. Its successful management inspired confidence both at home and abroad.

But this was not all. China made other material gains. The smooth transition from a metallic to a fiduciary currency made it possible to expand China's currency and credit when required by an emergency. The heavy outlays demanded by the present hostilities could not have been financed on a hard money basis; and under the conditions as they existed, a transition from the silver standard to an exchange standard could scarcely have been made without a serious shock to confidence. All these prewar developments provided effective resources and financial

[85]

machinery without which China's stubborn resistance to Japan's invasion would not have been possible.

STRENGTHENING THE FINANCIAL FRONT

Obviously, the primary problem of China's wartime finance is to raise funds to provide the sinews of war as well as to meet the demands of war relief and accelerate various projects essential to national defense and reconstruction. It has been said by Napoleon that the essential conditions of winning a war are "first, money; second, money; and third, money." Owing to the serious impairment of revenue receipts and unprecedented increase of military expenditures, China's wartime budgetary difficulties cannot be overestimated.

METHODS OF WAR FINANCING

There are as a rule four principal methods of war financing; namely, voluntary contributions, increased taxation, loan flotation and note-issue expansion — aside from those of requisition, mobilization of war fund reserve and conversion of State properties. Although China, like any country at war, has resorted to these usual means, the fundamental feature of its financial policy should be noted. Study of wartime financial policies of different countries shows that, with divergent backgrounds and objectives, they may be divided into two main groups: (1) countries with limited natural resources usually rely on reckless expedients to finance their military needs with the view to attaining quick decisive victory; and (2) countries with rich resources generally prefer cautious conservative methods of war financing with the minimum danger to national recovery in order to achieve ultimate victory after a protracted struggle.

In the present hostilities, China and Japan are poles apart in both their military strategy and financial policies. Being primarily an agricultural nation with abundant hidden wealth, China's economic structure in protracted hostilities is more conducive to the conservative policy of military and financial resistance, and the chances of its ultimate victory depend mainly upon playing for time and on the co-ordinated development of personal and national productive power. For China, this is the logical wartime policy from the standpoints of both military strategy and financial power.

PEOPLE'S PATRIOTIC CONTRIBUTIONS

A noteworthy fact in connection with China's war financing is the patriotic support of its people. The whole nation has responded readily to the government's call for needed funds and war relief materials. The loyalty and generosity of China's sons and daughters abroad are particularly praiseworthy. They have contributed hundreds of millions of dollars to the National Treasury, subscribed enthusiastically to the National War Bonds and invested considerable sums for the wartime development of mining and industries in China's hinterland. Moreover, their remittances home — increased from 300 million dollars annually in the prewar years to 600 million dollars since the hostilities — have been a helpful factor in reducing China's adverse balance of international payments.

Taxation Adjustments

The low per capita wealth of the Chinese people, coupled with the already heavy hardships brought upon them by the war's ravages, the government's lack of an adequate system of direct taxation, and the enemy's occupation of many important cities, has precluded any large reliance on increase of taxation as an effective means of raising war funds. Keeping in mind the necessity of conserving the people's economic strength, the government has so formulated its wartime taxation policy so as not to add undue hardship to the people's burden. Aside from the institution of the excess income (or war profit) tax and the inheritance tax, which are universally regarded as sound taxes, the government has made various taxation adjustments that are calculated to reduce the people's burden, particularly of those living in or adjacent to the wartorn areas, to encourage export trade, to assist industrial production and to promote thrift and economy.

Introduction of Public Treasury System

In connection with the reorganization of the nation's

fiscal system, the introduction of the Public Treasury System on October 1, 1939, is a distinct wartime improvement. The new system, which replaces the traditional decentralized system of handling public funds by various government offices, has the advantage of centralizing the receipts and disbursements of public funds, and at the same time, of separating the two functions. It will necessarily result in a closer co-operation of the nation's political and financial powers.

Issue of War Loans

Fiscal theory recommends that extraordinary wartime needs be financed largely out of revenue; nevertheless, experience has shown that where this is impossible the emergency can be met for a considerable period by relying largely upon borrowings. During the last World War, for instance, the United States contemplated the raising of war funds by increasing taxes and issuing bonds in equal amounts, but the proceeds of taxation amounted to less than 30 per cent of the total war expenditures. British war finance was singularly sound and stable, its system of direct taxation proving highly elastic and productive, and yet the total amount of its tax receipts occupied only about 17 per cent of its war budget. Since the outbreak of the present hostilities, China has had to depend upon continued borrowing to meet 70 percent of its war budget. Thanks to the people's patriotic support, and the banks' loyal co-operation, the government has been able to carry out the borrowing program smoothly and, up to the end of 1939, has authorized internal loan issues equivalent to the total of 2,780 million dollars.

COMPARISON WITH JAPAN

During the same period, loans issued in Japan amounted to about 12,600 million yen. In other words, Japan's new debt due to the "China Incident" is about five times as large as China's (at official rates of exchange), and the per capita debt is increased by about 6 dollars in China and 180 yen in Japan, the ratio being 1 to 30. Comparing the total national indebtedness of the two countries outstanding at the end of 1939, the figures would be roughly 7,280 million dollars for China and 23,600 million yen for Japan. That is to say, Japan's present national debt is more than three times China's burden, while the present per capita debt is about 16 dollars in China and 340 yen in Japan, the former being only about 1/21 of the latter. During 1940, new bond issues are expected to reach considerable figures in both countries. Although admittedly the per capita wealth is much lower in China than in Japan, yet in this race of mounting national indebtedness Japan may be expected to reach the end of its tether sooner than China will.

FOREIGN CONFIDENCE AND FINANCIAL ASSISTANCE

Appreciation must be recorded of the friendly assistance which different countries have extended to China in the form of credits during the present hostilities. These include the Wood Oil loan and Commodity Credit extended by America; the Export Guarantee Credit and Currency Stabilization Fund Credit extended by Great Britain; the Nan-Cheng Railway loan extended by France; the Barter Trade Credits of considerably larger amounts extended by Soviet Russia, and fairly huge amounts of private credits for purchases of materials in different countries. The extension of these credit arrangements, though mostly made on the basis of barter of goods, has been helpful in the stabilization of China's war finance while at the same time beneficial to the economies of the lending countries themselves. It bespeaks confidence in China's financial future and presents a striking contrast to the fact that in the world's financial capitals the doors of borrowing are closed to Japan.

WARTIME DEBT SERVICE

Outstanding in China's wartime financial record is the government's scrupulous anxiety to live up to its obligations. China's determination to uphold its credit has been such that for well over a year following the outbreak of the present hostilities, it continued to meet its debt service fully and regularly. Maintenance of debt service, in spite of the enormous urgent demands on the National Treasury, and enforced readjustment of the country's financial

[91]

and economic life as a result of the hostilities, explains why China's credit in both foreign and domestic markets has remained intact. That it imposed great hardships on the government and people to keep on paying could not be doubted. But without seizing upon some pretext for declaring a general moratorium, China girded its financial loins and paid.

CHINA'S PERFORMANCE VS. JAPAN'S INTERFERENCE

For the first twenty-one months of the war (July, 1937-March, 1939) China paid out not less than 530 million dollars for the services of external and internal obligations. This performance is all the more gratifying in view of the Japanese interference with the lion's share of the customs and salt revenues — the two principal securities of China's obligations. Between July, 1937, and December, 1938, the government advanced for the service of customs-secured obligations alone a total of 175 million dollars from other sources in order to make up for the revenues that should have been remitted from areas under Japanese occupation.

In the meantime, services of obligations contracted during the war have all been met fully and promptly. During the two and a half years from the outbreak of hostilities to the end of 1939, total disbursements for debt services amounted to 714 million dollars, of which 229 million was for payment of external obligations and

[92]

485 million for that of internal obligations. The fact must be recorded, on the other hand, that in respect of the customs alone, revenues forcibly detained by the Japanese in the areas under their occupation had accumulated to the extent of more than 380 million dollars by the end of 1939. China's wartime accomplishment in fulfilling its obligations, in contrast to Japan's highhanded interference with that honorable performance, is a record which China's creditors may not soon forget.

RELUCTANT SUSPENSION OF CUSTOMS AND SALT DEBT SERVICES

As a result of Japanese occupation of important salt-producing areas and routes of communication, and the seizure of salt revenue offices, particularly in Hopei and Shantung, China felt compelled in September, 1938, to suspend temporarily the amortization payments then due on the Crisp and Anglo-French loans, interest payments continuing to be met. Subsequently, in view of the forcible detention by the Japanese of the customs revenue in the war areas despite their assurances, and despite all efforts to induce them to allow remittances in respect of all China's obligations that were secured thereon at the time of the outbreak of hostilities, the Chinese Government was forced to the conclusion that the situation had become too anomalous to be continued and very reluctantly took remedial action on January 15,

1939. As from that date, the Ministry of Finance declined to make further advances to the Inspector-General of Customs, and instructed him to open special accounts in the Central Bank of China in which periodically are deposited a share of the long-term debt service proportionate to the collections in areas not subject to Japanese interference. For similar reasons, the government on March 26, 1939, took action in relation to the salt loans similar to the arrangements concerning the customs loans. It is gratifying to note that these temporary measures, adopted by force of circumstances, have been received with sympathy and understanding in the financial markets.

WARTIME CURRENCY

A most significant factor in the successful management of China's war finance, likewise of importance to foreign business interests, is the maintenance of exchange. Like any country at war, China has had to meet certain currency difficulties that are the necessary adjuncts of warfare, and has found it necessary to enforce certain measures of exchange control to permit adjustment to economic and trade conditions. Because of the existence of extra-territoriality and of foreign settlements and concessions, and in view of the extent of the areas affected by Japanese interference, particularly in Shanghai, which is China's commercial and financial center, the Chinese Government has found it difficult to enforce rigid measures of financial control such as other countries have adopted.

SUCCESSFUL MONETARY MANAGEMENT

Nevertheless, thanks to the strong foundation laid in the Currency Reform of November, 1935, and to appropriate wartime management, China has been able to maintain the exchange stability of its currency to a degree generally regarded as remarkable. The people's sustained confidence in the national currency has enabled the government to combat with notable success the Japanese sinister schemes to undermine it. During the first eight months of the hostilities, Chinese Government banks freely bought and sold exchange at the official rates. Although since then the government has been obliged to modify the procedure of exchange operations and to allow downward adjustment of exchange from time to time to a more reasonable level according to the needs of the national economy, yet it has persistently and consistently adhered to its declared policy of maintaining the national currency.

Throughout the period of hostilities, China has maintained both in "occupied" and unoccupied areas an acceptable medium of exchange which has consistently been demanded by the people in preference to the issues the Japanese and their puppets have attempted to circulate at the point of bayonets, and which has the distinct advantage of free convertibility into foreign currency. Although during the past year there were marked changes in the value of the national currency in the foreign exchange market, the fluctuations were due largely to speculation, and the government has continued to make exchange available to legitimate business requirements. The existence of the so-called "black market" in financial centers is not an uncommon phenomenon in countries subject to rigid exchange control, even in peacetime.

INCREASED CIRCULATION OF CURRENCY

There has been some misapprehension concerning the increase of note issue and its bearing on the position of the currency. Indeed, the volume of currency in circulation has expanded considerably since the opening of hostilities, from 1,444 million dollars in July, 1937, to 1,727 million a year later, to 2,627 million two years later, and again to 3,082 million at the end of 1939. Superficially, such a large increase might easily be mistaken as an evidence of serious currency inflation, but a closer analysis would suggest that the increase in note issue has been brought about more by economic reasons than by fiscal necessities. Even before the war, China's note issue was not sufficient to meet the needs of the entire country. As a consequence of hostilities, increased hoarding and holding of cash balances by the public to meet emergency requirements have entailed a larger volume of currency. Extended circulation of the national currency in areas formerly served by their respective local currencies, notably in the provinces of Yunnan, Szechuan, Kwangsi and Sikong, as well as in Sinkiang, has likewise resulted in a larger circulation. Moreover, circulation of the national currency has continued even in the areas occupied by the Japanese, especially in Central China, in the foreign-controlled areas in Shanghai and Tientsin, and in the territories where the Chinese guerrillas are active. Where the Japanese control is really effective, the legal tender notes, being prohibited from circulation, are in effect immobilized and not in active circulation at all. Besides, there has been large export of notes, either on government or private account. Insofar as these notes are exported, and particularly when they are kept in the vaults, they amount in effect to hoarding because they are no longer in active circulation. Rapidly increasing activities in connection with the economic reconstruction of the interior, such as the building of railways and roads, and the development of mines and manufactures, also require a larger amount of currency for pay rolls and retail transactions. Finally, increases in the level of prices have in themselves required a larger volume of hand-to-hand currency.

AVOIDANCE OF RECKLESS FINANCE

Whatever the increase in note issue may be, it is im-

[97]

portant to note that, fundamentally speaking, whether or not there is an excessive issue depends not on statistical figures but on the saturation point at which national currency requirements are adequately provided. Judging from this viewpoint, the present total volume of China's note issue cannot be said to have passed the point of saturation. Far from having plunged the country into the abyss of reckless inflation, the government has resolutely refused to imitate other countries in tampering with the issue of bank notes in wartime.

All in all, the surprise of the last three years' management is not that China's currency has been subjected to severe tests but that it has withstood so well the enormous strains imposed upon it by the hostilities and enemy's onslaught. Little wonder that such a showing has inspired confidence both at home and abroad in China's financial outlook.

FEVERISH ECONOMIC DEVELOPMENT OF THE HINTERLAND

Along with the successful management of China's wartime finance and currency, foreign friends should be interested to note the intensive economic development that is forging ahead in China's vast hinterland despite, or rather because of, the war. Remarkable progress has been made in removing factories and plants from the coastal cities to the interior, in establishing essential industries in the rear, in rehabilitating rural economy, in developing agricultural exports, in readjusting trade, in opening up natural resources and in improving means of communications. All these efforts, coupled with China's abundance of man power and natural resources, as well as successive excellent crops, which truly are God-sent assistance, have enabled the government to erect in China's vast hinterland — the Northwest and Southwest — a strong base for national resistance and reconstruction, and to adopt a policy of playing for time. The significant progress, moreover, is an undertaking in modernization, the economic possibilities of which are of immense importance to foreign and Chinese interests alike.

INTERNATIONAL DEVELOPMENT OF CHINA

In carrying out this vast program of economic development simultaneously with armed resistance, the Chinese Government continues to welcome the financial and technical assistance of friendly powers. The principle of "International Development of China," so wisely laid down by the Father of the Chinese Republic, the late Dr. Sun Yat-sen, remains and will remain the watchword of China's policy of national reconstruction. China appreciates foreign co-operation not only in maintaining its financial stability in wartime, but even more in tackling the still greater problems of economic rehabilitation that will follow in the wake of the present hostilities.

[99]

CHINA SHALL RISE AGAIN

At the outbreak of the Sino-Japanese hostilities in July, 1937, China under the National Government was continuing unprecedented achievements in its financial and economic development. It was my singular privilege and fortune to associate myself with this significant movement, under the leadership of Generalissimo Chiang Kai-shek, and with the support of the nation. The rapid progress achieved was yielding great benefits both to the Chinese nation and to foreign countries having friendly relations with it. Besides, China was fast becoming an important stabilizing factor in the international situation. Obviously it was because China's modern development was growing so rapidly that the Japanese militarists launched their brutal invasion. Undeniably the war has been a severe strain on China's economy, but in the madness of the Japanese aggression even the important interests of Western powers have been trampled upon with impunity. The interruption of China's progress is undoubtedly one of the greatest tragedies of history. Japan's slogan of creating a "New Order in East Asia" is but a camouflage for its twofold object of dominating China in its own interest and of expelling the interest and influence of Western powers from the Far East. But, thanks to the strong financial foundation laid during the few years preceding the hostilities and to the successful management of its wartime finance and currency, China has been able to main-

[100]

tain a financial front stronger and more durable than its enemy had conjectured. Committed to its dual policy of armed resistance and national reconstruction, China is confident of its ultimate victory.

CHINA'S FUTURE AND THE WORLD

In this great conflict, China is fighting not only to defend its own freedom and independence against the forces of aggression and lawlessness but also to establish conditions that will enable it to develop its vast economic possibilities for the prosperity and happiness of the world as a whole. The vital interests and security of the free nations of the world are intimately bound up with China's present struggle. Japan is now eager to end the "China Incident," but there can be no end to the fight until the Japanese troops are withdrawn from the Chinese territory. In the past, material assistance from friendly powers has been of great value to China in maintaining its economic and financial structure. Assuredly it is in the interests of China's friends that there be further strengthening of China's financial as well as military front.

XII

*CHINA'S STRATEGY IN THE WAR**

Japan's failure versus China's success in strategy during the first stage of the war from July 7, 1937, to the conclusion of the Wuhan (Wuchang-Hankow-Hanyang) battle in the winter of 1938.

The strategy decided upon by the Japanese Army at the time of the Lukouchiao outrage was to win a quick, decisive war, to be followed by the immediate conclusion of a dictated peace. The reasons are obvious. Japan is small in population and her material resources are limited.

Although preparations for this invasion had been made over a period of tens of years, Japanese militarists realized that in fighting a nation of China's size in territory and population, which enjoyed internal solidarity, they could maintain a relatively superior position only for a short period of time and over a small area. Once they exceeded these limitations, the situation would turn against them. Consequently, immediately after the hostilities broke out, the Japanese attempted to destroy the Chinese field forces and China's will to resist, in a lightning campaign.

* By General Ho Ying-chin, Minister of War

Their scheme was to force peace on China after one or at most several major engagements. They wanted to be spared the ordeal of prolonged warfare, which would shake Japan to its foundations. Such a Japanese "peace," being insincere, naturally could not last long. In reality, they planned to divide the entire course of war into a number of phases so that in the interim both their troops and people could rest and recuperate. Meanwhile, they would tighten their control in the "occupied" areas and seize more Chinese property and interests. Then, as soon as they had sufficiently recovered from the earlier losses, they would proceed to the next phase.

The Chinese faced an initial disadvantage because they had to begin their resistance before the preliminary preparations in their national defenses were completed. Furthermore, owing to the lack of adequate means of transport, it was not easy for large numbers of Chinese troops in the interior provinces to be concentrated at the fronts. It was, therefore, immediately realized that in the beginning the Chinese must fight against great odds; that places along the coast and rivers could not very well be defended; that inevitably the northern provinces would be invaded, and that it would be physically impossible for the Chinese to crush the better-equipped Japanese forces at places where the latter had convenient supply lines.

It soon became clear that it would be best for the Chinese to keep their military strength intact, while prolonging the war until a decisive battle could be fought in the hinterland. Hence the Chinese counter-strategy throughout the first stage of the hostilities was to fight according to the rules of a war of attrition. The purpose was to prevent the Japanese from winning a decisive battle and to frustrate their plan for a short war. At the same time, the national policy of "fight to the finish" was proclaimed as China's determined answer to the Japanese dream of concluding peace at an early date.

Altogether three major battles were fought during the first stage, in addition to 277 minor engagements. At the end of each of these battles, when the strength of the Japanese troops had been worn down as much as expected, the Chinese forces deliberately withdrew to avoid a final struggle. The purpose was to make it impossible for the Japanese troops — even with their superiority in numbers, equipment, and mobility — to annihilate the Chinese field forces and to confine them to a few places, despite the unusually high price they had paid.

Meanwhile, the Chinese troops made good use of their vast territory to keep the Japanese strength divided. They also took advantage of the difficult means of communications in the interior to checkmate the movement of the Japanese troops. The Chinese objective was to gain time by yielding space in order to strengthen the army and to prepare it for the second stage.

CHINA'S STRATEGY IN THE WAR

When the first stage (up to the withdrawal from Hankow) came to an end, the Chinese Army had not only succeeded in evading destruction, but had improved their tactics through experience. Simultaneously, the Chinese had had ample time to gather strength by increasing the number of fighting units and improving their organization and equipment. The determination of the Chinese forces and civilians to continue resistance became stronger, and their faith in ultimate victory became firmer. As a result, the Japanese had to admit that their strategy had been a complete failure, and they also began to give lip service to "prolonged warfare." Herein lies the foundation for China's ultimate victory.

Changes in strategy by China and Japan during the second stage of the war which began at the end of the Wuhan battle and was still unfinished up to July 7, 1940

At the commencement of the second stage of war, the Japanese military realized that the future of their war of aggression was beset with difficulties and that no prompt conclusion of the hostilities was in sight; that, instead, the war would be a protracted one, and that it would end in their own defeat. Yet they could not extricate themselves. Finally, they had to reshape their strategy into one of "feeding the war with war spoils." Thus they hastened to create puppet regimes, hoping such traitors as they could find could hold the "occupied" areas for them, thereby relieving them of the necessity of keeping a large garrison force behind the front. Meanwhile, they intensified their seizures of all Chinese human and material resources within reach to replenish their mounting military and financial losses.

Another phase of their changed strategy was to launch offensives on limited fronts; to cause disturbances along the coast, and to seek the closure of China's international routes. Tactics such as these show that the Japanese have been compelled to adopt a passive plan.

Chinese strategy in the present stage, designed to set at naught the Japanese plan, has demonstrated a greater initiative. The policy of "fighting to the finish" remains unchanged. Furthermore, an "all-front resistance" has been launched to accelerate the Japanese exhaustion by different forms of warfare. At the same time, all available human and material resources of the nation are being mobilized to build a stronger Chinese Army.

Owing to inadequate defenses along the coast, the Chinese tactics in dealing with Japanese troops who landed from warships, are to delay their progress as long as possible and then draw them inland before lashing out at them in fierce counterattacks. Japanese troops in central and north China provinces who have penetrated inland have been divided into many isolated units. The Chinese tactics are to block them from advancing any farther, and to deliver incessant onslaughts against them. On several occasions, full advantage has been taken of enemy pushes to launch fierce counterattacks against widespread Japanese units.

Furthermore, the "occupied" areas were divided into many war zones, into which large numbers of Chinese regular troops were sent to harass the Japanese, thereby keeping the Japanese garrisons busy, and immobilizing them for service at the front where they were needed most. To make the situation worse for the Japanese, Chinese masses behind the enemy lines have been aroused against the invaders. They not only refuse to have anything to do with the Japanese or their puppets in political, economic and cultural affairs, but those in possession of firearms have risen to engage the Japanese in extensive guerrilla warfare, in collaboration with Chinese regular soldiers. They are continually carrying on lightning raids on Japanese garrisons, cutting their lines of communication, setting fire to their military stores, all with a view to increasing their difficulties in obtaining supplies from their bases. These harassing activities, being incessantly kept up over wide areas, have had the effect of reducing the strength, and shattering the morale, of the enemy. From time to time, Chinese soldiers return to the rear for reorganization. Meanwhile an entirely new army is being trained for future counteroffensives.

Another encouraging fact is that the Chinese civilians in places away from the fronts all work hard and contribute their share toward the building up of new strength by producing more food and other supplies for the use of the army. Consequently, there is no longer any line of demarcation between Chinese troops and civilians at the front, in the occupied areas or in the rear. One and all, they are engaged in different phases of China's all-front resistance.

From January, 1939, to May, 1940, six major battles were fought: near Nanchang; in the Suihsien-Tsaoyang area in Hupeh; in northern Hunan; in northern Kwangtung; in southern Kwangsi; and east of the Han River in Hupeh. In addition, there were 194 other important engagements, and 6,718 others on a smaller scale. If the 5,009 guerrilla onslaughts are included, the total number of battles, large and small, will reach the amazing total of 11,927. With regard to the six major campaigns, the Japanese were successful only in the battle of Nanchang, while in the remaining five they met with great reverses. Then in every one of the 11,921 comparatively minor engagements, the Chinese succeeded in inflicting heavy casualties on the Japanese.

The present stage is not only characterized by the large number of battles fought, but also by the fact that the sphere of hostilities covers the enemy front and flank, as well as their immediate and distant rear. The Japanese troops are subjected to attacks from all directions, and their plan to exploit the human and material resources in the "occupied" areas has been foiled. On the contrary, their attempt to retain control in the "occupied" areas has resulted in a steady drain on their military strength and a slump in their fighting caliber. They are war weary and demoralized by the protracted warfare.

The all-front Chinese resistance made possible by the close cooperation between the armed forces and civilians has put the Japanese on the defensive and confined their control in the "occupied" areas to mere points and lines. The Japanese troops, deprived of their freedom of action, have sunk inextricably into the Chinese quagmire. Although the second stage is as yet unfinished, it has already become clear that the new Japanese strategy of "feeding the war with war spoils" is again a failure. Equally clear is the fact that the longer the Chinese troops fight, the stronger they become.

Statistics showing the progress of the Japanese troops from the beginning of the war to the end of May, 1940.

The following tables demonstrate that the progress of the Japanese troops has been sharply reduced as the hostilities moved from one phase to another.

During the first stage of the war

Table 1

From the Lukouchiao Incident to the fall of Nanking:

Starting points	Positions reached	Distance
East Hopei	Paotow (Suiyuan)	620 km.
Armistice line	Pingyao (Shansi)	600 km.
. . . .	Anyang (Honan)	480 km.
. . . .	Lokou (Shantung)	440 km.
Woosung	Chuhsien (Anhwei)	360 km.
. . . . .	Wuhu (Anhwei)	400 km.
. . . . .	Fuyang (Chekiang)	185 km.

Table 2

From the fall of Nanking to the end of the Hsuchow battle:

Starting points	Positions reached	Distance
Pingyao (Shansi) . . .	Fenglintu (Shansi)	370 km.
Anyang (Honan)	Kaifeng (Honan)	170 km.
Tsinan (Shantung) . . .	Chuhsien (Anhwei)	560 km.

Table 3

From the fall of Hsuchow to the Wuhan battle:

Starting points	Positions reached	Distance
Hofei (Anhwei)	Sinyang (Honan)	300 km.
Anking (Anhwei) . . .	Tsaoshih (Hupeh)	475 km.
Wuhu (Anhwei) . . .	Yoyang (Hunan)	690 km.
Bias Bay (Kwangtung) .	Canton (Kwangtung)	200 km.

During the second stage of the war

Table 1

From the fall of Yoyang to the end of the south Kwangsi battle:

Starting points	Positions reached	Distance
Tsaoshih (Hupeh) . . .	Chunghsiang (Hupeh)	75 km.
Swatow (Kwangtung) . .	Chaochow (Kwangtung)	50 km.
Yunghsin (Kiangsi) . .	Siangfukwan (Kiangsi)	110 km.
Yamchow Bay (Kwangtung)	Nanning (Kwangsi)	150 km.
Hangchow (Chekiang) .	Hsiaoshan (Chekiang)	30 km.

Table 2

From the south Kwangsi battle to the end of May, 1940:

Starting points	Positions reached	Distance
Suihsien (Hupeh) . . .	Tsaoyang (Hupeh)	70 km.

The foregoing figures show that during the first stage of the war, the minimum advance accomplished by the Japanese troops covered a distance of 170 kilometers, and the maximum progress was 690 kilometers. During the second stage, however, the Japanese progress was reduced to 150 kilometers at most, while the shortest advance was only 50 kilometers. This is concrete proof of the declining strength of the Japanese Army.

Japanese casualties since the war began

Japan has only a small population. Herein lies her fundamental weakness, because man power is one of the basic requirements of military prowess. Whether or not the Japanese are capable of sustaining prolonged warfare may be seen from a study of Japanese casualties which, up to May 31, 1940, totaled more than 1,640,000.

Period	Front-line troops	Troops in rear
July 7, 1937, to December 31, 1937	256,200	
1938	444,890	
1939	409,795	
January 1, 1940, to May 31, 1940	194,103	340,000
Total	1,304,988	340,000
Grand total		1,644,988

Thus during the first stage from July 7, 1937, to the end of 1938, front-line Japanese effectives, both killed and wounded, totaled 701,090. During the second stage from January, 1939, to the end of May, 1940, front-line Japanese losses numbered 603,898. On the surface it seems that Japanese casualties, during the second stage, have been smaller than in the previous period. Actually, when these casualties are read together with the distances covered by the Japanese Army during the two stages, it instantly becomes clear that Japanese losses were proportionately heavier in the latter period. This is another proof of the sharp decline in Japanese fighting power. It also goes to show that Japan, in view of her small population, is not capable of standing a prolonged war.

Size of Japanese military reserves

The fighting unit in the Japanese Army is the division. In time of peace, Japan maintains a standing army of 17

[113]

divisions. In time of war, enough men in active service can be called up to fill 68 divisions for operations outside of Japan. Following the invasion of Manchuria in 1931, Japan secretly organized eight more divisions. As these are new units, the available reservists number 140,000 men. A part of the reservists have to be mobilized simultaneously with those in active service. As a result, these eight new divisions can be expanded to only 12 divisions. Thus, the grand total stands at 80 divisions. During the last three years, Japan has trained 700,000 new recruits, but they have been more than offset by their casualties which reached 1,644,988. Aside from the 52 divisions which have been mobilized, and those which have to be employed for other purposes, or are unavailable because of one reason or another, Japan's fighting operatives have been greatly reduced. In the future, the Japanese will have to fill their depleted ranks by resorting to the following methods:

(1) To call up the first class of militiamen, composed mostly of ex-soldiers too old for active service or dismissed replacements.

(2) To prolong the years of military service beyond the age of 40.

(3) To lower the age limit of servicemen from 20 to 19.

These younger men may make good soldiers but their number is limited. According to an investigation, the Japanese can muster only 400,000 youths nineteen years old. When those who have to be used as replacements are deducted, the rest will be barely enough to make ten more divisions. If Japan should actually mobilize this class of young men and throw them into the battlefield in China, it will not only jeopardize Japan's home defense but will also hasten the collapse of their invasion in China.

The Chinese Army today

When the hostilities first broke out, the numerical strength of the Chinese Army did not exceed 2,000,000. Since then, it has been increased to 5,000,000. This does not include replacements still held in readiness in the rear or new divisions under training.

Not mentioning the expansion of infantry, the Chinese cavalry force has been enlarged 150 per cent; independent artillery units by 80 per cent; artillery units attached to army corps and divisions by 340 per cent; anti-tank guns by 1,000 per cent, and anti-aircraft guns by 76 per cent. In addition, more tank units and other special troops have been increased.

With regard to China's munition industries, operations in plants removed from the occupied areas, have been in full swing, capable of making all types of light and heavy arms used by the infantry, and enough of them to free China of reliance on external supplies.

These are all tangible improvements. Such gains, as in the spirit to attack and the faith in the ultimate victory, though they cannot be expressed in figures, are none the less real. Meanwhile, the Chinese troops, partly through fighting and partly due to better military education, have demonstrated an all-round improvement in their tactics. In the early days of the war, the Chinese were proportionately less in number and lower in fighting caliber. After three years of struggle, though greater efforts are needed to improve their equipment, the Chinese have attained a position of absolute superiority over the Japanese in numerical strength.

Conclusion

It is clear that during the past three years important changes have occurred in the relative size and strength of the two opposing armies. The initiative, formerly in Japanese hands, has since passed into the hands of the Chinese. Despite their superiority in armaments, the Japanese have never been able to deliver a decisive blow to the Chinese. Owing to the yet inadequate number of airplanes, field pieces, tanks and other attacking weapons in their possession, the Chinese troops have often found it hard to annihilate all enemy units they attacked or besieged. However, the Chinese troops have their own ways of fighting and winning battles. Consequently the most these defects can do is to prolong the war, but they will not keep China from emerging victorious in the end.

XIII

CHINA'S FOREIGN RELATIONS DURING THE SINO-JAPANESE HOSTILITIES 1937-1940*

In this resumé of China's foreign relations during three years of resistance against Japanese aggression (from July, 1937 to July, 1940), only the main diplomatic questions are touched upon, while matters of relatively minor importance are omitted.

How the Conflict Was Started

The Lukouchiao (Marco Polo Bridge) Incident was only the spark and not the actual cause of the present conflict, as the Japanese militarists had long dreamed of carrying out their plan of continental expansion and ultimately of world conquest.

It will be recalled that the incident was precipitated during the course of a maneuver conducted without the slightest treaty basis by Japanese troops on Chinese territory about twenty miles west of Peiping at ten o'clock on the evening of July 7, 1937. Under the pretext of searching for one of their missing men, they demanded entry into the walled city of Wanping. When their un-

* By Dr. Wang Chung-hui, Minister of Foreign Affairs.

[118]

reasonable request was refused, they shelled the city with their artillery, and our troops had no alternative but to resist in self-defense.

On July 12th, the Chinese Government proposed the mutual withdrawal of troops to their original positions pending a final settlement of the incident. This offer was flatly rejected by the Japanese, who continued to pour in reinforcements, and by July 15th it was estimated that they had more than 20,000 troops and more than 100 planes concentrated in the Peiping-Tientsin area. The enemy's preconceived plan for the invasion was probably unintentionally revealed when a spokesman of the Japanese Kwantung Army stationed in Manchuria made the bellicose declaration: "We are prepared to resort to the most extreme measures if further provocation is given."

CHINA'S STAND

China's case was clearly presented in a memorandum delivered on July 16, 1937, to the governments of Great Britain, France, the United States, the Soviet Union, Italy, Germany, Belgium, the Netherlands and Portugal. The memorandum pointed out that each attempt to reach a peaceful settlement was nullified by a fresh Japanese attack; that the invasion constituted "a clear violation of China's sovereignty, contrary to the letter and spirit of the Nine Power Treaty, the Paris Peace Pact and the Covenant of the League of Nations"; and that nevertheless

[119]

China was prepared to effect a settlement of the dispute by pacific means.

Although it was quite clear by this time that Japan was bent on aggression, China was still doing her best to bring about an amicable settlement. Accordingly, an Aide Memoire was presented to the Japanese Embassy on July 19, 1937, reiterating the Chinese Government's "desire for a peaceful settlement of the Incident as well as its intention not to aggravate the situation. It is, therefore, proposed that the two parties jointly fix a definite date on which both sides shall simultaneously cease all military movements and withdraw their respective armed forces to the positions occupied prior to the Incident. . . . In short, the Chinese Government is ready to exhaust all pacific means for the maintenance of peace in Eastern Asia. Therefore, all methods provided by international law and treaties for the pacific settlement of international disputes — such as direct negotiation, good offices, mediation, arbitration, etc. — are equally acceptable to the Chinese Government."

On August 20, 1937, the Ministry of Foreign Affairs issued a statement from which the following passage may be quoted:

Japan's present action in China is a continuation of her aggressive program started in Manchuria in September, 1931. Japan has now occupied the Peiping and Tientsin area and is bent upon the extension of her occupation to the whole of north China and the domination of other regions, in spite of all her assurances that she has no territorial designs on this country. She is attempting to destroy all the work of reconstruction which the Chinese nation has so steadily and assiduously undertaken during the last ten years.

CHINA'S APPEAL TO THE LEAGUE OF NATIONS AND THE BRUSSELS CONFERENCE

The Japanese invasion of China legally involved more than fifty nations since the Covenant states that "any war or threat of war, whether immediately affecting any of the Members of the League or not, is hereby declared a matter of concern to the whole League," and furthermore, "the Members of the League undertake to preserve, as against external aggression, the territorial integrity and existing political independence of all Members of the League."

On August 30, 1937, China sent a statement to the Secretary-General of the League of Nations for communication to the members explaining how the Marco Polo Bridge Incident took place and outlining events which followed the clash. The statement pointed out that in resisting Japan's "continuation of her aggressive program started in Manchuria in September, 1931 . . . China is exercising her natural right of self-defence."

In the Chinese Government's appeal to the League of

Nations on September 12, 1937, the attention of all Member States was called to the fact that the invasion "is an aggression against the territorial integrity and existing political independence of China, a Member of the League of Nations, and clearly constitutes a case to be dealt with under Article X of the Covenant. The grave situation which Japanese aggression has thus created also falls within the purview of Article XI of the same instrument, and therefore, is a matter of concern to the whole League."

The Assembly of the League of Nations "adopted a Resolution on September 28, 1937, condemning the bombing of open Chinese towns and cities by Japanese aircraft" and declaring that "no excuse can be made for such acts, which have aroused horror and indignation throughout the world." In a further resolution adopted on October 6, 1937, the Assembly:

"Expresses its moral support for China, and recommends that Members of the League should refrain from taking any action which might have the effect of weakening China's power of resistance and thus of increasing her difficulties in the present conflict, and should also consider how far they can individually extend aid to China."

On October 6, 1937, the Assembly adopted two reports of the Far East Advisory Committee and requested "its President to take the necessary action with regard to the proposed meeting of the Members of the League which are parties to the Nine Power Treaty." Brussels was chosen as the seat of the conference, and accordingly, invitations were sent by the Belgian Government on October 15 to the signatories and adherents of that treaty, namely, the United States, United Kingdom, Union of South Africa, Australia, New Zealand, Canada, India, Italy, France, China, the Netherlands, Portugal, Japan, Bolivia, Mexico, Sweden, Norway and Denmark. All the accepting States agreed that invitations should be sent to Germany and the Soviet Union. The invitation was accepted by the Soviet Union. Germany, on the other hand, did not send any representative on the ground that she is not a party to the Nine Power Treaty, but "is prepared at any moment to take action for the pacific settlement of the dispute, as soon as it has been proved that conditions indispensable for achieving this object exist."

Japan rejected Belgium's invitation with the farfetched argument that her invasion of Chinese territory is a "measure of self-defense . . . that an attempt to seek a solution at a gathering of so many Powers . . . will only serve to complicate the situation still further." The conference took issue with the Japanese contention, and on November 15, 1937, after twelve days of deliberation, issued a declaration which reads in part: "It is clear that the Japanese concept of the issues and interests involved in the conflict under reference is utterly different from the concept of most of the other nations and governments of the world. The Japanese Government insists that, as the conflict is between Japan and China, it concerns those two countries only. Against this, the representatives of the above-mentioned States now met at Brussels consider this conflict of concern in law to all countries party to the Nine Power Treaty of Washington of 1922, and to all countries party to the Pact of Paris of 1928, and of concern in fact to all countries members of the family of nations."

On November 24, a further declaration was issued, the more important passages of which are as follows:

The Conference is convinced that force by itself can provide no just and lasting solution for disputes between nations . . . It further believes that a satisfactory settlement cannot be achieved by direct negotiations between the parties to the conflict alone, and that only by consultation with other Powers principally concerned can there be achieved an agreement the terms of which will be just, generally acceptable and likely to endure.

This Conference strongly reaffirms the principles of the Nine Power Treaty as being among the basic principles which are essential to world peace and orderly progressive development of national and international life.

Legally, the conference is still in existence, as its sittings have only been suspended, and may "be called together again whenever its chairman or any two of its members shall have reported that they consider that its deliberations can be advantageously resumed."

Since Japanese aggression continued unabated, more resolutions were adopted by the League Council on February 2, 1938; May 14, 1938, and September 29, 1938, giving moral support to China. The report adopted by the Council on September 30, 1938, declared that Article XVI of the League Covenant was applicable to Japan. This article provides *inter alia* for the application of sanctions by all Member States by withdrawing all credits, stopping all financial and trade relations, and ceasing to use the ships of the aggressor or aggressors. According to this report, "the provisions of Article XVI are, under Article XVII, paragraph 3, applicable to present conditions, and the Members of the League are entitled not only to act as before on the basis of the said finding, but also to adopt individually the measures provided for in Article XVI."

The Council's resolution of January 20, 1939, recalled the terms of the resolution of February 2, 1938, which expressed the Council's confidence that "those States represented on the Council for whom the situation is of special interest will lose no opportunity of examining in consultation with other similarly interested Powers the feasibility of any further steps which may contribute to a just settlement of the conflict in the Far East." The Council also "invites the Members of the League . . . to

examine in consultation . . . with other interested Powers
the proposals made in the statement of the representative
of China before the Council on January 17, 1939, for
the taking of effective measures, especially measures of
aid to China." With regard to the above-mentioned measures, "The Chinese Government desires that the Council
recommend that the Member States should extend financial and economic assistance to China, among other purposes, for the development and reconstruction of China's
southwestern provinces and for the relief of civilian refugees."

On May 21, 1939, on the eve of a meeting of the
Council, I as Chinese Minister for Foreign Affairs, in a
public statement urged the Member States to take collective action to check Japanese aggression on China, to
cease supplying war materials as well as suspend financial
and trade relations with the aggressor, and enforce the application of Article XVI, in accordance with the Council's
report.

On the following day, Dr. Wellington Koo, China's
chief delegate to the League, proposed that certain measures be adopted by the Council. There were:

First, a recommendation to the Member States to extend
financial and material aid to China for fortifying her power of
resistance and for assisting her to give help and succor to the
millions of Chinese refugees driven away from their homes and

rendered destitute by the Japanese invasion; to refrain from doing anything which may weaken China's power of resistance; to withhold from Japan the supply of instruments of war and raw materials necessary for the continuation of her aggression against China, particularly aeroplanes and oil; and to restrict the importation of Japanese goods, and adopt other means of retaliation against Japan's deliberate violation of the treaty rights of Member States.

In the second place, the setting-up of a general committee — or, if preferred, a special limited body of the Powers directly interested in the Far East — for the purpose of co-ordinating the foregoing measures.

In the third place, further implementing of the Assembly and Council Resolutions already adopted with a view to extending aid to China and restraining the aggressors.

According to its resolution of May 27, 1939, the Council continued "to view with great concern the grave situation in the Far East created by Japanese aggression," and renewed "its expression of profound sympathy with China in her heroic struggle for the maintenance of her independence and territorial integrity threatened by the Japanese invasion, and in the suffering which is thereby inflicted on her people." The resolution further deemed it "desirable that measures of aid to China, including relief measures, and such other measures as may from time to time be found practicable should be made as effective as possible" and expressed "the hope that such measures will be continued."

[127]

In December of the same year when the League met to discuss the Soviet-Finnish dispute, China, seeing that there was no opportunity to renew her appeal, reserved the right to bring it up at the appropriate moment.

FOREIGN ASSISTANCE

Although China was disappointed by the fact that no concrete action was taken by the League to enforce sanctions on the aggressor, she welcomed the individual assistance rendered by the Powers, besides the contributions in money and medical supplies from foreign sympathizers all over the world.

During the past three years, the Chinese Government had obtained loans and credits from America and Great Britain. China's arrangement with the United States for gasoline and motor trucks in exchange for tung oil worked very satisfactorily, while the Sino-British Currency Stabilization Fund was an important factor in maintaining for a time the stability of the Chinese legal tender. And it cannot be doubted that the Sino-Soviet barter agreement has proved mutually beneficial to both countries.

REFUTATION OF "NEW ORDER IN EAST ASIA"

In the hope of misguiding the Japanese people at home, and deceiving the world as to the true nature of the invasion of China, the sugar-coated phrase "a New

Order in East Asia" was coined by the Japanese militarists and their underlings.

In a masterly rebuttal of Premier Konoye's statement of December 22, 1938, in which it was alleged that the ultimate objective of the so-called China Incident was to achieve "a rebirth of China and the erection of a New Order in East Asia," Generalissimo Chiang Kai-shek said on December 26 that what Konoye meant by a China reborn was that "independent China was to perish and in its place an enslaved China created." In answer to Konoye's statement that a new China is to be brought about through "the establishment of linked relations of mutual assistance in matters political, economic and cultural, between Japan, Manchukuo and China," the Generalissimo reminded us of "links of forged chains" designed to drag us down to a pit from which there can be no escape.

Touching on the economic aspect of the so-called "New Order in East Asia," Generalissimo Chiang Kai-shek pointed out that "by urging the elimination of economic barriers, Japan aspires to exclude American and European influence and dominate the Pacific . . . the so-called 'economic unity' of Japan, Manchukuo and China is the instrument she intends to use for obtaining a stranglehold on China's economic arteries. . . . We are then to become their slaves and cattle, and the whole of our nation will thus be dissolved beneath the lash of tyranny . . . The 'New Order in East Asia' is a term for the overthrow of international order in East Asia and the enslavement of China as the means whereby Japan may dominate the Pacific and proceed to dismember other countries."

In conclusion, the Generalissimo made it clear that:

Our object in prosecuting this war of resistance, is to complete the task of national revolution and secure for China independence, liberty and equality. Internationally, our object is to secure righteousness and justice, restore the prestige of treaties, and re-establish peace and order.

NONRECOGNITION DOCTRINE

The nonrecognition doctrine was first expounded by Colonel Henry L. Stimson during his term of office as American Secretary of State, when the United States refused to recognize the puppet regime created by Japan in Manchuria eight years ago. The note of January 7, 1932, addressed to both China and Japan, declared that "the American Government . . . cannot admit the legality of any situation, *de facto* or *de jure*, nor does it intend to recognize any treaty or agreement entered into between those governments or agents thereof which may impair the treaty rights of the United States or its citizens in China, including those which relate to the sovereignty, independence or territorial and administrative integrity of the Republic of China . . . and that it does not intend to recognize any situation, treaty or agreement which may be brought about by means contrary to the covenant and obligations of the Pact of Paris of August 27th, 1938, to which both China and Japan as well as the United States are parties."

The nonrecognition doctrine enunciated during Japan's first undeclared war on China has exerted a profound influence on the attitude of other powers toward the Far East. The League Assembly implemented this doctrine by adopting a resolution on February 24, 1933, calling upon its Members to "abstain from taking any isolated action with regard to the situation in Manchuria."

It was in line with the established American principle of nonrecognition that the American Ambassador to Japan, Mr. Joseph Clark Grew, said in the course of a speech made in October, 1939, that the "New Order in East Asia" had been "officially defined as the order of security, stability, and progress," but it "appeared to include, among other things, depriving Americans of their long-established rights in China, and to this the American people are opposed."

The abrogation of the 1911 American-Japanese Treaty of Amity and Commerce as well as the application of the moral embargo on various supplies shows the real American attitude toward Japanese aggression.

With regard to Japanese-sponsored puppet regimes in

China, it goes without saying that ever since their establishment, the Chinese Government has consistently denounced them as being illegal and traitorous.

On December 20, 1937, following the appearance of the so-called "Provisional Government" in Peiping, the National Government of the Republic of China solemnly declared that "the establishment of any bogus regime in Peiping or other localities under Japanese military occupation constitutes a violation by Japan of China's sovereignty and administrative integrity. Any action taken by such puppet regimes, whether of an internal or external nature, is *ipso facto* null and void."

This stand was again made known immediately following the installation of Wang Ching-wei as the chief puppet of the bogus "National Government" in Nanking by the Japanese, when the Foreign Minister addressed identic notes on March 30, 1940, to the foreign embassies and legations in China calling attention to the following:

The Chinese Government desires to take this opportunity to repeat most emphatically the declaration already made on several occasions that any act done by such an unlawful organization as has just been set up in Nanking or any other puppet body that may exist elsewhere in China, is *ipso facto* null and void and shall never be recognized by the Chinese Government and people. The Chinese Government is convinced that all self-respecting States will uphold law and justice in the conduct of international relations and will never accord *de jure* or *de facto* recognition to Japan's puppet organization in China. Any manifestation of such recognition, in whatever form or manner, would be a violation of international law and treaties and would be considered as an act most unfriendly to the Chinese nation, for the consequences of which the recognizing party would have to bear full responsibility.

The attitude of the Powers in this respect is significant. Mr. Cordell Hull, American Secretary of State, clarified the position of the United States in a statement issued on March 30, 1939. Criticizing the "setting-up of a new regime in Nanking," he said that this appeared "to be following the pattern of other regimes and systems which have been set up in China under the aegis of an outside Power, and which in their functioning especially favor the interests of that outside Power." He further pointed out that "the attitude of the United States toward the use of armed force as an instrument of national policy is well known," and "that attitude and position remain unchanged." Continuing, Mr. Hull said:

Twelve years ago the Government of the United States recognized, as did other governments, the National Government of the Republic of China. The Government of the United States has ample reason for believing that that government, with its capital now in Chungking, has had and still has the allegiance and support of the great majority of the Chinese people. The Govern-

[133]

ment of the United States, of course, continues to recognize that government as the Government of China.

Other nations have adopted a similar attitude and continue to recognize the National Government at Chungking as the only legally-constituted government of China.

THE SHANGHAI CUSTOMS ISSUE

On May 3, 1938, an agreement was reached between Great Britain and Japan regarding the deposit of customs revenue. The Central Bank of China and the Hongkong and Shanghai Bank have been the depositories for customs revenue throughout China, but under the new arrangement all revenues collected in areas under Japanese occupation have to be deposited with a Japanese bank, namely, the Yokohama Specie Bank.

The Ministry of Foreign Affairs lodged a protest on May 6, 1938, which concluded with the statement: "China is not in any way bound by the arrangements concerning the Chinese Customs just concluded between the British and Japanese Governments and fully reserves her rights and freedom of action in matters relating to the Customs."

THE TIENTSIN SILVER QUESTION

Since July, 1939, the silver question had formed a bone of contention between Britain and Japan. Japan, on the one hand, demanded the surrender of the reserves of Chinese silver stored in the British Concession; while Britain, on the other hand, taking cognizance of China's position, refused to give in to the Japanese demands.

Negotiations had been going on between the Chinese and British Governments, and upon the settlement of this question, the Chinese Government issued a declaration on June 21, 1940, which reads:

With regard to the silver now stored in the British Concession at Tientsin, the Chinese Government desires to place on record the point already repeatedly emphasized in the recent conversations between the Minister for Foreign Affairs and the British Ambassador on the subject, to the effect that the silver in question is the property of the Bank of Communications and part of the reserve fund for *fapi*. The Chinese Government further records its view that the British Government are acting as trustees for the interest of the Bank of Communications and the Chinese Government in respect of the balance of the silver after a quantity equivalent to £100,000 sterling has been set aside by the Chinese Government for relief purposes in North China. Consequently the arrangement now made for sealing the silver does not alter its status in any respect.

THE CLOSING OF THE INTERNATIONAL TRADE ROUTE THROUGH INDO-CHINA

As a sequel to the sudden turn of events in Europe resulting in the Franco-German armistice, France yielded to Japanese pressure and stopped traffic of every description between China and the outside world *via* Indo-China. The Chinese Government immediately lodged a strong protest with the French Government on June 21, 1940, and a second one on June 24. On the day before the second protest was lodged, the Minister of Foreign Affairs issued an official statement, which, because of its importance, is reproduced below *in extenso:*

Owing to their geographical proximity, China and French Indo-China have long had relationships of an intimate nature. For many years their commercial and economic needs have been complementary to each other. Today, as a channel of international trade, Indo-China is of vital importance not only to the commerce between China and foreign countries but also to the security of this country.

China and France have concluded several agreements, concerning this region, the most recent of which is "La Convention Reglant les Rapports entre la Chine et la France relativement a l'Indo-Chine Francaise et aux Provinces Chinoises Limitrophes," signed on May 16, 1930. Under this Convention, France agrees to the transportation through Indo-China of all kinds of merchandise, including arms and ammunition. In view of the above-mentioned commitment on the part of the French Government, the Chinese Government has the right to request France to live up to her obligations and to keep the Indo-China route open for international trade. However, during the past year or so the Chinese Government has not made use of this route for the transit of arms and ammunition out of consideration for any possible difficulty in which a friendly nation might become involved.

Unfortunately, the militarist government of Japan, taking full advantage of the international situation in Europe, has openly or otherwise coerced the French Government to close the Indo-China route to international trade. The Chinese Government considers it most regrettable that the Japanese demands have not been categorically rejected, for the object of these demands is to compel France to blockade a country with which she is at peace and on friendly terms. Such a blockade cannot be justified from the standpoint of the Sino-French Convention or of international law.

The failure of the French Government to take a strong stand against the Japanese demands can only encourage further disturbance of the peace in the Far East on the part of the Japanese militarists. This the Chinese Government cannot but view with the gravest concern. The Chinese Government is fully convinced that any military movement of the Japanese in furtherance of their plan of aggression on any part of Asia or the Pacific will be carried out with the view of utilizing their aggressive gains for attaining their principal object of conquering China. It is obvious that should Japan invade Indo-China, her goal would not be limited to the seizure of the French colony, but also to make use of Indo-China as a base for attacking China. Therefore, in case of an armed Japanese invasion of Indo-China, the Chinese Government, in order to preserve China's existence and independence will be constrained to take such measures in self-defense as may be deemed necessary to cope with the situation in pursuance of its fixed policy of resistance against aggression.

[137]

CONCLUSION OF NEW TREATIES

During the period under review, China has concluded several treaties with foreign countries on a basis of equality and reciprocity. The first in point of time was the Non-aggression Pact with the Soviet Union signed on August 21, 1937. In Article I, the two countries "agree to refrain from any aggression against each other either individually or jointly with one or more other Powers." Article II stipulates that:

In the event that either of the High Contracting Parties should be subjected to aggression on the part of one or more third Powers, the other High Contracting Party obligates itself not to render assistance of any kind, either directly or indirectly, to such third Power or Powers at any time during the entire conflict, and also to refrain from taking any action or entering into any agreement which may be used by the aggressor or aggressors to the disadvantage of the Party subjected to aggression.

The following treaties of amity were concluded:

(1) The Sino-Liberian Treaty of December 11, 1937.
(2) The Sino-Estonian Treaty of December 21, 1937.
(3) The Sino-Dominican Treaty of May 11, 1940.

The last-mentioned treaty is similar in wording to the other treaties, except that there shall be no discriminating provisions in the laws of either country against the nationals of the other.

REORGANIZATION OF MINISTRY OF FOREIGN AFFAIRS

In order that China's wartime diplomatic functions may be better co-ordinated, the Ministry of Foreign Affairs was reorganized in the month of April, 1940. There were originally five departments, namely, the General Affairs Department, the International Department, the European and American Department, the Asiatic Department, and the Intelligence and Publicity Department, and also a Treaty Commission, a Counsellors' office and a Secretariat.

As a result of the reorganization, the International Department was abolished. The Treaty Commission was absorbed by the newly organized Treaty Department, which, besides taking care of treaty relations and legal matters, has charge of affairs connected with the League of Nations. The European and American Department was split into a European Department and an American Department. The Asiatic Department was reorganized into an Eastern Asiatic Department and a Western Asiatic Department.

Recently the Chinese diplomatic and consular service was expanded. A Chinese Legation was established in

Rumania. The Chinese consulates in Rangoon, Burma, and Wellington, New Zealand, were raised to the status of consulates general. A consulate was established in Jidda, Saudi Arabia; while consular offices were opened in Haiphong, Indo-China, and Melbourne, Australia.

Conclusion

In this brief summary of events relating to China's foreign relations during the past three years, it is clear that the Chinese Government has adopted a consistent foreign policy throughout this entire period.

Although the Chinese people are peace-loving by nature, yet in the face of invasion they do not hesitate to take up arms in self-defense. Today, China is not only defending her national existence, independence and integrity, but also upholding the sanctity of the Nine Power Treaty, and other international treaties. In defending herself, China is at the same time defending the position of the Western powers with interests in the Far East, by frustrating Japan's plan of utilizing the man power and resources of this vast country to realize her ambition of dominating Asia and ultimately the world.

Irrespective of international developments, we are determined to continue our war of resistance until final victory is achieved.

XIV

INDUSTRIALIZATION OF
*WESTERN CHINA**

BEFORE 1937 there was little modern industry in the western provinces of China. Almost all the industrial plants with modern equipment, such as cotton mills, flour mills, etc., were concentrated in a number of places along the eastern coast, the Yangtze River, or in some other few centers in eastern China.

At the very beginning of the war, the government instructed a number of departments to plan and carry out the industrialization of the interior provinces along lines compatible with the practical conditions (such as capacity of transport) prevailing during wartime.

The plan chiefly comprised the establishment of a number of industrial centers, the particular location of which cannot now be published as the war is in progress. In each center necessary effort has been made for the supply of power.

In order to utilize the mechanical equipment already existing in the eastern provinces, a number of factories owned by private persons or companies were moved to the interior.

* By Wong Wen-hao, Minister of Economic Affairs.

The total weight of the machinery of more than 400 factories thus dismantled, and transported with government help, amounted to more than 70,000 tons. These factories represent many kinds of industry. They include machine works, metallurgical plants, chemical works, cotton mills, flour mills, paper factories.

In addition to the equipment of these factories iron and steel furnaces and much related materials of the Han Yeh Ping Company were also sent into the western area from Han-Yang and Ta-Yeh.

The Liuhokou blast furnace, originally built in Hankow, was also dismantled and moved to the interior.

Several coal mines had their original plants transported, the most important being the Chung Fu Joint Mining Administration of Honan Province. Their hoisting, pumping and other equipment were mostly sent to the southwestern provinces for the operation of a number of coal mines. The total weight of the materials from the mines and furnaces thus moved is about 50,000 tons, making a grand total, together with the equipment of the factories above mentioned, of 120,000 tons.

To supplement these plants, the government started a number of new factories, including electrolytic copper plants, electrical apparatus factories, and machine works. The entirely new equipment which has been imported from abroad, or supplemented in China, totals at least 10,000 tons in weight.

INDUSTRIALIZATION

Further effort is being made to encourage the establishment of factories for woolen clothes, rubber tires, alcohol making and so on.

IRON AND STEEL

In order to supply the iron ore required by the iron and steel furnaces re-established in the interior, efforts have been made to open up, on a large scale, two iron mines in Szechuan Province. Discoveries of rich iron ore deposits have also been made in Yunnan and Kweichow provinces, and a scheme has been outlined for the exploitation of these mines. There will be an ample supply of iron ore for the iron and steel furnaces.

The increasing demand for iron also gives much impetus to the native iron mines and furnaces (smaller in size, but larger in number than the modern ones) to increase their production to a figure already more than double the prewar scale. Statistics cannot be given during this period of war.

NON-FERROUS METALS

The copper refineries erected since the war have been put into operation, and are producing electrolytic copper for ammunition purposes. The zinc and lead smelting plants in Hunan Province have been moved to a safe locality to carry on production.

With regard to mineral products for export, the situation is considered satisfactory. Tin production shows an appreciable increase as a result of the improvement and enlargement of the smelting plants. Production of tungsten and antimony has attained good results by the maintenance of normal output in the original places of production and new discoveries of deposits in other localities. In spite of transportation difficulties, the exportation of these mineral products is still being carried on in considerable quantities. Mercury is being produced in greater amount than before the war.

Machine Works

Machine works constitute a very large percentage of the factories moved westwards. The Central Machine Works, and the Electrical Equipmental Manufacturing Works, both owned by the National Resources Commission, and more than 100 privately owned machine shops of various sizes render help in the manufacture of ammunition and other war supplies. Meanwhile, they are pursuing their own line of production, including machine tools, boilers, steam engines, gas producers and engines, generator sets, transformers, motors, and other industrial equipment. The Central Machine Works also includes a motor truck assembling plant.

Chemical Industry

Caustic soda, soda ash, bleaching powder, sulphuric,

hydrochloric and nitric acids can all be produced in the hinterland of China nowadays. With abundant supply of common salt, pyrites, Glauber salt, and saltpeter, we can enlarge the production considerably, provided additional equipment for such industry is available.

Cement was being produced in Szechuan Province before the war. In order to meet the increasing demand, cement works of smaller sizes are being built in Yunnan, Hunan and Kwangsi provinces. The production campaign will be spread over various localities in western China, to establish small units to meet this demand. Glassware, firebricks and other ceramic products are also supplied locally at present.

The western provinces of China are well known for their abundance in oil and tallow production. The method of manufacture of tung oil, which is a very important item of Chinese exports, especially to the United States, has been improved by introducing modern machinery to this industry for drying and pressing, thus giving a better color and quality to the oil.

Rapeseed and tung oils are being used to make gasoline, kerosene, diesel, and lubricating oils, to supplement the supply of mineral oils. Soaps are entirely supplied locally nowadays by utilizing vegetable and animal tallows as raw materials. Furthermore, the development of the paint and varnish industry is gaining speed by using vegetable oils and pigments obtainable in interior China.

Tanning has also become a very important industry. In addition to a number of small tanneries already existing in the interior, several modern tanneries have moved in, and, together with a newly established one, are already in operation. Vegetable tanning is especially encouraged as a means to reduce the quantity of tanning materials which must be imported from abroad.

Sugar production in Szechuan Province is the second largest in China, only next to that of Kwangtung Province. Even the molasses — the residue of sugar manufacture — is very valuable in wartime, inasmuch as it can be used as raw material for the manufacture of alcohol.

As the need for liquid fuel is increasing, there has been a mushroom growth of alcohol plants all over the western provinces, using either molasses, kaoliang, or potatoes as raw material.

Two paper factories of considerable size were moved in, and are being re-erected with the government's help. Pending their completion, the present supply consists of paper manufactured by two paper factories of small size, and by several papermakers who use half machinery and half handicraft. It is estimated that the total output, when all the paper factories are in full operation, will amount to about fifteen tons a day. This will be quite sufficient to meet the wartime demand.

At present, bamboo, scrapped paper, and rags are the principal raw materials used. In order to provide an adequate supply of raw materials for the bigger factories, a mechanical wood pulp factory is under erection, and a chemical pulp factory is also under planning.

The production of dyestuff and medicine of organic nature has to await the establishment of the coal distillation industry, which is also being planned. Meanwhile, bismuth and mercury compounds, and extracts from herbs and salt brine, are already available for medical purposes. As for dyestuff, the revival of the use of vegetable extracts is also noteworthy.

The erection of a rubber tire factory in Yunnan Province designed to manufacture tires for trucks and airplanes has been started. This factory will also undertake the manufacture of gas masks, naval portable boats and other rubber articles as its auxiliary output. Other rubber factories of smaller size have been in operation, chiefly making common articles of daily use.

TEXTILE INDUSTRY

The recent development of the textile industry in western China may be discussed under the headings of cotton, woolen, silk, and ramie.

In China, before the war, there were a total of more than 4,000,000 spindles in the cotton-spinning industry, all of which were located in coastal and Yangtze ports, and North China, with the exception of 25,000 spindles in Sian, 50,000 spindles in Changsha, and 5,000 spindles in Kunming. Since the war, along with the factories moved in with the government's help, approximately 240,000 spindles were dismantled from cotton mills in Chengchow and Hankow and transported to Szechuan and Shensi provinces.

The first cotton mill ever erected in Szechuan Province was able to start operation in January, 1939, and the working capacity will increase daily as soon as additional machinery is installed and is in operating condition. New spindles have been added to the cotton mills in Yunnan Province. Besides these cotton mills, improved wooden spinning machines and the "Ghosh" spinning machines have been introduced to increase the production of yarn to meet the present requirements.

Woolen spinning is another new industry in western China. There are at present three woolen spinning mills under erection. The total capacity of all three is about 4,000 spindles, including woolen and worsted.

The silk of Szechuan Province was formerly an item of export. Now that several silk weaving factories have been moved in, Szechuan silk is woven into cloth for daily wear, and tests are also being made to decide its usefulness for making parachutes. In Yunnan Province, silk production is a comparatively recent development, and, according to the opinion of experts, there is a very good prospect for future growth.

Ramie fiber in Szechuan Province is woven by hand

into linen cloth which is very extensively used for summer wear. Improvements have been recently made in regard to the degumming and softening of the fiber, and Madame H. H. Kung is actively working to have plants erected and operated in favorable localities to supply local needs as well as fill future export demands. The erection of a ramie factory using modern spinning machinery is now under planning as it is generally believed that this is the fundamental solution for the future development of the industry.

FLOUR MILLS

Only flour mills of small size were in operation in the interior before the war. The chief reason is that Szechuan Province is a rice-growing province, and the people in this part of the country are not in the habit of consuming flour for regular daily meals. Since the war, flour has become a wartime necessity for the army, and the demand is increasing. In anticipation of such possibilities, flour mills in Hankow, Shasi, and Chengchow were instructed by the government to dismantle and move their machinery to Shensi and Szechuan provinces. Furthermore, efforts have been made to manufacture locally machinery of simpler types for flour mills, and these are now installed in Kwangsi, Kweichow and Kansu provinces. When the erection of these flour mills is completed, the output of

[149]

all the mills in western China will be above ten thousand bags of flour daily.

COAL MINES

Native coal mines operated with very primitive methods are scattered all over the western provinces. With the mining machinery that has been moved in, it has been possible to modernize some of the native mines and also open new mines on a modern basis. The total output of the coal mines in Szechuan Province alone had already reached 1,500,000 tons during 1939 — more than double the output of two years ago.

While the actual work of industrialization has been proceeding serious efforts have been made to investigate the natural resources of the interior provinces. The geological condition of the main mineral resources such as coal, iron, copper, etc., is, of course, better known. Several minerals — asbestos, phosphate and beauxite (aluminum ore) — the existence of which in China was not known before, have been recently discovered.

China is by nature not very rich in some common metals like copper, lead, and zinc, but she possesses particularly rich reserves of tin, wolfram, antimony, mercury, bismuth, arsenic minerals, phosphate, etc., which can be supplied to friendly countries. Of the minerals already better developed, their export has assumed an importance now well known to the world. Those which

[150]

need further development to make them utilizable are receiving the special attention of the government.

From the agricultural point of view, western China includes vast areas which can yield abundant crops of various kinds. During the past fifteen years or so, successful results have been obtained in the growth of a large amount of cotton of distinctly better quality, so that China has become one of the few main cotton-producing countries in the world.

The distribution of cotton growing in China cannot, however, be equal. So far as west China is concerned, cotton growing is chiefly concentrated in Shensi Province, but very poorly represented in the southwestern provinces. The government doubled its effort for the last three years in Szechuan Province where large amounts of delfos and other better seeds of longer fibers have been freely distributed to the farmers.

In Yunnan Province there was no silk industry before the present war. Experts found, however, that the climate and other conditions particularly suited the rearing of silkworms which produced silk of a better quality than in other provinces. In a number of districts serious encouragement has been given to the growth of mulberry trees and to the production of silk. One silk-weaving plant is already completed while another one is being installed. There is thus a brilliant prospect for the silk industry in that province.

In the northwestern area, where the rainfall is too scanty, a number of irrigation works have been carried out, giving sufficient water to fields of over 350,000 acres.

These are a few instances to illustrate the work of investigation and development of resources that is being done in free China. In addition it is worth while to mention the great resources of water power which exist chiefly in the southwest provinces. An active survey is being carried out on the topography, rainfall, etc., in order to make concrete plans for a number of hydroelectric stations. Actual construction work has already been started in a few places. Such work is deemed necessary to supply abundant and cheap power to the industrial plants required for the economic development of the country.

*　　　*　　　*

Since this chapter was written the intensified indiscriminate bombing by Japan to beat us to our knees has destroyed many of the factories referred to. But that destruction will not deter us. We are picking up the pieces and will persevere with them.

XV

FREE CHINA'S RECONSTRUCTION WORK IN THE FIELD OF COMMUNICATIONS, JULY, 1937 to JUNE, 1940*

THE foregoing portrayal of the Sino-Japanese conflict as a result of aggression by Japan would be incomplete without giving here a summary of reconstruction work accomplished by the Chinese National Government in the field of communications since the beginning of the present hostilities.

HIGHWAYS

The achievement in this field by the Chinese National Government is greater than it appears, for not only did the blockade of most of the coast embarrass transport of articles not procurable inland, but workers carried on with all the dangers and inconveniences that go with bombing attacks and war conditions. Despite all this, construction was rapid and efficient.

One instance may be given: Kansu Province, one of the most distant from the coast, and thus backward, had till recently been denied modern roads and has even now not a single kilometer of railway line. One can visualize

* By Minister Chang Kia-ngau, Minister of Communications.

[153]

the peasants on the unsurfaced paths that passed as roads watching the survey team in December, 1937, mapping out the highway between Tienshui and Fenghsien, 230 kilometers long. By the following January, thousands of laborers, with men carrying strange instruments, and some speaking the unfamiliar dialects of coastal provinces, had begun the great road that was to revolutionize the lives of those worthy Kansu countryfolk.

In five months, the highway was open to traffic, and the isolation of thousands of years was over. Great motor trucks roared past hamlets that had seldom seen a stranger, and farm produce could be readily sold at good prices.

Free China has now four fifths as much road mileage as the entire country possessed before hostilities, although Japanese propaganda would have the world believe that the National Government of China is isolated in a mountainous and unproductive area of small extent.

To say that new roads covering 3,600 kilometers have been constructed in the last two years loses force if we do not consider that these highways are carrying education, modern hygienic knowledge, and the intellectual stimulus of newspapers, to peasants whose isolation was beyond imagination.

This ferment of new ideas is guaranteed by many kilometers of roads now under construction, and this is only the beginning of a great program. Poverty and superstition disappear before these great arterial highways.

RECONSTRUCTION WORK

One of the most spectacular is the road from Chengtu to Kangting, also known as Tachienlu, which is now nearing completion under the most severe handicaps. Kangting is the town where caravans are made up for Lhasa, Tibet.

The traveler sees from a height of nearly 10,000 feet along this new road great peaks of eternal snow, thrusting up at one point to 24,000 feet above sea level. Fast motor trucks will startle the patient yak, for so many centuries the chief beast of burden, and will relieve the Chinese tea coolie of his amazing load of 350 pounds, destined to slake the thirst of Tibetans on the great wind-swept plateaux of the land of mystery.

China was carrying on a great interior traffic before George Stephenson invented the locomotive, or Robert Fulton experimented with the steamer; China had its silk road to Persia two thousand years before either invention startled the world.

The aim of the Chinese National Government is to use modern methods wherever possible, but not to retard trade by refusing to utilize the 25,000 camels in the northwest, the yak of Sikang, and in all provinces the coolies with their wheelbarrows and bamboo carrying poles.

By these primitive means a transport trade, vast in the aggregate, can be carried on as it was 1,500 years before Columbus made his epochal voyage.

Free China has now 80,000 kilometers of modern roads,* compared with 110,000 in all China before the Japanese aggression. Bridges are being strengthened and in many cases replaced by steel or concrete structures. Ferryboats are rapidly disappearing as new bridges take their place. In general, the slogan is bigger, better, and more numerous roads.

It is now possible to go by motor vehicle from Chungking to Chengtu in one day, while only seven years ago express freight and passengers took at least ten days by foot path.

The Burma Road, 2,296 kilometers from Chungking to Lashio, the nearest large town in Burma, is one of the major achievements of road construction in China. The final section of 960 kilometers from Kunming to the Burmese border was completed in eleven months, by utilizing short sections of old roads near Kunming.

The cost of road construction in Free China today ranges from $10,000, Chinese currency, per kilometer, in level country, to $40,000 on the most difficult mountainous stretches — a silent tribute to the policy of combining foreign engineering experience with old and tried Chinese methods, and with the unlimited and excellent Chinese labor.

There are now 300,000 Chinese laborers working on road construction in Free China.

* See Map No. 1: "Free China's Trunk Highways."

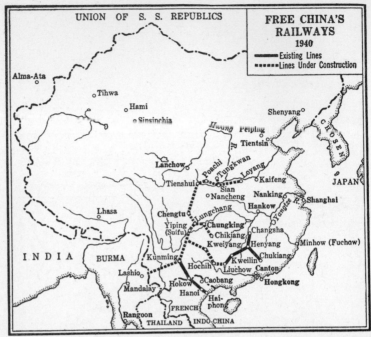

FREE CHINA'S
RAILWAYS
1940
━━━ Existing Lines
┅┅┅ Lines Under Construction

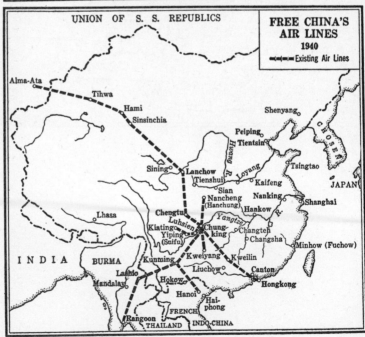

FREE CHINA'S
AIR LINES
1940
━◄━ Existing Air Lines

Connections with the outside world are vital, and hence after the fall of Nanning in Kwangsi Province, a new road was rushed through from Hochih, in Kwangsi Province, to Caobang, in Indo-China. This highway was opened to traffic in an unsurfaced condition, but long before these words are read the new artery of commerce will be surfaced and ready for the heaviest traffic.

Another road going to Indo-China is now under construction. It runs along the French Railway from Kunming to Hokow on the frontier, supplementing the railway as a means of international transportation. A part of this new road has already been put into service unsurfaced, but by the end of this year, the entire distance will be up to the standard of modern highway construction.

RAILWAYS

China is an ideal country for railway construction, cutting transit times from months to days and from weeks to hours. Construction is cheap and maintenance cost always low, and Chinese take at once to the convenience of the "fire cart," as the locomotive is popularly called.

Unfortunately, Japan's attack on China deprived the National Government of 7,300 kilometers of railways.

This did not quench the spirit of the people, for already 635 new kilometers have been completed, while many more are under construction to make an extensive network of railways in Free China.

The new line from Hengyang, in Hunan Province, to Kweilin, in Kwangsi Province, 360 kilometers long, was completed only eleven months after the first spade of earth was turned; this line has since been extended to Liuchow, over 170 kilometers beyond Kweilin.

The Yunnan-Burma Railway, 880 kilometers long, tapping a territory rich in coal and many other resources, has already over 30 per cent of earthwork completed; and a section of 130 kilometers from Kunming westward will be open to traffic this year if rails are available.

This is a line of considerable engineering difficulty, with many tunnels, one of them 610 meters long, and its energetic construction is symptomatic of the spirit that animates Free China.

This railway will run through some of the finest scenery in the world, and its value is by no means confined to the period of hostilities.

With its extension to Suifu on the Yangtze River, already under construction, the Yunnan-Burma Railway will affect a vast territory in Free China of 500,000 square miles, and a population of 75 millions.

As with the highways, the railway program* briefly outlined has been possible only through the intense loyalty of the staff and construction laborers, who are not deterred at all by any hazards of war.

* See Map No. 2: "Free China's Railways (Existing and under construction)."

NAVIGATION

Utilizing the many navigable rivers in Szechuan, Hunan, and Kwangsi Provinces, the National Government has added 2,000 kilometers of steam navigation to her inland total, and another 1,500 kilometers are under consideration.

Just before the aggression of Japan, China had 500,000 tons of steam-propelled vessels, many of which have been destroyed by the enemy. Fortunately, 60 ships, specially constructed for the dangerous navigation of the Upper Yangtze River, were beyond the reach of Japan, and have been doing yeoman service in carrying on the trade of the great river. From October, 1938, to May, 1939, these steamers, supplemented by old-type wooden junks, moved 150,000 tons of cargo from Ichang into Szechuan Province.

Steamers for the Upper Yangtze traffic must be of special construction and power to perform the journey unaided, but when Hankow had to be evacuated, there were some 160 down-river steamships unable to make the journey up the rapids under their own steam.

The National Government constructed steam-driven cable pulleys near the chief rapids, and the valuable fleet of down-river steamers was hauled over the rapids and was thus saved. In addition, at the eight stations so far erected, assistance was given to 4,500 junks at the rapids, and on 500 occasions steamers have also utilized the steam-driven pulleys.

But steamers could not cope with the vast traffic of the Upper Yangtze and many other rivers, on which junks of types unchanged for centuries maintained communication between populous towns. The National Government evolved a streamlined junk, of a type suited to Chinese navigators, and more than 10,000 tons of this new type of craft are plying on waterways of Free China which are unsafe for steam navigation, or where this modern innovation has not yet been fully developed.

The Chinese have been navigators for thousands of years, and their natural aptitude is responding to the improvements made on the many inland waterways by the National Government.

AIR ROUTES

Despite Japanese seizure of air bases, the air lines controlled by Free China now total 12,000 kilometers,* almost as many as before the hostilities, and will soon climb to a record figure. The air route from Chungking, via Hami, to Alma-Ata, in Russia, is itself 3,800 kilometers long.

Over territory that would have taken months of travel only a few years ago, a visitor to China can now leave

* See Map No. 3: "Free China's Air Lines."

Rangoon in Burma by plane from Chungking, and continue his journey the same day to Hong Kong, a total distance of 3,340 kilometers.

Other countries have seen the gradual replacement of rough paths by modern roads, then the coming of the locomotive, and finally the highest speed of transport, the airplane.

China has in many cases eliminated the transitional stages, and jumped from primitive sedan-chair and mule transport to the fast Douglas plane, for most of the air fleet in China is of American make. From a speed of three miles an hour by sedan chair to two hundred miles an hour by airplane represents a gain in speed to suggest the magic carpet of our childhood's tales.

It has not been without incident. On several occasions passenger planes have been attacked by Japanese aircraft. On August 24, 1938, the Chinese-American aviation company, called the China National Aviation Corporation, with 49 per cent of its capital from American sources, operated the passenger airplane *Kweilin* from Hong Kong to Chungking. When just outside Hong Kong territory, enemy planes attacked the *Kweilin,* which carried thirteen passengers including three women and two children. Not satisfied with the forced landing of the civil plane in the water, the Japanese military planes bombed and machine-gunned the helpless *Kweilin,* killing all the occupants except one of the pilots, the radio operator and one pas-

[161]

senger, who managed to swim ashore in a wounded condition. As many as thirteen bullet wounds were found on one of the bodies. Under such risks has the aviation service in Free China been conducted, and enormously developed. Planes are always booked long in advance, and pressure on space is so great that excess baggage is seldom carried.

POST OFFICE

The manifold activities of communications embrace posts and telegraphs. Post offices and postal agencies under the control of Free China number 66,000, of which 6,000 have been recently opened. The domestic letter rate is five Chinese cents, the cheapest in the world, and postal routes now total 502,000 kilometers. China uses all methods that suit the conditions; fast Douglas planes and efficient motor trucking are as necessary in their fields as the overland day-and-night courier service, mule transport of parcels over mountain trails, or rafts of inflated skins on rivers not navigable but which must be crossed by the mail courier.

China has its pony express, like the famous American counterpart immortalized by Mark Twain. "The old order changeth yielding place to the new" is one of Tennyson's well-known lines, and of nothing is it more true than the Chinese Post Office. It also sponsors a modern savings bank with the usual banking facilities.

RECONSTRUCTION WORK

TELEGRAPH

The prewar figure of 95,000 kilometers of telegraph lines for all China will soon be surpassed in Free China by the rapid development that has been proceeding for the last three years. The courage displayed in the other fields of communications has not been found wanting in the devoted staff of the telegraph service.

New telegraph lines established cover a distance of 33,000 kilometers, those under construction, 12,000 kilometers, and those under contemplation, 11,000 kilometers. Old poles and old wires have been replaced on many lines.

TELEPHONE

The Japanese assault on China took away almost 30,000 kilometers of long-distance telephone lines, being about one half of the total at that time. But intensive effort has brought the kilometrage in Free China up to the highest figure for the whole country before hostilities, no less than 9,000 kilometers having been added in the last six months alone. The equipment of city telephones is, where possible, being improved.

A network of telephone lines has been completed, with Chungking and Kweilin as the center in the south and Hanchung as the center in the north, stretching out to almost all important cities in Free China, as far as Fukien and Anhwei and many places in the guerrilla areas. Many duplicate or parallel lines have been established. Radio telephone has been used, where necessary, to supplement ordinary long-distance telephone service.

RADIO

Large stations have been built, or are nearing completion, at many points in Free China. Radio is also being developed in Sikang, the territory adjoining Tibet, and in Kwangtung and Kwangsi Provinces.

Great improvement has been made in international radio service. Chungking is now connected with Manila, Hanoi and Moscow. International radio stations have been erected at two major cities in Free China, and another new one will soon be established. Thus, Cathay is brought to the door of the outside world.

This brief summary of the achievements of the National Government of China in the field of communications will show that hostilities have not interrupted progress in Free China, but rather stimulated it. This recent vast development has had its effect on the population and commerce of the southwest, which, once so backward, is now the most progressive part of China.

XVI

CHINESE CULTURE AND EDUCATION DURING THREE YEARS OF WAR*

EDUCATION is one of the fundamental requirements for the existence of a nation. The Ministry of Education, therefore, in undertaking to provide for the nation's literate masses, intelligent and upright citizens, learned persons, experts and specialists on the one hand, and to reconstruct our agelong culture on the other, shoulders a grave responsibility.

The gravity of this responsibility is further increased, at this moment, by the fact that the entire structure and personnel of our educational system must adjust to the needs of war. That is, while trying its best to devise means of protection for the cultural and educational institutions

* By Chen Li-fu, Minister of Education.

NOTE: This chapter was written while Japanese bombers were busily destroying more educational establishments in Chungking and its vicinity. The following cultural centers have just been destroyed or damaged: The National Central University, The Szechuan Provincial Chungking University, Fu Tan University, The National Kiangsu Medical College, The Szechuan Provincial Normal College, The National Pharmaceutical College, The Central Industrial Vocational School, The National Chungking College, Fu Tan Middle School, Ta Kung Vocational School, The China Vocational Training School, The Szechuan Provincial Vocational School for Women, The Szechuan Provincial Chuan Tung Normal School, The Ministry of Education, the Number Three War Area Teachers' Service Corps.

[165]

of the entire nation against the armed attacks and aerial bombardments of our enemy, the Ministry of Education should redouble its efforts, modify its means and methods, and concentrate every bit of its resources, to help strengthen the conviction of the entire people and increase our power of resistance, spiritual as well as physical; so that the people of China will be able to stand whatever tests they may encounter during the war, know where to direct their might and how to economize the use of it in order to hold out for protracted hostilities; so that they will be firm in their resistance and wholly and unconditionally confident of their ultimate victory, so essential to national revival and cultural reconstruction.

It is most impressive and inspiring to see our educators, scholars, artists, teachers and students — prompted by their sense of patriotism, and under the leadership of the Ministry of Education — bravely hold to their responsibilities in various capacities, irrespective of their sufferings. Some sacrificed their lives for the protection of their schools; some marched on foot for months from north to south before they reached their destinations; some built with their own hands sheds for their studies, classrooms, laboratories, libraries and dormitories, in which they work and live; some take part in service at the front, while others serve in the rear.

In extending guidance to all such groups, in translocating the cultural and educational institutions, in organizing nationwide relief and assistance, besides its regular duties, the Ministry of Education has on hand a program three times as heavy as that in times of peace.

The task is difficult, but our spirit is high. And together with my colleagues and the culturists and educators of the entire nation, I have come to the conclusion, after a long period of deliberation and experiment, that illiteracy must be wiped out at once; that higher learning must be further promoted; that our national classics must be systematically studied; that character education must be universalized; that a better system of technical education must be built up. These and other realizations have led us to formulate proper plans and projects in accordance with the resolutions adopted by the National Congress of the Kuomintang convened in April, 1938, which resolved upon a dual program of "armed resistance and national reconstruction." The damage and losses sustained by our cultural and educational institutions and the work of the Ministry of Education in detail are as follows:

THE LOSSES OF INSTITUTIONS OF HIGHER EDUCATION

Before the war, there were in the country 108 colleges and universities. The grounds and buildings of 91 of these have either been occupied or damaged by the enemy. Of them 14 have been completely destroyed. As it has been the set policy of the enemy to destroy our educational and cultural institutions, even the schools situated far behind in the interior have not been spared by the enemy bombers. What the losses will be up to the end of the first three years of war cannot yet be estimated, but up to the end of December, 1939, the losses sustained by the institutions of higher learning amounted to more than $37,-003,367. Tables I, II, and III, below show the distribution of such losses.

Table I

Property Losses of National Universities and Colleges in the War Areas (to the end of December, 1939)

Name	Property Losses	Remarks
National Central University	$3,383,400	
National University of Peiping	1,922,317	
National Normal University	1,502,871	
National Peking University	1,628,515	This sum includes only the equipment; cost of the premises is not included.
National Tsin Hua University	6,050,000	University premises and buildings, $3,500,-000; library, $2,500,-000; branch in Changsha bombed, $50,000.
National Shantung University	3,611,663	Buildings in Tsingtao, $2,912,580; laboratory, $181,764; premises in Tsinan, College of Agriculture, $287,584.
National Sun Yat-sen University	6,638,964	Damage by aerial bombardment.

CULTURE AND EDUCATION

Name	Property Losses	Remarks
National Tungchi University	1,480,000	
National University of Chekiang	1,560,000	Premises, $1,300,000; other equipment, $260,000.
National Hunan University	700,000	Damage by aerial bombardment.
National Amoy University	1,288,202	Buildings, $972,700; libraries and laboratories, $80,907; machinery, equipment, and museum pieces, $4,189,595.
National Peiyang Engineering College	629,063	
National Chung-Cheng Medical College	1,200	Damage by aerial bombardment.
National School of Pharmacy	49,000	
National School of Physical Education of the Central Institute of National Physical Exercise	179,814	
Woosung School of Commercial Nagivation	290,700	Buildings and equipment, $196,500; machinery, $19,400; library and laboratories, $24,000; losses of faculty and students, $50,800.
National School of Fine Arts of Hangchow	$81,030	
National Chinan University	413,000	
National Wuhan University	2,875,937	
National Chaotung University	2,369,650	

Name	Property Losses	Remarks
National Commercial College of Shanghai	183,066	
National School of Music	159,975	
National Medical College of Soochow	5,000	
National School of Fine Arts of Peiping	——	No details
National School of Dentistry	——	No details
National College of Law of Kwangtung	——	No details
National Medical College of Shanghai	——	No details
TOTAL	$37,003,467	

Table II

Property Losses of Provincial Universities and Colleges in the War Areas

(to the end of December, 1939)

Name	Property Losses	Remarks
Provincial University of Anhwei	$3,088,607	
Provincial University of Hunan	1,600,000	This includes only the cost of the premises; library and laboratory equipment not included.
Provincial University of Shansi	366,770	
Provincial University of Kwangtung	——	No details

CULTURE AND EDUCATION

Name	Property Losses	Remarks
Provincial University of Jang Ching	951,837	
Provincial College of Medicine and Political Science of Kiangsu	325,106	
Provincial College of Technology of Hopei	800,000	
Provincial Girls' Normal College of Hopei	696,000	
Provincial College of Agriculture of Hopei	152,353	
Provincial College of Medicine of Hopei	186,930	
Provincial School of Medicine and Pharmacy of Chekiang	698,794	
Provincial School of Technology of Shansi	14,589	
Provincial School of Medicine of Kiangsi	70,000	
Provincial School of Technology of Kiangsi	——	No details
Provincial School of Commerce of Shansi	——	No details
Provincial School of Hydraulic Engineering of Honan	45,530	
Provincial School of Silk Manufacture of Kiangsu	64,051	
Provincial School of Physical Education of Peiping	——	No details
Provincial School of Village Reconstruction of Shantung	——	No details
Provincial School of Physical Education of Kwangtung	58,022	
TOTAL	$8,045,919	

Table III

Property Losses of Private Universities and Colleges in the War Areas

(to the end of December, 1939)

Name	Property Losses	Remarks
University of Nanking	$15,384,834	
Fu Tan University	2,316,310	
Kwang Hua University	544,975	
Great China University	800,000	
Soochow University	550,000	
Shanghai University	1,510,000	
Fu Jen University	——	Without details
Sino-French University	——	Without details
Nankai University	3,750,000	University, $3,000,000; Middle School, $750,000.
Cheloo University	957,350	
Lin-nan University	3,800,000	
Central China Union University of Wuchang	392,397	
Chung Hua University of Wuchang	431,910	
Kuo Min University of Kwang-tung	383,080	
Canton University	199,444	
Ginling College	6,306,225	
Shanghai College of Law	510,000	
Chih-Tze University	511,100	
Chao-Yang College	247,750	
Chung Kao College	433,800	
Cheng-Feng College of Arts	100,000	
Peiping Union Medical College	——	

CULTURE AND EDUCATION

Name	Property Losses	Remarks
Min Kuo College	215,000	
Tientsin Engineering and Commercial College	1,200,000	
Nan-Tung College	307,810	
Tsekiang College	600,000	
Kwang Hua Medical College	169,926	
Chao-Tsao Engineering College	184,452	
Girls' College of Medicine of Shanghai	34,651	
Tung-Teh Medical College	160,000	
Southwestern Medical College	270,000	
Shanghai College of Law and Jurisprudence	50,000	
Wuchang School of Fine Arts	1,045,953	
Far East School of Physical Education	240,000	
Soochow School of Fine Arts	92,000	
Hsin Hwa School of Fine Arts	180,000	
Shanghai School of Fine Arts	123,000	
Wusih School of Chinese Classics	110,000	
Wen Hua School of Library Science of Wuchang	26,000	
Chuan Tze School of Medicine of Shansi	102,988	
Railway School	30,988	
TOTAL	$44,771,897	

Our cultural and educational institutions have, of course, sustained tremendous losses, but they are striving to maintain their regular courses with an undaunted spirit,

[173]

CHINA SHALL RISE AGAIN

despite the almost insurmountable difficulties. As a result of the war, most of our cultural and educational institutions in the coastal provinces have been removed into the interior, and have been playing an important part in developing those provinces. For instance, before the war there were only 33 universities and colleges in the interior, now there are 101.

It must be borne in mind that the losses sustained by our institutions of higher learning cannot be entirely evaluated in terms of money, such as the material for economic research possessed by Nankai University, the modern history documents of Tsinghua University, and the geological fossils of the National University of Peiping.*

OTHER CULTURAL AND EDUCATIONAL INSTITUTIONS

The losses sustained by the vocational schools, primary and secondary schools, and kindergartens are, because of their large number, even greater than those sustained by the colleges and universities. In the districts now occupied by the Japanese there were formerly 110 middle schools with more than 41,700 students. Of the 3,264 middle schools that existed in the country prior to the aggression, 1,296, or 40 per cent, are now in the areas occupied by the enemy.

* The losses of the following institutions have not yet been reported: University of Shanghai, Yenching University, and Southwestern School of Medicine.

CULTURE AND EDUCATION

Property losses of the middle schools alone amount to more than $65,567,783. As a result, 20,510, or one third, of the middle school teachers and staff members, and one half of some 571,800 middle school students, of the entire country have suffered.

Before the war, China had more than 294,000 primary schools. In recent years these schools have been improved both in quantity and quality, as indicated by the increase in enrollment, the improvement in the standard of courses of instruction, the modification in the methods of teaching and training, the increase in the salaries of teachers, etc. Since the commencement of the war, 129,700 primary schools have been forced to close down, and more than 259,000 teachers and staff members, and 6,483,000 children of school age have become idle.

THE LOSSES OF LIBRARIES, MUSEUMS, ETC.

The losses sustained by the libraries, popular reading centers, and museums are also great. There are altogether 2,118 libraries and 835 popular reading centers and 54 museums in the occupied and war zones. Supposing that the average number of books in each library is 5,000 volumes, then the books thus lost would be more than 1,000,000 volumes, to say nothing of the value of the rare books of the Peiping National Library and the other libraries in Nanking, Tientsin, Tsingtao, etc.

The losses of the museums are even greater, and can-

[175]

not be estimated in terms of money. For instance, the Palace Museum of Peiping was looted of 214 cases of rare articles by the enemy; the Library Hall of Peiping, of 1,737 cases of documents and manuscripts; the Office of the Secretariat of the former National Peiping Palace Museum, of 826 cases; the Summer Palace, of 88 cases; the Library, of 5 cases; the Museum of the Ministry of Interior, of 114 cases, making a grand total of 2,984 cases.

Roughly expressed in terms of money, the National Central Library suffered a loss of $550,000; the National Central Museum, $665,000; the Kiangsu Provincial Library of Chinese Books, $300,000. As far as can be gathered, China's losses in these items during the war have thus far amounted to more than $18,150,000.

LOOTING OF PRIVATE COLLECTORS

Equally great were the losses sustained by private collectors of manuscripts, books, and curios. Most of the famous private collections of books and curios were kept in cities like Peiping, Tientsin, Shanghai, Soochow, Hangchow, Wusih, Wuchin, etc. As no severe fighting ever took place in Peiping, the losses of private collections there were small as compared with those in the other cities mentioned above which were the scenes of large-scale battles. The losses suffered by the private collectors in these cities are enormous and irretrievable.

CULTURE AND EDUCATION

To mention just one or two instances, the rare manuscripts of Chia Yeh Hall, of the Liu family, in Nanshun, Chekiang, with its incomplete copy of *Yung Lo Ta Tien* were looted by the Japanese; also, the bronzes of the Pan family in Soochow, and the valuable collections of scrolls and paintings of the Ku family in the same city.

Indeed the Japanese have inflicted such heavy and widespread losses on China's cultural and educational institutions that it is difficult to estimate them in terms of money, even approximately. To the best of our ability, these losses, excluding those suffered by colleges and universities may be assessed as roughly equivalent to $209, 182,382 as per Table IV below:

Table IV

Property Losses of Middle Schools, Primary Schools and Institutions of Social Education in the War Areas

(up to the end of December, 1939)

Chekiang	$3,972,775
Kiangsu	43,479,398
Kiangsi	397,274
Hupeh	553,510
Szechuan	106,467
Kwangsi	632,300
Yunnan	91,000
Shansi	1,303,052
Shensi	44,220
Fukien	1,790,300

Anhwei	9,063,760
Hunan	19,616,015
Kwangtung	6,362,464
Hopei	22,775,264
Shantung	44,146,957
Honan	12,992,782
Chahar	2,447,905
Suiyuan	994,748
Nanking	5,246,915
Shanghai	8,704,882
Peiping	13,128,308
Tientsin	7,164,061
Weihaiwei	756,022
Tsingtao	2,164,051
TOTAL	$209,182,382

EMERGENCY RELIEF

Enormous as are the material losses, the human suffering and complications caused by the war have given rise to a host of problems that have taxed to the extreme both the resources and the energy of the educational authorities. Naturally the first problem is that of relief. Take, for instance, the case of colleges and universities. Before the war, 41,922 students were enrolled in our colleges and universities; and there were some 11,850 faculty and staff members. After the war broke out one half of that number joined either the army or the service of other wartime activities. But for those students who chose to continue their studies, the Ministry of Education had to

[178]

provide accommodations in regions of safety; while for the former professors and staff members of the colleges and universities that had been destroyed or forced to close down, the Ministry had to provide employment.

This task, difficult even in ordinary times, becomes almost impossible during the war. The problem, for instance, of providing equipment and library books for the colleges and universities from the war areas and of housing them in new premises in the rear is a tremendous one.

The relief of university and college students constitutes another serious problem. The Ministry of Education has, from the very outset, decided that students who lost their former schools may be allowed upon application to join other existing schools as temporary or auditor students. Up to the present, 1,106 students have applied for transfers and been accepted. The smallness of this figure is explained by the fact that, through the efforts of the government, 83 out of a total of 108 institutions of higher learning have been able to maintain themselves — that is to say, only 25 institutions have been actually forced to close down. It must be remembered, of course, that a number of students have joined the fighting services. Besides, there are 464 students who have been assigned by the government to various kinds of work. For those students who have found schools in which to study but whose incomes have been cut short as a result of the war, the government has appropriated large sums for relief.

Thanks to the contributions of organizations in foreign lands, this fund has been greatly increased. Up to the moment of writing, 2,709 students have received relief from the government in the form of individual loans. Altogether $66,884 have been distributed.

The Hunan Education Department has just announced that it will offer 333 scholarships of $60 each semi-annually, totaling $40,000 for this fiscal year, to needy Hunan students studying in colleges in any part of the country who are above average intelligence and of good deportment.

RELIEF OF STUDENTS STUDYING ABROAD

China has a considerable number of students studying abroad. As their expenses continue to be a drain on China's foreign exchange reserve, the Ministry of Education and the Ministry of Finance have jointly formulated regulations restricting the purchase of foreign exchange and the issuance of passports only to those students whose courses of study directly concern the problems of national defense, such as science, engineering, medicine and military science. To those who were studying these subjects abroad, but who experienced financial difficulties as a result of the war, the Ministry of Education managed to remit varying amounts of relief funds so that they might complete their studies. There was also promulgated a set of regulations governing the sending of students to study abroad. It is as follows:

1. The sending of students abroad, both government and self-supported, is limited to those who intend to study military science, pure science, engineering, medicine, and those subjects of direct use or immediate concern to our war and national defense.

2. Any student, government or self-supported, must possess one of the following qualifications before he or she can be admitted:

   (a) Having continued research work or served in the government for at least two years with distinction after graduation from one of the recognized government or private universities;

   (b) Having continued research work or served in the government for at least four years with distinction after graduation from one of the recognized government or private colleges or technical institutes.

3. With the exception of students taking courses in military science, engineering, medicine, or subjects of direct use or immediate concern to our war and national defense (which must of necessity be continued), whose accomplishments are endorsed by the institutions in which they study and by the Chinese embassies concerned, those who are at present studying abroad with study permits, who have stayed in the countries specified or chosen for three or more years, should return to China before September of this year (1938); no remittance permit will be granted them in case of further delay on their part.

4. Those students who are studying abroad without any study permit will not be endorsed by the Ministry of Education in case they should petition for remittance permits. In case they wish to return at once, they may, with an endorsement from the Chinese embassies concerned, petition the Ministry of Education for remittance permits to cover their return passages.

Up to the end of December, 1939, students to the number of 543 have received relief from the government. The table is as follows:

Relief for Students Studying Abroad

(to the end of December, 1939)

Country	Given Allowance for Living	Given Return Passage Fee	Total
Great Britain	35	35	70
Germany	61	103	164
United States	70	84	154
France	13	91	104
Belgium	8	8	16
Egypt	—	28	28
Turkey	—	1	1
Japan	—	1	1
Italy	2	2	4
Switzerland	2	—	2
Denmark	—	1	1
Total	191	354	545

CULTURE AND EDUCATION

On account of the war, as many as 2,000 teachers in the educational institutions have lost their positions. To relieve them, the Ministry of Education has, in spite of considerable difficulties, appropriated large sums of money. Teachers in the universities, colleges, and other institutions of higher learning, who have lost their means of livelihood, may apply for relief at the Ministry of Education. Of course, many of them have since been employed by government or private institutions for work directly or indirectly connected with the war. But there are others who are still unemployed. To these the government offers as relief a monthly allowance, and work suitable for them.

So far, 10,671 persons have applied and received work from the Ministry of Education. Of these 169 are engaged in editing and writing books and textbooks. The remaining persons have taken up positions in the Bureaus of Education of the provincial governments. The mere fact that so far only 10,671 persons have applied for relief from the government shows that the proportion of teachers who have found employment elsewhere must be a large one.

Relief for teachers in the secondary and primary schools has assumed a great variety of forms. First, many of these teachers have found employment in the middle schools recently established by the Ministry of Education. As a

[183]

rule, middle schools were established by provincial governments or by private persons. There was, before the war, no national middle school. The Ministry of Education has, since the early part of 1938, established 13 national middle schools which are distributed over the provinces of Szechuan, Kweichow, Honan, Shansi, Kansu, Hupeh, Shensi, and Anhwei, each school having, on the average, 150 teachers and 1,200 to 1,500 students. This move was undertaken because it was thought that this would be an improvement upon the old system, and because it would afford relief to teachers and students coming into the interior from the war areas.

In the second place, 2,551 school teachers have been organized into War Service Corps to be despatched for duty in the various provinces. Their main duties are to look after the dressing, feeding, housing and transportation of the wounded soldiers and refugees; to educate the Chinese masses behind the lines by means of lectures, songs, plays and wall posters; to mobilize the populace into transportation units in order to help the fighting force. Some of them are even doing intelligence work, or leading guerrilla units. There are seven of these War Service Corps, one in each of the provinces of Szechuan, Kweichow, Honan, Hupeh, Shansi, Kansu and Shensi.

In the third place, 8,476 school teachers have been distributed by the government among the various provinces to do educational work. Others to the number of

307 have been sent by the Ministry of Education to work in the Training Schools for the Teaching of Elementary Chinese by the use of character cards, or through Child Relief Associations, Child Welfare Associations, Committees for the Education of Refugees, etc. These forms of relief have so far benefited 8,883 persons in all, the distribution of whom is shown in the following table:

Table VI

Relief for Middle and Primary School Teachers from the War Areas

(to the end of December, 1939)

Educational work under different Provincial Governments:

Hupeh	4,672
Szechuan	708
Hunan	1,387
Kwangsi	319
Kwangtung	6
Anhwei	173
Yunnan	47
Kiangsu	228
Honan	122
Shansi	217
Chekiang	300
Kweichow	190
Kansu	34

Educational relief organizations:

Character card training classes	97
Child welfare associations	81

Child relief associations 99
Refugees' education committees 30

Others;

Teachers of the National Language . . . 79
Editors of children's reading manuals . . 27
Mass reader of children's reading manuals . 17
Teachers distributed to Yunnan Province . 46

TOTAL 8,883

Table VII

Relief for Social Education Workers

(to the end of December, 1939)

Social Educational Corps 262
Social Educational Second Corps 489
Theaters in Circuit 69
Educational Cars 5
Educational Inspectors and Guides in the
several provinces 85
Social Educational Workers sent to the
Bureaus of Education in the several
provinces 376

TOTAL 1,788

The Ministry of Education also gave much needed relief to 1,788 social-education workers by assisting them to work in circuit theaters, circuit education cars, social education corps, etc., in the different provinces.

REDISTRIBUTION OF COLLEGES AND UNIVERSITIES

The problems of relief confronting educational authorities in China should be tackled in the light of reconstruction; that is to say, while we are engaged in relief, we seek to improve our educational system at the same time.

Before the war, most of the colleges and universities were concentrated in a few cities along the coast. As the severest battles were fought in China's maritime provinces, these institutions suffered terribly, as already shown above. In our effort to re-establish a new system of higher education for the country, we took care to correct this mistake by redistributing the new institutions in different cities in the rear on a more geographical basis, so that areas formerly considered backward may be benefited by the maintenance of one or more institutions of higher learning.

Meanwhile, the Ministry of Education took advantage of the opportunity to amalgamate those colleges or universities whose functions duplicated each other, in order to raise their standard and efficiency; for instance, the National Tsinghua University, the National University of Peiping, and the private Nankai University. The present National Northwestern United University is derived from the combination of the former National Peiping University, the National Normal University of Peiping

[187]

and the National Peiyang Engineering College. There are other cases of amalgamation, and, it is gratifying to note, the results have proved beneficial both in respect to finance and administration.

For the improvement of the teaching staff of the middle schools, the Ministry of Education has established a normal college in Hunan Province and added five normal colleges to five universities, namely, the National Central, the National Northwestern United, the National Southwestern United, the National Sun Yat-sen, and the National University of Chungking. Graduation in these colleges will take one year in addition to the regular college course.

Military training is required in all schools above the secondary grade. In the summer the students are required to attend training camps for a period of three months. In the primary schools, boy scout training is emphasized.

In order to realize the ideal of triple emphasis on morals, knowledge and physical culture, the Ministry of Education has set up a Training Research Commission to study the problem. Among the measures recommended by the Commission is the introduction of the tutorial system, which is to be enforced in schools above the secondary grades.

Under the system each tutor will undertake personally to look after the general training of from ten to fifteen students in addition to giving lectures in the classroom, thus making him not only a transmitter of knowledge, but also, a guardian to the students in helping them to solve many of their life problems. At the same time, an outline for normal education is formulated, detailing its course so that the different grades of schools can follow accordingly. For physical culture, too, detailed regulations have been laid down, with special attention to the students' life, food, and hygiene, in order to build up in them good healthy habits, and ultimately to raise the health standard of the entire people.

SPECIAL VOCATIONAL EDUCATION

In co-operation with the Ministries of Interior, Finance, Communications, War, and the Commission on Aeronautical Affairs, the Ministry of Education has drafted a plan for vocational education that will prepare the students for work in the different government departments. The Ministry of Education has also assigned a group of experts to study the needs of the different provinces in connection with reconstruction, and to advise them in the establishment of schools, and the assignment of teaching staffs. Since the war started, the Ministry of Education found employment for 2,000 out of 4,494 of the total number of college graduates.

Our vocational education aims at building a sound middle cadre for the various professions and industrial enterprises. There are training schools and short-time classes for mechanics, electrical communications, metal work, etc. Also, special classes are opened in more than ten colleges and universities for advanced studies along such lines.

Our attempts to introduce practical courses into the middle school curriculum, as well as in the vocational schools, have been very successful. In the lower grade of middle school, woodworking, gardening, and elementary courses on agriculture are taught, and in the upper grade of the middle school, foundry and blacksmithery. The results are evidenced by the increasing number of specialists, technicians and experts taking part in our war of resistance, and by the percentage increase in the number of students of science and engineering taking college entrance examinations. In 1938, for example, only 53.9 per cent of the students who took the examinations were enrolled in the science and engineering courses. In 1939 the ratio jumped to 59.4 per cent.

PEOPLE'S EDUCATION

The promotion of people's education, which is one of the most important undertakings in our educational program, has received a great impetus since the war started. Whenever possible the work is carried on as part of the program of the People's Military Training Corps; that is, those attending free schools for people's education are urged to join the Military Training Corps. The aim of the Free School for People's Education is to give the masses an elementary knowledge of the Chinese language as well as training in citizenship. Before the fall of Hankow, 1,500 classes were conducted in Wuhan. The experiment was later extended to Chungking, Chengtu, and to the Provinces of Kansu, Kweichow, Yunnan and Fukien.

At the National Conference on People's Education held from March 12 to 16 in Chungking, the *five-year plan for people's education,* adopted by the Executive Yuan, was further deliberated. The proper enforcement of this plan will help to convert at least 140,000,000 adult illiterates into intelligent citizens for China within the coming five years.

At present, there are already 44 per cent — 19,800,000 — of the entire number of children of school age (from 6 to 12) in school. By the enforcement of this plan, there should be, during the first two years, at least one people's school in every three "pao." The "pao" is at once a civic and a military organization for both peace and wartime. Each "pao" consists of from ten to fifteen families. Ten "pao" make a village, or a village consists of from ten to fifteen "pao." In this way there should be at least more than 260,000 people's schools for the 800,000 "pao" of the entire nation at the end of the first two years.

Each people's school consists of three divisions, or classes, namely, the children's division, the men's division, and the women's division. During the second two years there should be at least one people's school in every two "pao." In the fifth and last year there should be at least one people's school in each "pao." That is to say, at the end of the fifth year there should be at least 800,000 people's schools providing education for at least 90 per cent of the children of school age. As a matter of fact, certain provinces have already succeeded in establishing one or even two people's schools in each "pao." Kiangsi Province, for instance, has at present one people's school in each "pao," while Fukien Province has two people's schools in each "pao." The fulfillment of this five-year plan needs at least $2,932,000,000 and 1,600,000 teachers — properly trained teachers.

CHINESE CULTURE

Chinese culture, old, rich, cosmopolitan, is essentially humanistic. Humanistic, because to Chinese culture, the entire universe, constant in matter but variable in form, exists as a regenerating process capable of transmutations, one of whose microscopic forms is man. Slowly progressing on a way paved by both materialism and spiritualism, it maintains well the balance between man and nature, between the universe and its composite elements, between that which is dynamic and that which is static, between that which is weak, yielding, and that which is harsh and violent, thus achieving the golden mean.

In its approach to life, Chinese culture begins with

self-perfection, as it exerts influence upon both nature and other human beings: from those who are dear to those who are less dear and from man to all things. In his attempt to be nature's equal in essence, man ventures to enlarge his highly limited being intellectually and morally through the constant increase of knowledge, which in turn enables him to acquire spacial and durational adjustment with the rest of the universe.

The universe, conductive of the spiritual endeavors as well as the material achievements of man, is thus conceived in terms of human life, and the chief purpose of man's life is to discover its relation and harmony with the rest of the universe.

This atoneness between the universe and human life characterizes every phase of Chinese life, every achievement of the Chinese people.

Chinese culture does not indulge in the purely metaphysical, or the vague and aloof; nor does it engage itself in study merely for the sake of study, but for the expression and perfection and simplification of human life. It attempts to reconcile the countless entities composing the universe by finding a balance between extremes. It does not seek to question nature's verdict upon man, but to understand how to effect self-control and mutual tolerance. Above all, it identifies the beautiful with the true and wise.

This theory of knowledge and of life is, of course, Confucian, and serves as the foundation for the Confucian doctrine of "cheng," the sophi-conscience of mind; that is, the interpenetration of intelligence and morality upon which wisdom is born. From wisdom come peace, harmony and universal happiness.

Confucianism, with its nonconditional motive for life and living, its ethical conception of human relations and its emphasis on social political benevolence and cosmopolitanism, has gathered and held together the divergent groups of which the Chinese people are composed and given them unity and inner tranquility through centuries of turmoil. Because it does not preach the gospel of reward like other religions or philosophies, Confucianism is able to transcend the bounds of utilitarianism; because it conceives of life in terms of ethical relations, it is free from material unrest and religious despair in its view of the present life of man. Because it advocates benevolence of government, democracy, and leadership, Confucianism does not have to rely upon either tradition of policy or any ruling mechanism; because it calls for a universal ethico-social fellowship, Confucianism takes the entire world under Heaven as a family, not in the patriarchal sense, but in the sense of love and co-operation.

With such a cultural background the educational system of China naturally shuns extremes, deviations, one-sided developments, while striving to secure the balance between knowledge and virtue, between man and nature, between the old and new, between that which is physical and that which is mental. The chief task of the Ministry of Education today, as already said, is to protect and reconstruct this culture, to enlighten the illiterate masses, and to train character as well as create specialists. This undertaking is imperative in face of the determination of our enemy to annihilate both our culture and our race.

To sum up, the duties of the Ministry of Education, multifarious and complex as they are, are represented by three objectives: to meet the needs of our war environment, to reform our educational system, and to protect and reconstruct our culture.

The nationwide organization for relief and assistance, the translocation of cultural and educational institutions; the inauguration of the auditor-student system, the enforcement of military drill, etc., constitute the emergency measures, to which certain measures of reconstruction are allied — such as the establishment of the thirteen national middle schools, the centralization of the experts, and educators in refuge in order to raise the cultural level of the interior provinces.

Among the emergency measures are certain experimental features, such as the circuit theaters and street plays. These have been most effective in educating the masses during the war.

The chief measures of reformation are the enforcement of character education, the widespread introduction of technical and productive courses, the establishment of normal colleges, the creation of the national conformity college entrance examination, the standardization of the courses of study, etc.

The character education advocated by Generalissimo Chiang Kai-shek, and instituted by myself, serves as the basic point of our program. Building upon the eight cardinal virtues of loyalty, filial piety, benevolence, love, faithfulness, righteousness, peace and harmony, upon our agelong conception of ethics, upon the new moral ideas incorporated in the Three Peoples' Principles, it links together the old and new ideas of character and intellectual development and physical culture. Its purpose is to build upright and able individuals who may become intelligent, law-abiding citizens of their own country as well as useful members of the world at large.

The new system of normal college is an improvement upon the old one by virtue of its lengthened period for resident study, its well-distributed courses, and the grant of free tuition which helps to draw numerous promising youths to the teaching profession. The national conformity college entrance examination helps to standardize admission requirements, thereby avoiding inconvenience and confusion.

The attention paid to music, both Chinese and Western, the establishment of Fu Shin Shu Yuan, or Academy of Chinese Classics, the National Council of Higher

Learning, the National Academy of Music, the vast translation and compilation projects suggest other major efforts of the Ministry. Hereafter, while venturing to maintain its regular course, it will redouble its efforts on the following six points:

1. The extermination of illiteracy.
2. The enforcement of character education.   .
3. Close relationship between education and actual life.
4. The universalization of technical and productive education.
5. Mutual adjustment between education and our national programs of defense and reconstruction.
6. The protection and reconstruction of our culture.

XVII

THE CHINESE NATIONAL HEALTH ADMINISTRATION DURING THE SINO-JAPANESE HOSTILITIES*

FOLLOWING the aggression by Japan which began on July 7, 1937, and the opening of the war of resistance, the Chinese National Government immediately set up a Ministry of Health. The aim was to put all the medical and health activities of the nation under one administration, divided into two sections — the Army Medical Administration for the army, and the National Health Administration for the civilian population. The Ministry was, however, short-lived.

In January, 1938, the Army Medical Administration was affiliated with the Ministry of War, while the National Health Administration was placed under the Ministry of Interior.

In April, 1940, the National Health Administration was formed to function directly under the Executive Yuan. Following the Generalissimo's policy of prolonged resistance and national reconstruction, the activities of the National Health Administration have been accord-

* By Dr. P. Z. King, Director-General of the Chinese National Health Administration.

[198]

ingly adjusted to fit into the dual program of meeting both the emergent wartime needs and the permanent public health reconstruction.

WAR-TIME EPIDEMIC PREVENTION AND MEDICAL RELIEF

(1) *Epidemic Prevention and Control:*

Realizing the danger and possibility of epidemic outbreaks among both army and civilian camps of laborers and refugees, the National Health Administration lost no time in organizing measures for prevention and treatment.

Among epidemics of communicable diseases claiming attention during the past two years may be mentioned the epidemics of cholera, which spread rapidly during the summers of 1938 and 1939 in the Yangtze Valley and South China; plague in Fukien Province and along the border of Chekiang; malaria during 1938 in Central and South China, especially in Kwangsi, Kweichow and Yunnan provinces; diphtheria during the spring of 1939 in Ninghsia Province; and typhus and relapsing fever in the Northwest. Other diseases such as smallpox, typhoid and dysentery were sporadic, but did not assume serious proportions.

To meet the vast needs, the National Health Administration, immediately after the outbreak of war, co-operated with the Army Medical Administration in organizing two army anti-epidemic units. The National Health Administration also organized an Anti-Epidemic Corps, which, at present, maintains twenty-three anti-epidemic units, five isolation hospitals, one sanitary engineering unit, one diagnostic laboratory unit, and four supply depots. As all the units are mobile in nature and each unit is divisible into four subunits to function independently, they have been mobilized from time to time for service in afflicted areas. During 1939 their work extended to more than a hundred localities in the provinces of Shantung, Kansu, Shensi, Honan, Hupeh, Hunan, Kiangsi, Anhwei, Chekiang, Fukien, Kwangtung, Kwangsi, Kweichow, Szechuan, Sikang, and Yunnan.

Among the preventive measures for the control of epidemics, the units have conducted preventive inoculations on a large scale; built delousing stations; disinfected wells and drinking-water supplies. The clinics provide ambulatory treatment, while serious cases are isolated in the hospitals. In all this work, the National Health Administration is grateful to the League of Nations, which has collaborated with the Chinese Government by detailing an Epidemic Commission to China since November, 1937, giving us technical and material assistance.

Table I summarizes the more important activities of the National Health Administration Anti-Epidemic Corps during the period July, 1938, to December, 1939.

CHINESE HEALTH ADMINISTRATION

Table 1

*Statistical Summary of the More Important Activities of the National
Health Administration Anti-Epidemic Corps from the Period from
July 1938 to December 1939*

Service	1938 (July-Dec.)	1939	Total
Preventive Inoculations:			
Cholera	818,711	774,446	1,593,157
Typhoid	74,478	972,425	166,903
Smallpox	32,585	371,700	404,285
Meningitis	0	4,931	4,931
Plague	0	12,449	12,449
Curative Service:			
No. first visits	158,494	445,378	603,872
No. subsequent visits	86,556	559,816	646,372
No. patients admitted to hospital	2,822	9,435	12,257
Health Service:			
Physical Examinations	2,530	15,009	17,539
Deliveries	1	267	268
Health Talks	2,144	10,426	12,570
Attendance at health talks	772,476	671,726	1,444,202
Sanitation			
No. persons deloused	0	8,684	8,684
No. pieces clothing and bedding deloused	0	38,384	38,384
Sanitary inspections and improvements	10,586	16,133	26,719
No. wells disinfected	24,589	235,621	260,210
No. barrels river water disinfected	0	172,996	172,996
No. times latrine disinfected	24,166	10,276	34,442
Laboratory Examinations:			
Bacteriological and parasitological examinations	0	9,166	9,166
Clinical diagnostic examinations	0	1,895	1,895
Examinations of foods and drinks	0	62	62

(2) *Health Protection for Refugee Children*

For relief of the large number of orphans created by the war, many institutions have been established and maintained under the auspices of Madame Chiang Kai-shek, the National Child Welfare Association, the National Relief Commission, and other social welfare organizations. The National Health Administration gives assistance in the medical care in these orphanages and is taking direct charge of it in twenty such institutions.

(3) *Medical Care of the Wounded*

In addition to the medical service for the wounded soldiers undertaken by the Army Medical Administration and the Medical Division of the Ministry of Military Supplies and Transport, medical units organized by the National Red Cross Society of China, under the supervision of the National Health Administration, have rendered technical and material assistance to the military hospitals. During the period January, 1938, to June, 1939, 76 units were in operation, of which there were 34 curative units, 23 ambulance units, 11 nursing units, 7 preventive units and 1 X-ray unit with 20 attached subunits, composing a total of 1,847 doctors, nurses, pharmacists, sanitary engineers and assistants. Motor and boat convoys were kept in operation for the transportation of the wounded, while supply depots were maintained to prepare and issue medical supplies to these units. Table

2 gives a summary of the medical services performed by the Red Cross Medical Relief Corps during the period January, 1938, to June, 1939.

Table 2

Medical Service Performed by the Red Cross Medical Relief Corps During the Period January, 1938, to June, 1939.

X-Ray examinations		15,417
Operations		19,755
Reduction of fractures		15,216
Dressings		1,782,452
Medical treatments		227,915
Preventive Inoculations		594,739
Smallpox	160,967	
Cholera	265,181	
Cholera and typhoid	157,969	
Tetanus	10,622	

For the medical relief of air-raid victims, special units and hospital facilities were organized with the co-operation of local medical and health organizations and private practitioners.

[203]

(4) *Medical Service in Mission Hospitals for the Wounded and Sick in War Zones*

This work has been accomplished mainly through the
missionary doctors who have courageously stood by their
posts and who are doing their best to meet the medical
needs in war zones. With a special subsidy from the National Health Administration, the mission hospitals have
been enabled to give both hospital and ambulatory treatment to more wounded soldiers, air-raid victims and sick
refugees free of charge. At the end of year 1939, 71
hospitals have been receiving such subsidies with a total
bed capacity of 3,650. A sum of $632,279.19 was dis-
bursed for this purpose, including the purchase of drugs
and medical supplies for distribution.

PROJECTS OF PUBLIC HEALTH RECONSTRUCTION

(1) *Development of State Medicine*
    (a) *Adoption and Promotion of the Hsien (County)
    Health System:*

For the promotion of rural health, a hsien health system
has been worked out and adopted as an integral part of
the hsien administration. This system provides a health
center for each hsien, a district health center for each district (a hsien usually has four or five districts), a health
station for each town, village or group of villages, and a
health worker for each "pao" (an average of 100 fami-

lies). The hsien health center is provided, besides the health function, with a 20 to 40-bed hospital, a laboratory and a mobile clinic. The district health centers and health stations have a clinic and the health workers are provided with a first-aid outfit. It is expected that this system, when universally adopted throughout the country, will provide a solid foundation for the state medical service.

With this aim in view, the National Health Administration has subsidized the provincial health authorities in form of medical personnel and medical supplies for the development of local health organizations. Three model hsien health centers are being established in each province for the purpose of demonstration. Table 3 gives an idea of the development of local health organizations and the increase in budget for health work in certain provinces during the period 1937-1939.

Owing to the large field open for the development of health work in the northwestern provinces, the National Health Administration in May, 1939, established a Special Health Commissioner's Office in Sian. This office has maintained 12 health corps, a hospital of 300 beds, and is supervising and directing all health activities in the seven Provinces of Shensi, Shansi, Honan, Kansu, Chinghai, Ninghsia and Suiyuan. (See Table 4 for a summary of activities undertaken under the Special Health Commissioner's Office in Sian for the period May to December, 1939.)

Table 3

Comparative Table Showing the Development of Local Health Organizations and Increase in Budget for Health in Certain Provinces During the Period 1937-1939

Province	Health Budget			No. Hsien Health Organizations		
	July 1936-June 1937	Jan.-Dec. 1939	Comparison	July 1937	Dec. 1939	Comparison
Chekiang	$ 106,864	$ 403,404	+$ 296,540	14	6	— 8
Kiangsi	599,613	566,547	— 33,066	83	83	0
Hupeh	67,174	233,549	+ 166,375	0	8	+ 8
Hunan	114,009	186,487	+ 72,478	6	68	+ 62
Shensi	281,466	57,494	— 223,972	8	14	+ 6
Fukien	161,920	447,074	+ 285,154	15	62	+ 47
Kwangsi	1,077,310	1,579,868	+ 502,558	88	99	+ 11
Yunnan	—	—	—	3	37	+ 34
Kweichow	62,248	699,965	+ 637,717	0	64	+ 64
Kansu	83,774	142,289	+ 58,515	0	5	+ 5
Szechuan	—	320,000	—	0	9	+ 9
Kwangtung	—	114,000	—	0	39	+ 39
	$2,554,378	$4,750,677	+$1,762,299	217	494	+ 277

Table 4

Important Activities of the Northwest Special Health Commissioner's Office* During the Period May to December, 1939

Activity	Number
Preventive Inoculations:	
Cholera	282,675
Typhoid	23,955
Smallpox	37,255
Curative Service:	
No. treatments at clinic	406,950
No. patients admitted to hospital	278
Health Service:	
Physical examinations	11,218
Deliveries	300
Sanitation:	
No. persons deloused	34,217
No. pieces clothing and bedding deloused	206,143
Sanitary inspections and improvements	473
Disinfections	8,574
Laboratory Examinations:	
Bacteriological examinations	482
Serological examinations	179
Parasitological examinations	4,151
Clinical diagnostic examinations	3,096

* This office was established in May, 1939.

Table 5

Summary of the More Important Activities of the Highway Health Stations Under the National Health Administration during the Period April to December, 1939.

Activity	Number
Preventive Inoculations:	
Smallpox	103,793
Cholera	277,083
Cholera and typhoid combined	5,679
Curative Service:	
First visits	101,982
Subsequent visits	151,465
Emergency cases	3,066
Patients admitted to hospital	813
Health Service:	
Physical examinations	13,374
Investigation of communicable diseases	2,200
Prenatal examinations	2,653
Deliveries	719
Postnatal examinations	814
Health Education:	
Health talks	2,856
Attendance at health talks	157,131
Home visits	14,514
Individual health advice	16,801
Environmental Sanitation:	
Sanitary inspections	2,839
Well disinfection	240,063
Latrine disinfection	3,657
Laboratory Examinations:	
Urine	659
Stool	278
Sputum	130
Blood	1,639

(b) *Establishment of Highway Health Stations:* Another project to stimulate the development of the hsien health system in the provinces consists of the establishment of highway health stations at the important points along different highways. The organization, size and composition of staff of such a highway health station approximates that of the permanent hsien health center. Housed in uniform buildings with 30-bed wards, an outpatient department and a small diagnostic laboratory, each station is expected to undertake the curative and preventive services over a distance of 100 kilometers. Fifteen such stations, each with one or two substations, were established during 1939, besides 13 stations and 15 mobile units for the highways still under construction, at the request of the Ministry of Communications. Table 5 gives a summary of the work carried out by these highway health stations during 1939.

(2) *Unification and Expansion of the Medical Service on the Yunnan-Burma Highway and Railway*

Owing to the growing importance of the Yunnan-Burma Highway and Railway, and in order to meet the need of medical service for the large number of laborers and floating population along this route, the Central Government has just approved a plan to centralize the available medical service there under the National Health Administration whereby the few existing medical organizations may be co-ordinated and the medical facilities may be extended to important points of the route where such are lacking. Preparations are being made to establish eighteen additional stations, six of which, with hospital accommodations. A supply depot will also be established for the distribution of drugs and material for sanitary improvements.

(3) *Anti-Malaria and Anti-Goiter Campaign in Yunnan*

Because of the devastating effect of malaria in Yunnan, incapacitating at least 30 per cent of the laborers engaged in highway and railway construction, and the high prevalence of goiter affecting over 25 per cent of the population, the Central and Provincial governments have jointly started a five-year anti-malaria and anti-goiter campaign in that province. A malaria research institute, and four anti-malaria stations have already been organized during the first year, and twelve such stations will be established at the completion of the program.

From December, 1939, to May, 1940, the United States Public Health Service has despatched a mission of malariologists to the province. As a result of their survey of the disease in Hsiakwan, Yungping, Paoshan, Mangshih, Chefang, and other important malaria centers in western Yunnan, they have recommended valuable control measures based upon local conditions, including camp location, larvacides, irrigation, and organization of the campaign. This work is being continued by the Weishengshu Anti-Epidemic Unit and experts detailed to the province by the Rockefeller Foundation, who are working on the spot in close collaboration with the Yunnan Malaria Research Institute.

Simultaneous with this anti-malaria campaign, the National Health Administration is co-operating with the Yunnan Provincial Salt Administration in anti-goiter work by iodizing the large salt cakes and the provision of prophylactic doses of potassium iodide to the school children.

(4) *Training of Wartime Medical and Public Health Personnel*

With the extension of hostilities to the interior provinces, the need for medical personnel for wartime service has become increasingly greater. Besides conscripting the newly graduated doctors and pharmacists, a special Wartime Medical Service Training School was established in June, 1938, for the purpose of training medical and public health workers for wartime service. The types of workers trained include surgical officers, assistant medical officers, nurses, nursing assistants, X-ray technicians, and sanitary technicians. By the end of 1939, a total of 3,631 persons received training from this school.

The Public Health Personnel Training Institute, established in 1935, continued to carry on its function of training candidates sent by local governments. During 1939, twelve classes were conducted for the training of a total of 287 medical officers, sanitary engineers, maternity and child health workers, and public health nurses.

(5) *Provision for Drugs, Vaccines and Other Medical Supplies*

The National Health Administration wishes to extend its thanks to friendly nations, various helping organizations and individuals, and overseas Chinese who have continuously and generously contributed funds and medical supplies to the National Red Cross. The need nevertheless has been very great. With the war in Europe, which further restricts the source of supply, and with increased difficulty of transportation, attempts were made to encourage the manufacture of drugs and instruments at home. While many private small drug factories have come into existence utilizing native raw material, a Central Pharmaceutical Manufacturing Company is being established for large-scale production. The production of vaccines and sera in quantities sufficient for the requirements of the whole country has been achieved, as will be seen from Table 6.

Table 6

Important Biological Products Prepared by the National Epidemic Prevention Bureau and Northwest Epidemic Prevention Bureau During 1939

Product	Quantity
Bacterial and Virus Vaccines:	
Smallpox	24,102,884 doses
Concentrated cholera	4,785,780 cc.
Cholera and typhoid combined	15,260,760 cc.
Typhoid, triple	378,410 cc.
Others	520,071 cc.
Sera and Antitoxins:	
Diptheria antitoxin	51,336,500 units
Tetanus antitoxin	11,026,000 units
Antimeningococcus serum	107,560 cc.
Antiscarlatina serum	36,050 cc.
Others	50,010 cc
Rinderpest and other vaccines for animal use	99,805 cc.

Thanks to the response to the call of our medical personnel, it has been possible for the National Health Administration to meet the urgent medical needs to an appreciable extent in spite of the tremendous difficulties. In the public health reconstruction of a great nation, three years are but as one day. The little that has been accomplished since the war began will only serve to stimulate our greater effort toward this difficult task.

[213]

At the Fifth General Conference of the Chinese Medical Association (2,886 members) which opened at Kunming, Yunnan Province, on April 2, Dr. King took occasion to express his satisfaction at being able to note the important part played by members of the association in medical relief work, especially by those participating in the work of the Army Medical Service, the Chinese Red Cross Society, and the International Red Cross Committees. He praised the doctors and nurses of mission and private hospitals who have courageously stood by their posts in the "occupied" as well as war areas. They have met an important need for the provision of free medical care of wounded soldiers and the poor and sick in these areas.

For the co-ordination of this work, emergency offices were opened by the association in Kunming, and by the Council on Medical Missions in Chungking, while the general secretary and directors of these offices made extensive visits to the local medical relief organizations and hospitals.

Immediately after the fighting began in Shanghai in August, 1937, the headquarters of the association organized emergency hospitals for wounded soldiers. In addition, other medical work was co-ordinated, such as sending out appeals for donations of medical supplies and finding medical workers and assistants for such agencies as the Red Cross Society. The Hong Kong branch acted as the receiving depot of donated medical supplies, while other branches in the interior served as agencies of distribution.

Many members of the association have been instrumental in spreading local health organizations during the past three years, especially in the southwestern provinces.

With a large increase in the number of health organizations in the interior provinces, the Chinese Medical Association co-operated in securing men and women medical workers to operate the new endeavors. Under the auspices of the Council of Public Health of the association, two health demonstration centers were organized and maintained in Shanghai and Kutsing, Yunnan Province. In addition to medical work among the local people, instruction in public health was given, and many of the personnel served as teachers in the different medical colleges.

In the great trek of colleges and universities from the war-affected areas, a number of China's medical schools from Kiangsu, Shantung and other provinces, gradually moved to the interior. They were eventually concentrated in three centers: Kunming, Kweiyang and Chengtu.

Consequent upon these moves, many more doctors became affiliated with the association, and a branch was organized in Chengtu.

In addition to their ordinary teaching duties, members of the association are frequently called upon to participate in conducting special courses to meet emergency needs.

They have been busy training doctors and nurses for the new medical and public health centers.

The Council on Medical Education made a special appeal to medical colleges in America for assistance in personnel, books and equipment for the three medical college centers in Free China, since most of the schools which moved to the interior were greatly depleted in medical equipment, books and journals, as well as in staff.

Large consignments of books, charts and journals were shipped from Shanghai for the use of the medical students in the interior.

At the same time, the Council on Publications continued its editorial work. There was no interruption to the printing of the National Medical Journal and the Chinese Medical Journal, and a new magazine, the National Health Journal of China, was started. Two new books were published, fifteen others are in the hands of the printers, and eleven more are being prepared for publication.

Other activities of the association since the Fourth General Conference in 1937 include many additions to the museum and a special history number of the National Medical Journal. The Council on Research has continued its investigations of foods, dietary conditions and standards in China.

The Council on Pharmacy and Chemistry has continued its program of introducing new drugs which have been scientifically tested. This has been of great importance, since transportation difficulties and high exchange rates make it extremely difficult to import drugs from abroad. Members of the association were urged to make special studies of all raw materials in the interior which might be utilized for medicines.

XVIII

*THE CHINESE ARMY MEDICAL SERVICE**

AT THE commencement of the present Sino-Japanese conflict the Chinese Army Medical Service had comparatively little difficulty in coping with the situation because of the limited war front. With the rapid spread of hostilities there was a corresponding need for expansion of the service and the question of shortage of qualified technical personnel presented itself for serious consideration. The call to the colors was quickly answered and many doctors and nurses left their private and institutional practice to join the Army Medical Service. However, the need of medical and auxiliary personnel was greater than what the country could supply. Fortunately, compatriots and friends from at home and abroad, came singly, and in organized groups, with technical skill and medical supplies, rendering much valuable aid to the Army Medical Service.

During the three years of war, there have been established about 650 military medical units, including hospitals, casualty receiving stations, surgical operating teams, anti-epidemic corps, and various transport and supply

* By Surgeon-General C. T. Loo, Director, Army Medical Administration.

organizations. Suffice it to say that these establishments are designed for the maintenance of the health of the fighting forces, and the facilitation of the speedy return to active service of those who have become wounded or sick.

In war, aside from humanitarian considerations, prompt diagnosis and treatment of the wounded and sick among the troops is of self-evident tactical importance. The issue of first-aid packages to the rank and file, the establishment of aid posts in and near the battlefields, and provision for evacuation to places of relative safety of those who require a longer rest and more thorough treatment all constitute the first-line activities of the Army Medical Service.

Credit should be given to our womenfolk at home and abroad for the preparation of first-aid packages for the use of our heroic defenders. These little gifts have saved many a limb and life.

Close to the fighting line, at the battalion or regimental aid posts, where the wounded receive their first proper medical attention, one may sometimes find foreign volunteers assisting our medical officers. For us to take such a risk is duty, but for these foreign friends it is perhaps something more sacred.

The evacuation of the wounded and sick from the front to the rear for better care requires an elaborate system of organization. In the early stages of the present war, when railways and highways could be utilized to our advantage, there was not much difficulty encountered as far as the evacuation was concerned; but following the change of our military tactics in the past year, when much of the fighting now takes place in roadless areas, it has been as difficult for us to evacuate our wounded and sick as for the enemy to use their mechanized forces.

As it is man power that we rely upon to win this war, so it is this same power that will solve our evacuation problem. Hundreds of stretcher-bearer companies have been organized for the transportation by relays of the wounded and sick from the field of action. As the distance to be covered on foot by these bearers is oftentimes over one hundred kilometers, there have been established rest stations at intervals of about twelve kilometers at which food, lodging and first-aid are provided. A large number of these establishments are under the management of groups of young enthusiastic workers sponsored by the National Christian Service Council for Wounded Soldiers in Transit.

To bring up a large number of regular army stretcher-bearers from the rear to the front is quite an expense in time and energy; but this has been very much reduced because local civilian volunteers have not been difficult to find in the war areas. The "pao-chia" system (an organization consisting of ten to fifteen families) is utilized, especially in guerrilla warfare. The wounded and sick are usually entrusted to the villagers for transportation and sometimes temporary care. From one "pao" to another under the charge of the respective "pao" villagers, the wounded and sick are sent away to places of relative safety for better medical care. All necessary provisions are gladly offered to the wounded and sick comrades.

The stretcher-bearers are responsible for the evacuation from the combat zone to the communication zone; and from this point on to the rear the journey is continued by railway, highway or waterway. In connection with highway transportation, thanks are due to our overseas compatriots and friends for the donation of a large number of ambulances and trucks, and of the services of many drivers and mechanics.

At strategic points, receiving stations have been established where large groups of wounded and sick are collected and given temporary housing and care; but it is in the regular military hospitals that more elaborate diagnosis and treatment facilities are available.

Attached to some of these military hospitals are medical and nursing units of the Chinese Red Cross Medical Relief Corps, the New Life Movement Association, and other voluntary organizations. These units consisting of highly qualified doctors and nurses have served well in the technical field.

The frequent visits of Madame Chiang Kai-shek to these hospitals have inspired many young nonprofessional men and women to come to these institutions to do whatever they can for the comfort of the patients. Some come to serve as attendants in the ward; others cook food, wash clothes and write letters for the patients. These little services are well appreciated by the patients who unquestionably deserve a great deal more.

According to hospital statistics, of the total admissions in the last three years of war, casualty cases constituted about 64 per cent and sickness cases 36 per cent. About 52 per cent of the total number have returned to active service; 2 to 3 per cent have become incapacitated; and 10 per cent have succumbed to disease or wounds.

Although the war is still going on, it is not premature to consider the problem of rehabilitation of the crippled and disabled soldiers. Crippled and disabled soldiers' homes have been established in different parts of the country, and vocational training of various types is given.

In addition to the regular pensions that the wounded soldiers are entitled to have, the government has set aside vast tracts of land for those who are capable of agricultural pursuit; others have been admitted to work in cotton mills, match factories, and other workshops; still others have been employed as office clerks, doorkeepers, night watchmen, etc., depending upon the extent of their injury.

It should be pointed out here that Chinese society has welcomed the return of the disabled soldiers, and has given them an opportunity to earn a more or less independent living. In fact, many employers, industrial or otherwise, prefer them to able-bodied men because of their steadiness and interest in their jobs.

In Kweiyang, an Orthopedic Center has been established under the joint auspices of the Emergency Medical Field Service Training School and the Chinese Red Cross Medical Relief Corps. The Center is a place where the services of expert orthopedic surgeons and physiotherapists are available, where the disabled may be restored to various degrees of usefulness, and where they may be given vocational training. Aside from those routine services, the Center aims to train orthopedic surgeons and auxiliary personnel with the hope that similar centers may be established elsewhere. The Center is also equipped for the production of orthopedic appliances, such as splints, crutches, and artificial limbs.

That war breeds epidemics is a well-known fact. Through the combined effort of the Army Anti-Epidemic Corps, the Weishengshu (National Health Administration) Anti-Epidemic Corps, the Chinese Red Cross Preventive Units, and the Provincial Health Administrations, most of the serious epidemic diseases have been kept more or less in check. In the last three years there were comparatively few cases of smallpox as a result of widespread vaccination campaigns. Cholera broke out in many places in 1938 and 1939, but there were relatively few cases occurring in the army, proving that the millions of doses of cholera vaccine and the hundreds of tons of bleaching powder used did produce results.

That this war against the cholera vibrio as against our national enemy requires the co-operative endeavor and grim determination of all doctors, nurses, sanitary engineers, sanitary inspectors, and men of all walks of life, is clearly indicated.

As for the control of relapsing fever which ravaged the northwestern provinces in 1938, and somewhat less severely in 1939, a widespread campaign against lice has been launched. Many delousing stations have been established, especially in military hospitals, at which facilities for individual bathing, destruction of lice by heat, and scabies treatment, are provided. Scabies is a prevalent condition among the troops, and this mass treatment is an answer to the urgent need.

The control of malaria is a herculean task because of the magnitude and complexity of the problem; it has cost millions of dollars in other parts of the world. Under the existing conditions, with limited financial and material resources, it is hoped that through the proper use of quinine therapy and simple sanitary and hygienic measures, malarial infections may be partially controlled.

The donation of quinine in large quantities by overseas Chinese and foreign friends in the last three years has lessened our difficulty considerably.

CHINESE ARMY MEDICAL SERVICE

Malnutrition is another evil that war brings forth. The shortage of food supplies in general, or of certain essential articles of food, usually lead to all sorts of nutritional diseases, besides predisposing the individual to infections. That "an army marches on its stomach" is a well-founded truth; hence the nutrition of the soldier should be seriously considered and studied.

At the invitation of the Army Medical Administration, nutrition experts on the staffs of the Emergency Medical Field Service Training School, the National Tsing Hua University and the Chinese Red Cross Medical Relief Corps, are now working jointly on this problem among the troops. It is hoped that their investigations will lead to the improvement of the nutritional status of the army.

It may also be added that in the military hospitals in the last two years, under the guidance of the nutrition experts, special diets have been served to patients suffering from nutritional deficiencies, and these have helped to hasten recovery and have saved many lives.

The Friends of the Wounded Soldier Society has raised large sums of money to finance a good part of the special diet program in the military hospitals.

It has been previously mentioned that the shortage of medical and auxiliary personnel in the Army Medical Service has been somewhat remedied by the enlistment of many voluntary workers from at home and abroad.

Among the volunteers from abroad, there are many overseas Chinese doctors and nurses from Java, Straits Settlements, the Philippine Islands, the United States, and other parts of the world. A number of foreign friends from India, Australia, New Zealand, Canada, the United States, Germany, Spain and other countries have also come to help under the Red Cross banners. As of old, when in face of human suffering, the missionary hospitals have readily responded to the call for help and many civilian victims of war have received their care.

Voluntary workers have indeed been a great help to the Army Medical Service, but many more are required to meet the essential needs. Local training has to be conducted to make up the deficit; hence the establishment of the Emergency Medical Field Service Training School in 1938.

The basic training, aiming to equip all trainees for field service, is completed in two months, a period admittedly too short for advanced instruction, but that is all that can be afforded for the present. All technical methods and procedure as taught in this school are designed from the standpoint of practicability, usefulness, and availability of supplies, not neglecting the scientific aspects. Courses in orthopedic surgery, laboratory technique, roentgenological diagnosis, field sanitation, and other special subjects, are also offered and the period of training varies from three to twelve months.

To date, about 4,000 trainees have completed their training in this school at Kweiyang and in its branch at Paocheng, Shensi Province. In addition to these emergency establishments, the Army Medical School, serving as another training center, offers similar short-term courses besides the regular five-year course.

Because of importation and transportation difficulties, especially since the outbreak of the European War, the problem of medical supplies and equipment has become increasingly perplexing. As doctors in this country differ by reason of their previous training — e.g., German, French, British or American — the drugs prescribed usually vary. To have a large assortment of medicines ready for use in accordance with individual preferences is well-nigh impossible under the existing conditions.

In an attempt to meet this situation, all methods of diagnosis, treatment and prevention have been simplified and standardized; and the medical and sanitary supplies required are consequently reduced to an essential minimum. To facilitate the issuing and distribution of supplies to the various field units, they are prepared and packed in standard sizes and shapes. It is gratifying to report that a large variety of medical and surgical supplies can now be produced locally. For example, Industrial Co-operatives and cotton mills, employing large numbers of refugees and disabled soldiers, have produced gauze for surgical dressing; and the manufacture of pharmaceutical products is a new industrial enterprise in Free China.

In conclusion, under present war conditions, the Army Medical Service is experiencing numerous difficulties. Most of them are, however, not insurmountable.

On account of financial and material limitations, some of the outstanding problems regarding personnel, supplies and transport facilities are being solved in a rather inadequate manner. Voluntary service and generous donation from at home and abroad have been most helpful and are very much appreciated.

As the war will go on for some time, there will surely be more and more difficulties confronting the Army Medical Service. It is hoped that moral support and material aid will continue to come from all parts of the world.

XIX

*THE CHINESE RED CROSS
MEDICAL RELIEF CORPS IN
THREE YEARS OF WAR**

NORTH CHINA BACKGROUND

Following their armed invasion of China's four north-eastern provinces (Manchuria) in 1931, the Japanese struck their second blow at Jehol Province in 1933 and attacked China proper along the Great Wall. At that time the army medical units were unable to give adequate care to the wounded. The Chinese Red Cross therefore tried to meet the need, in so far as it could, by instituting the North China Medical Relief Commission, which in turn organized a Medical Relief Corps of twelve medical units, a motor ambulance service, and a medical supply depot. The Corps operated between Peiping and the Great Wall during the eleven weeks of fighting and for some time afterwards, being liquidated when the wounded in the northern hospitals were evacuated. Two medical units, however, remained as a training nucleus in Peiping.

In pursuit of their strategy of subjugating China by occupying it piecemeal following "local incidents" cal-

---

* By Dr. K. S. Lim, Director of the Chinese Red Cross Medical Relief
  Corps.

[229]

culated not to arouse the nation's suspicions, the Japanese next struck at Hopei Province. At Lukuochiao (Marco Polo Bridge), south of Peiping, on July 7, 1937, however, they met unexpected and most determined resistance, and inadvertently lit the torch of national struggle. This resistance, which the Japanese boasted they could destroy within three months and with no more than fifteen divisions, has now continued for three years. Instead of fifteen divisions the Japanese now have more than double that number in China, while over a million Japanese have been killed, wounded or otherwise invalided.

Soon after the battle of Marco Polo Bridge the Chinese Red Cross organized a mobile surgical unit and sent it to Hopei to serve the wounded there. The two Red Cross units in Peiping were also mobilized, but were prevented by the Japanese occupation of Peiping from rendering any field service.

THE BATTLE FOR SHANGHAI AND NANKING

Five weeks after the battle in the north began, the Japanese turned to attack the main body of China's best-equipped armies at Shanghai, gateway to Nanking, the national capital. Here the Chinese Red Cross Headquarters, supported by practically every Chinese medical worker and by the patriotic people of Shanghai, established a number of temporary Red Cross hospitals. The majority of medical workers and civilian volunteers had other means of support, and so accepted no remuneration. Besides the free offer of services for all kinds of Red Cross work, including preparation of dressings, transport of the wounded by stretcher and motor vehicles, large contributions of money, medical and other supplies poured in.

After three months of resistance against overwhelmingly powerful enemy land, air and naval forces, the Chinese armies retreated from Shanghai and Nanking. The loss of those cities deprived the Red Cross not only of hospitals with their equipment, but of the greater part of their personnel and other assistance such as motor vehicles. However, in an effort to evacuate supplies, equipment and personnel from the fighting zones, there was many an unwritten saga of heroism and determination. Some evacuating Red Cross ambulance workers, with their ambulances, were annihilated; and in Nanking, Red Cross doctors and nurses who had remained to care for the wounded who could not be evacuated were slaughtered together with the wounded, adding horror to the savage massacre of some 20,000 civilians and unarmed soldiers in that city. In the three years of warfare that have followed since then, other Red Cross workers have been repeatedly bombed out of hospitals in which they were caring for the wounded, while a number have been killed or wounded while on duty. Others have died from disease contracted in the performance of their humane

[231]

work. Red Cross trucks and ambulances displaying the Red Cross emblem have been bombed or machine-gunned time and again from the air.

In the early months of the war the Red Cross became acutely aware of the technical deficiencies of the army hospitals and of the various medical units in the field. The Red Cross at the time had no corps organization, so there was no machinery for the operation of mobile field units which could be moved from place to place to strengthen the poorly staffed and equipped military hospitals and to care for the masses of refugees. Therefore, from its new base after the fall of Shanghai and Nanking, the newly formed Red Cross Medical Relief Commission of the National Red Cross at Hankow faced the necessity of establishing operations on a nationwide scale. The task of organizing small mobile units of qualified doctors, nurses, and dressers, and later units of first-aid workers for service at the fronts, began; as well as the organization of a central supply station, with sub-branches, and of a transport system to serve not only the Red Cross mobile units in the field, but army and civilian medical units.

MOBILE MEDICAL UNITS ARE BORN

Fortunately, after the fall of Nanking, there was a lull in fighting for about three months. The Chinese armies, withdrawn westward and northward, were being reorganized, replenished, and re-equipped. The Japanese were also exhausted and had to bring replenishments from Japan, while the Japanese forces halted to loot and slaughter.

At that time, about 800 Red Cross doctors, nurses, and dressers had evacuated to Hankow, and, in the manner of refugees, were massed in a great warehouse, waiting for service, while only 17 Red Cross motor vehicles had been evacuated to Changsha. From these new bases, the Red Cross Medical Relief Commission began the organization of its Medical Corps. Small mobile units of 15 to 20 persons were organized. These were of various types: curative (or operating) units, nursing units and preventive units, to be sent for service behind the fronts as soon as they could be organized and equipped, and arrangements made for their maintenance and for regular supplies from a central supply station in Changsha. Later, seven substations to keep them regularly supplied were organized. Groups, consisting basically of two curative, two nursing (later incorporated into the curative units), and one preventive unit, served by a depot and one motor convoy, were assigned to particular lines serving the major fronts. The purpose of the group units, established in military hospitals and receiving stations, was the continuous care of the wounded from the moment of injury until convalescence. The units fulfilled their duties in so far as was humanly possible, though it is clear that qualified personnel volunteering for Red Cross service was far from sufficient.

The need for large numbers of first-aid and other auxiliary workers was overwhelming, and in the following months the Red Cross Medical Relief Corps called for volunteers of educated youth, primarily men with a high school or junior high school education. Such volunteers, who came in by the hundreds, were given a six-weeks' intensive training in the essentials of first aid and nursing, stretcher-bearer and anti-epidemic work. The training was insufficient, but time and need did not permit more. Such workers were organized into ambulance units, in charge of one doctor, and sent to receiving stations near the fronts or to service on hospital trains or boats. The foremost ambulance units at the fronts established contact with the Army or Divisional Headquarters. Some were accompanied by a small operating team detached from the nearest curative unit, so that emergency treatment could be adequately given to the severely wounded as near the fronts as possible. The evacuation of the wounded, particularly the severely wounded, was to be assisted by Red Cross motor convoys. But the number of such vehicles at the disposal of the Red Cross at the time was almost ludicrous, while the funds at the disposal of the Red Cross were totally inadequate to meet the needs of its own units for more than two or three months in advance.

EDUCATION OF MEDICAL WORKERS

While this work was proceeding, the Red Cross Medical Relief Commission was called upon to collaborate with the National Health Administration (and later with the Army Medical Administration), to draw up plans to meet another basic need in the care of the sick and wounded — that of the education of doctors, nurses and orderlies in the various medical organizations, both civil and military, connected with war. Also, for the education of preventive medical workers to cope with epidemics; and of auxiliary workers already mentioned and sent out as ambulance units. Therefore, in June, 1938, six months after the fall of Nanking, the Emergency Medical Service Training School was established at Changsha. Its primary task at that moment was to train preventive workers, after which anti-epidemic units were to be sent to the field. Soon this training was extended to the other groups mentioned. The Director of the Red Cross Medical Relief Commission was made Director of the Training School. The commission assigned a number of its best consultants as staff, and several Red Cross units to do duty as teaching staff. The Army Medical Administration assigned a large hospital for the severely wounded as a training hospital attached to the school.

This first training school has become one of the most important institutions developed in China during the war. Its staff investigates basic problems in the care of the sick and wounded, and in epidemic prevention; devises local methods, using native materials, wherever possible; and has been the first to standardize medical supplies and equipment. It prepared, and later published, manuals of standing orders on the following subjects for the guidance of personnel in all medical units serving the sick and wounded: (1) Medical Service — Organization and Tactics; (2) Surgery; (3) Medicine; (4) Nursing; (5) Preventive Medicine; (6) Sanitation; (7) X-ray; (8) Field Laboratory Technique; (9) Standard Medical Supplies. The preparation of such manuals, as teaching material to medical personnel in the field, is of the utmost importance, since the distribution of practical technical information among medical workers is still the most vital need and essential to improving the medical services.

The training school started work with contributions from the British Boxer Indemnity Commission, the Rockefeller Foundation, the National Council for Reconstruction, and the National Health Administration. After a few weeks it received a large contribution from Madame Chiang Kai-shek. And one month after its founding, it was able to extend the scope of its work to include the retraining of personnel from military hospitals, by a military order issued by Generalissimo Chiang Kai-shek.

The scope of the work of the training school can hardly be gauged by the number of medical personnel it has trained and retrained, yet figures are suggestive. From

June, 1938, down to the first of June of 1940, it has given wartime emergency training to 4,230 persons. These include doctors, nurses, auxiliaries, orderlies, sanitary inspectors, X-ray technicians, and even midwives. This number includes 729 trained in a branch of the training school established many months later in Hanchung, in southwestern Shensi.

JAPANESE ATTACKS — THE RED CROSS TO THE FRONT

Following the fall of Shanghai and Nanking, the Japanese Army halted to rest and receive replenishments, but its armies in our northwest continued fighting. After the occupation of Taiyuan and Linfeng in Shansi Province, the enemy directed drives against southern Shansi, toward Tungkwan, the strategic pass guarding the approaches to Sian, in Shensi Province, China's main center in the northwest. During that period, Red Cross units were distributed along the northwestern front, some in Sian and some as far north as Yenan, in Shensi Province.

In April and May, 1938, the Japanese began their drive on Hsuchow, the junction city on the Lunghai and the Tientsin-Nanking railways. Major battles were fought in regions approaching that city, the Chinese armies scoring a great victory in the battle of Taierchwang. Finally, outflanked, the Chinese armies withdrew to the west and southwest, and in early June the enemy occupied an almost empty and destroyed city.

[237]

During the Hsuchow campaign, Red Cross units were distributed on main lines of communication around Hsuchow, four of them within Hsuchow itself. Units were transferred from rear to field hospitals near the front, and were withdrawn twelve hours before the fall of Hsuchow. These units left the region on the last hospital trains loaded with wounded, and continued their service en route though these trains were repeatedly bombed by the Japanese.

At this time, the Red Cross Medical Relief Corps consisted of but 24 curative, 18 nursing, five preventive, and one X-ray units — a total of 48 units in all — in the field. It was only after this period that the first ambulance units were organized and sent to the fronts. But throughout the battle for Hsuchow, Red Cross units extended their services to include air-raid victims and refugees and other civilians in need. Special first-aid stations were set up to carry out this work.

THE DEFENSE OF WUHAN

For three months following the fall of Hsuchow, the Japanese advanced westward along the Lunghai Railway, against Chengchow, junction city on the Lunghai and the Peiping-Hankow railways. The flooding of regions east of Changchow, by the Yellow River, halted their advance, after which they transferred their main forces to the Yangtze River along which their land forces could be supported by naval craft. New divisions from Japan arrived in China to re-enforce the enemy. Their drive against Wuhan along the Yangtze was further supported by columns advancing through Anhwei and Hupeh Provinces from the northeast.

Though the Central Government had officially moved to Chungking, in Szechuan Province, still the Wuhan cities constituted the administrative, military, industrial and cultural center of the nation at the time, and against it the enemy concentrated all their land, naval, and air forces. For a while they made fairly rapid progress, but were halted for weeks when they reached mountain barriers. Enemy losses were heavy not only in wounded, but also in sick. Chinese main armies, though with inferior equipment, used mountainous regions as natural defenses to halt and attack the advancing enemy. In the meantime guerrilla forces in the enemy rear harassed their routes of communication, attacked their rear garrisons, and inflicted serious losses upon them while forcing them to keep ever heavier garrisons in the rear. In the north and northwest, mobile and guerrilla forces had recovered large areas behind enemy lines. These forces reached up to the walls of Peiping at times, destroying Japanese-controlled railways, highways, and industrial establishments.

Since the Yangtze Valley and the northwest were the main theaters of war, the Red Cross Medical Relief Corps concentrated its units at these fronts. Its 17 trucks grew to 60. Still the corps had insufficient vehicles, tires, gas and spare parts; insufficient medical supplies and hospital equipment, and inadequate funds to meet all its needs. Above all it had insufficient personnel.

The corps bent every effort to meet its responsibilities in the care of the sick and wounded of the armed forces, in epidemic prevention, and in the care of air-raid victims and refugees. It is difficult to describe in words the trials encountered by the units in the field. Japanese bombers aimed not merely at military objectives, but at towns and villages, schools, universities and other cultural institutions, also at military and mission hospitals caring for the sick and wounded. Many hospitals were totally destroyed, with heavy loss of life. Wounded men refused to ride in any vehicle displaying the Red Cross emblem. Red Cross units, bombed out of hospitals, their supplies destroyed, moved to new locations, replenished their stores, and continued working at night. On the main fronts the wounded could be evacuated only at night.

Many problems were solved, to the limit of capacity of the Red Cross, and the morale of the units in the field was generally very high. The influence of these units in many military hospitals was great, many hospitals being transformed by their presence. The morale of the troops was higher when they knew they would be given adequate care if wounded. However, the problem of insufficient medical personnel was and remains the most serious.

Chinese medical workers were not conscripted, and relatively few qualified Chinese doctors and nurses volunteered for Red Cross service, while practically none volunteered for the Army Medical Service. Calls for foreign volunteers have brought a total of 24 foreign doctors to the Red Cross, of whom 17 who had served with the Spanish Republican Government have done excellent work at the front.

To enable the Red Cross doctors and nurses to meet emergency wartime conditions, many of them were passed through the training school, which taught them wartime methods and enabled them to introduce training classes in military hospitals in which they served. This role of teacher has proved of inestimable value and perhaps has no parallel in history. These Red Cross units introduced the first real medical and nursing system in the military hospitals, the first special diet service for the severely sick and wounded, the first D.B.S. (delousing-bathing-scabies treatment) stations, and other more technical procedures. For the first time in military hospitals educated men and women did hard physical labor, washing and bathing and feeding the wounded, sweeping and keeping the wards clean. After three years of warfare, the Red Cross Medical Relief Corps constituted the only qualified medical service caring for the sick and wounded in military hospitals and stations. Letters and reports from nurses and doctors are generally dry, revealing little of this great drama. Yet some give moving reports of fearful conditions which they have changed, or grateful and contented faces of the wounded at the end of the day, of bodies slowly built up, men recovered to take up the struggle of national liberation once more. Red Cross units, and in a less dramatic form the Emergency Medical Training School in the rear, were making history. Yet how limited this service was can be estimated by the fact that until the first of June, 1940, the Red Cross had but 69 mobile units in the field.

THE FIGHT AGAINST EPIDEMICS

In the summer of 1938, when the Wuhan cities and the city of Nanchang were being defended, dangerous epidemics were rife among the troops at the front and among civilians, particularly refugees, in the front areas of Central China and in the south. Malaria, dysentery, and other diseases spread through the war zones, while cholera and typhoid broke out in a number of South China provinces. More than half the troops in some divisions at the front were sick. The Red Cross and Army Medical inspectors confirmed reports that 40-60 per cent of the sick had malaria, 20-30 per cent dysentery, and the remainder were suffering from other ailments. Malnutrition added to the sorry plight of the wounded.

To meet this situation and to make preparations to

cover the entire year, the Red Cross Medical Relief Corps laid down a five-point Anti-Epidemic Program, as follows:

1 — Control of typhus, relapsing fever, and scabies
2 — Control of malaria
3 — Control of cholera, dysentery and typhoid
4 — Control of smallpox
5 — Control of nutritional deficiency diseases.

The program was limited to objectives which were more important and could be definitely achieved with the personnel and materials available. D.B.S. stations were to become, in the winter months, an important factor in preventing epidemics of typhus and relapsing fever. As typhus vaccine could not be obtained, prophylaxis by delousing was the only effective measure of control. Typhus did make its appearance to a limited extent, in the north during spring and summer, and in the south during the winter seasons. Relapsing fever was probably far more prevalent than was apparent, particularly in roadless zones in the enemy rear, where many men may have died. Lack of knowledge on the part of army medical personnel prevented correct diagnosis and treatment of this and other diseases, and lack of microscopes and accessories hindered the Red Cross units in their work.

To meet the cholera menace, inoculation of troops and civilians was carried out wherever cholera was likely to appear. The work by Red Cross units in epidemic regions may best be demonstrated by one example:

In late June, 1939, an epidemic of cholera was reported from a small township in central Hunan. Red Cross preventive and ambulance units were rushed to the scene and more than 12,000 soldiers and civilians were inoculated with anti-cholera vaccine within a few days. Chlorination of water was instituted, special wards organized, and by July 2nd the epidemic was halted. Epidemic-prevention measures continued. Highway quarantine stations were set up, and by the end of July, 50,000 individuals had been inoculated. Only 80 persons died of the disease. This achievement was due to the efficient leadership of Red Cross group leader, Dr. Lin Ching-chen, who, a short time before, had distinguished himself during a typhus and relapsing fever epidemic in the military hospitals at Hengyang, a city south of Changsha. Two members of his unit came down with typhus, and he himself contracted relapsing fever. Fearing that a knowledge of his condition would undermine the confidence of the sick and wounded, Dr. Lin continued to work while treating himself, refusing to take to his bed.

Before introducing its anti-epidemic campaign, the Red Cross Medical Corps made provisions to supply its own units in the field with vaccine, anti-malaria and anti-dysenteric drugs. At the time it had supplies to care for 60,000 sick. The Army Medical Administration established three special base hospitals behind each of the three important fronts for the treatment of the sick only. Red Cross units served in these.

RED CROSS UNITS IN NEW FIELDS

In the autumn of 1938, one curative and one preventive unit of Red Cross volunteers penetrated to the rear of the enemy in Shansi Province to care for the sick and wounded of the 8th Route Army which was fighting by mobile and guerrilla warfare. This was the first time Red Cross units had left the main fronts and penetrated the enemy rear. The journey of these two units took nearly three months and was a veritable saga in long-distance walking and endurance in the bitter cold, across Japanese lines of the northwest. Their supplies were transported by a special convoy of pack mules and horses. Arriving at their destination, they took charge of a 600-bed hospital and opened a clinic in which 100 civilians were treated daily. Letters from unit members stated that civilians had unlimited trust in them, believing that they could cure any disease that existed. A few months later, the first Red Cross curative unit to enter the guerrilla region in the enemy rear along the banks of the Yangtze around Wuhu and Nanking began work in that region, and was later joined by an ambulance unit. At the same time a Red Cross unit was sent to join a guerrilla detachment that fought around the city of Hangchow, south of Shanghai.

All of these units have remained with the guerrilla forces.

In Wuhan, Changsha, Nanchang, Canton and other cities, the Red Cross erected special rescue stations for the care of air-raid victims, until they could be transferred to foreign and Chinese civilian hospitals and to military hospitals. Air-raid cases transferred to military hospitals were paid for by the Red Cross Medical Relief Corps at the rate of 20 cents a day for food — the same as that of soldiers. Many of those transferred to civilian hospitals were paid for by the International Red Cross Committee, a branch of the Chinese Red Cross.

Though relatively few at the time, Red Cross trucks and ambulances played an important role in the evacuation of the wounded from the fronts to the rear, and also of air-raid victims. The transportation of supplies from Hong Kong and their distribution to the various fronts, combined with other transport duties, taxed the Transportation Department to the limit. Twenty junks and two launches hired or bought by the Red Cross helped solve some transport problems, but were a drop in the ocean of need. There was gasoline on hand to last for not more than two or three months. Due to bad roads, tires lasted 5,000 miles instead of 10,000 and more. Yet Red Cross trucks were responsible for the transport not only of the wounded, but of supplies to its own units for helping branch societies of the Chinese Red Cross, military hospitals, medical departments of the armies, provincial health departments, and numerous wartime governmental and private relief organizations.

Records for the year of 1938 show that Red Cross trucks and ambulances covered 752,061 kilometers; transported 23,500 wounded and 21,684 personnel of its own and other organizations. This was apart from the transport of supplies of various medical organizations. Red Cross trucks also transferred a number of hospitals from one line to another.

With the fall of Canton and then the imminent fall of Wuhan (October 25, 1938), the Red Cross Medical Relief Corps began the evacuation of its personnel and supplies from Hankow to Changsha, and later from Changsha to Chiyang, in southwestern Hunan. The disastrous fires that began in Changsha on November 12th and destroyed the city caused the further evacuation of all that remained of Red Cross Headquarters in Changsha, of supplies, and units. All military hospitals had already been evacuated, some 400 wounded remaining on the station platform and many of them perishing in the flames that spread too rapidly for them to be rescued. When the evacuation began, the Red Cross had only 100 gallons of gasoline left in stock. As if in answer to its need, the Scottish Red Cross sent a contribution of £750 to the corps, thus enabling it to purchase gas and to continue its transportation service.

AFTER HANKOW — THE NATIONAL SITUATION

With the fall of Wuhan, conditions under which the war was being waged underwent great change. All national institutions had been evacuated from Wuhan, great factories with all their personnel, and with the families of their personnel, were moved to the west or northwest to build up new industrial centers. Much of Wuhan was burned or dynamited as the enemy approached. The main forces of the national armies had withdrawn to the west, though some were left on the enemy flanks and in the enemy rear to continue resistance.

The Japanese occupation of Wuhan did not result in China's surrender, as the Japanese had boasted, and the Japanese armies were too weak and exhausted to make further progress after the consolidation of their positions in and around the cities. Their airplanes continued to bomb open towns and cities, cultural institutions, and even boats loaded with refugees. And American industrialists continued to betray the cause of democracy in China and, it may turn out also, in America, by supplying Japan with over 70 per cent of its war material.

The Japanese Army was now drawn out, long and thin, along China's main lines of communication. Removed from these lines, they occupied only such cities as were surrounded by high walls which served as strong defense works. Vast areas in the enemy rear which were referred to as "occupied territory," were not occupied at all, but were in the hands of regular Chinese armed forces, guerrillas, and local government officials.

The chief armies were redistributed — a part to various fronts to impede any Japanese advance; a part to the Chinese rear for retraining and re-equipment; a part to the enemy rear. Roads behind all fronts were thoroughly destroyed for great depths (100-150 km.) in order to prevent the enemy from using their mechanized forces and bringing up artillery. Thereafter the Japanese were forced to wage war on more equal terms, a situation reflected in casualties which henceforth became about equal. However, such conditions also greatly hampered army and Red Cross medical forces from evacuating or caring properly for the wounded. The enemy attempted sporadic offensives in which they were generally driven back with heavy losses. Their mopping-up campaigns against guerrillas in their rear had no results except that more and more territory was cleaned of them. They began to abandon their dead and wounded, and many Japanese captives fell into Chinese hands and were put in concentration camps or training institutes to teach them the first fundamentals of humanity and the meaning of China's war of defense.

New Problems of the Red Cross

Due to the destruction of roads and parts of railway lines, the Red Cross faced serious difficulties in the evacuation of the wounded, the transportation of its units and their supplies. To reach the fronts, long routes over roadless areas had to be traversed. The wounded had to be carried by stretcher over vast areas. The lightly wounded and all but the seriously sick had to walk, sometimes for a month, before they reached a field hospital. The severely wounded in the enemy rear, where medical organization hardly existed, and those from the main fronts where highways had been destroyed, practically all died before they could be carried to a hospital. Many of the lightly wounded failed to survive. The one saving factor was that there are fewer wounded in mobile and guerrilla warfare than in positional.

On the main fronts, military hospitals were reorganized. Most were too large and cumbersome to operate in roadless territory. Many were therefore subdivided or reduced in size. Small mobile teams of personnel drawn from military hospitals or from the Red Cross were assigned to divisional hospitals, or to stations within calling distance. Attempts were made to place these within twelve hours' relay behind regimental positions, some within five hours' distance by stretcher-bearers.

Special rest stations every ten miles to provide food, water, shelter, and sometimes a change of dressings had already been established on the routes of communication from the fronts to the rear, before the fall of Wuhan. Civilian volunteers manned these stations, and not only the walking wounded and sick received care in them, but also swarms of refugees passing to the rear. Following the fall of Wuhan, Red Cross ambulance units were stationed in these rest stations to give medical care, and were maintained in them until the end of March, 1939. In addition, the dressing stations and stretcher-bearer battalions of the Army Medical Service for the specific care of the wounded took on greater importance though bearers were too few.

Congestion and insanitary conditions in the stations and hospitals on the way down from the Hunan front gave rise to much sickness. One out of every five wounded was seriously sick, most such serious cases being afflicted with nutritional edema, dysentery, enteritis, relapsing fever, malaria, or lung infection. Scabies and lice were widespread.

These conditions led the Red Cross to begin its anti-epidemic program. First the Red Cross called for contributions of bedding and hospital clothing, and for volunteers to aid in hospitals. In response, the first group of the "Friends of the Wounded" was organized to help in the hospitals in Hengyang. D.B.S. stations were built and put into operation. Red Cross senior nurses, doctors, and sanitary engineers, were sent far and wide as consultants and supervisors to carry out the program, and all Red Cross units were instructed to install special diet kitchens and to use a part of their expense allowance to pay for special or supplementary diet for the severely sick and wounded.

Toward the end of 1938, all national institutions were again instructed to move further westward, and in the following weeks the Red Cross, together with the Emergency Medical Training School, the training hospitals, and the main supply depot of the Red Cross, were moved to Kweiyang, Kweichow Province, and housed in newly constructed bamboo-thatched buildings.

GENERAL REVIEW —
THE SCOPE OF RED CROSS MEDICAL WORK

War experience on the many fronts has resulted in great progress in the fighting ability of the armed forces, but as in the case of other long wars, there is a tendency for sickness and disease steadily to increase in the army and among the people. This situation is reflected to some extent in a general summary of the number of cases of wounded and sick treated by Red Cross units. Reports from January, 1938, to the end of 1939 — a period of two full years — show the following cases treated in various military hospitals alone:

Surgical cases treated

Operations performed 33,910
Fractures treated 19,915
Dressings applied 3,227,200

THE CHINESE RED CROSS

Medical Cases treated

    Sick soldiers treated 344,814

    Sick civilians treated 508,913

These records show that Red Cross units cared for many sick civilians, and that sick soldiers in hospitals outnumbered the wounded requiring operations. Of the sick cases in military hospitals and in out-patient clinics established by Red Cross units, Red Cross units treated 65,372 cases of malaria alone. Many more cases of malaria were treated in military hospitals of every category, and in civilian medical units, with quinine supplied by the Red Cross, all of which was contributed by overseas Chinese — primarily in Java — and foreign Red Cross organizations. Only the most serious cases of malaria were hospitalized. From the summer of 1938 down to June 1, 1940, the Red Cross Medical Relief Corps alone distributed 12,929,600 quinine tablets to its own units, various military hospitals and armies, and to civilian medical groups.

Malaria is now so universal that its control is one of the gravest problems of the country. Considerations of time, economy, and inadequate medical personnel and sanitary engineers, make it impossible at the present time to eradicate the sources of the disease.

Next to malaria, dysentery ranked very high in the scale of diseases coped with, both among the troops and

[253]

refugees. In the year 1939, and the first five months of 1940, Red Cross medical units treated 12,500 such cases, and further distributed anti-dysenteric drugs to military and civil medical units.

Of other diseases, bronchitis ranked next to scabies among the minor ailments. About 12 per cent of the respiratory infections were cases of pulmonary tuberculosis, the greatest number being among soldiers of the northwest who lack sufficient clothing and food. Records show very high incidence of pulmonary tuberculosis among all guerrilla forces in the enemy rear. These forces are generally local civilians, large numbers of whom are sole survivors of families wiped out by the Japanese. The bitterness due to such a state can hardly be imagined.

Regarding preventive work by the Red Cross Medical Relief Corps, statistics from January, 1938, to June, 1, 1940, record the following:

Smallpox vaccinations . . . . 449,838 individuals
Cholera inoculations 953,737   "
Cholera and typhoid inoculations . . . 202,755   "
Anti-tetanus inoculations 12,151   "

The small number of individuals treated against tetanus was due to the relatively small amount of serum available, and the distribution of the bulk of this to the various hospitals and armies by the Relief Corps.

THE CHINESE RED CROSS

The extent of work done by Red Cross units in the prevention of louse-borne diseases and of scabies, by the erection of D.B.S. stations, may be gauged by the following figures from 1939 to June 1, 1940:

D. B. S. stations erected	208
Soldiers bathed	272,895
Clothing and bedding disinfected	1,578,932
Soldiers treated for scabies	212,185

The further scope of Red Cross work is indicated by records of the Transportation Department of the Relief Corps for the entire years 1938 and 1939, and down to June, 1, 1940.

Wounded and sick evacuated	67,873
Medical supplies transported (1938-1939 only) .	408,439
Personnel of Red Cross, various medical and civil units transported	46,025
Mileage covered in kilometers, by ambulance and trucks	2,470,743
Trucks, cars and ambulances in service, June 1, 1940	278

Apart from the above, many hospitals were transported from one front to another.

In speaking of wounded transported, special mention must be made of the high record established by 25 ambulances and trucks on the Kwangsi front during the fighting around Nanning in December, 1939, and January, 1940. Of some 20,000 wounded evacuated from that front, around 17,000 were evacuated by the 25 Red Cross vehicles. The efficiency, courage, and hard labor involved showed up the fine leadership of Chang Hung-tao, ambulance group leader on the Kwangsi front. Mr. Chang was also responsible for the educational work among truck drivers and mechanics, which kept their morale to the highest pitch.

The care of the sick and wounded in China is far from what it should be. The reasons for this are historical on the whole, with all that word connotes — social, economic, scientific. During the war, military and political progress has been greater than the scientific care of the wounded. Despite all difficulties, however, in many military hospitals there has been slow but steady improvement. Hospitals are better provided with bedding and other equipment while a steady though inadequate supply of drugs has been maintained; and to the best of its ability the Red Cross Medical Relief Corps has provided qualified personnel, medical supplies and other services as recorded above. General improvement has been due to a variety of factors, such as the following:

(1) The training of thousands of unqualified doctors and other medical personnel in or through the Emergency Medical Training Schools; more than 4,200 such personnel have been passed through short-term emergency

training. Red Cross units have demonstrated how medical work should be done, and many have conducted training classes wherever they have been assigned.

(2) An awakened national consciousness concerning the strengthening of national resistance consequent upon the adequate care of the sick and wounded. This consciousness has expressed itself in the development of such an organization as the "Friends of the Wounded," a civilian volunteer organization under the aegis of New Life which originated in close association with the Red Cross Medical Relief Corps. It aids the Army Medical Service with funds and personnel to establish D.B.S. stations, to provide special and supplementary diet, laundry and mending services, and sanitary supplies in military hospitals.

(3) The patriotism of overseas Chinese as expressed in the support of the Red Cross by funds, drugs, and vehicles.

(4) Widespread publicity in the Chinese and foreign press concerning conditions and needs in military hospitals and receiving stations, resulting in aid in funds, drugs and equipment. Foreign aid to China has further expressed itself through the International Red Cross Committee in China which has played an important role in the care of refugees and air-raid victims, and which co-operates with the Red Cross Medical Relief Corps.

(5) The special concern of Generalissimo and Ma-

dame Chiang Kai-shek for the welfare of the sick and wounded — a concern that has expressed itself in many ways, from personal tours of inspection, the appointment of better medical administrators in the army, military orders concerning the care of the sick and wounded, the retraining of army medical personnel, and in the severe punishment of responsible army hospital administrators for any corruption or default of duty. Without such concern, the special Emergency Medical Training School could never have played the educational role it has, nor could Red Cross units have worked so well in hospitals.

ORTHOPAEDIC HOSPITAL AND CENTER

In the past year, the Red Cross Medical Relief Corps has turned its attention to reconstructional surgery. This has been due to the increase of deformed and disabled soldiers, of whom some 30,000 have been listed for possible treatment. At least another 30,000 are unlisted, while the number of civilians deformed and disabled by Japanese air raids must now constitute a formidable number. Consequently the Red Cross tried to approach this problem, and attempt its solution. In August, 1939, it organized a 300-bed orthopaedic hospital as part of a center for treatment and rehabilitation of the disabled. Lack of qualified orthopaedic surgeons, and the difficulties in transporting patients to the hospital, have resulted in slow progress. However, a start has been made. During treatment, soldiers undergo vocational training along various lines — for instance, in sulphur refining, soapmaking, shoemaking, stocking knitting, tailoring and sewing, artificial limb making, barbering, etc. During the first nine months of its existence, 391 deformed or disabled soldiers have been under treatment and training in the Center.

FOREIGN AUXILIARY OF THE CHINESE RED CROSS

In the past year, the Red Cross Medical Relief Corps has been materially aided by the organization, in Hong Kong, of the Foreign Auxiliary of the Chinese Red Cross. The Directors and Advisory Council include the most prominent officials in the Chinese and Hong Kong governments and in the foreign diplomatic corps. Bishop Hall, of Hong Kong, who has helped so much to relieve distress in China, is the chairman. Mrs. Hilda Selwyn-Clarke, the Honorary Secretary, has been its moving spirit, and her voluntary, selfless labor for China has been very valuable. The Auxiliary collected considerable sums of money, and quantities of drugs, clothing and other supplies, for the Emergency Medical Training School and the Orthopaedic Center in Kweiyang, Kweichow Province, as well as for other medical organizations.

CONTRIBUTORS TO THE RED CROSS
MEDICAL RELIEF CORPS

The names and donations of overseas Chinese, foreign

organizations and individuals, and organizations and individuals in China, to the Medical Relief Corps are too many to list. Details have been published in many Red Cross reports. Aid has come from most of the leading countries of the world. The heaviest contributions have come from Chinese organizations in Java. Without their monthly supply of funds and drugs the Medical Corps could not have planned its work and functioned. Cash came from the Soviet Union; cash and medical supplies were sent by various international Red Cross societies, such as the British, American, Scandinavian, French, Swiss and German. The Indian National Congress sent drugs, and also five volunteer surgeons. The League of Nations Health Section helped. Two thirds of all trucks and ambulances, much medical equipment and supplies, especially quinine and vaccines, were donated by Chinese and American organizations throughout the whole of the United States, and some from Canada, through the American Bureau for Medical Aid to China, of which Col. Theodore Roosevelt, Jr. is President, and Dr. Co Tui the Vice-President. Without such aid the Red Cross never could have played the role it has, and without the continuation of that aid it will be unable to function. The Red Cross therefore expresses its thanks for all contributions of every kind, and its sincere hope that these will not cease so that it may continue to play its role in the struggle for human liberation.

[260]

XX

*THE CHINESE INDUSTRIAL CO-OPERATIVES**

IT WAS after the first year of war, when it began to be evident that China's struggle would be long-drawn-out, that the Central Government decided to encourage the widespread distribution of small industry throughout the country.

To do this, it set up the organization known now as Chinese Industrial Co-operatives, which proceeded to gather a staff of technicians, organizers, and accountants, and to encourage Chinese artisans, worker refugees, and crippled soldiers, to form themselves into co-operative units for the production of consumer goods to replace those that had come in from the coast in former times.

The scheme was to finance these solid, dependable people; give them a workable system of organization based on that which had stood the test of experience in the best co-operatives of the world so far; provide them with a simple system of cost accounting; improve their processes with the best technical knowledge available, and, as the

* By Rewi Alley, Technical Adviser to the Chinese Industrial Co-operatives.

plan progressed, to organize the co-operatives into federations which would manage their own marketing and supply agencies. The result would be a linking of the whole productive effort throughout the country into a chain of co-operative industry which would stand all the strains likely to be placed upon it.

The evacuation of women from Hankow industry by Madame Chiang Kai-shek before the fall of that city provided many of the first workers for the Industrial Co-operative Movement in the regions toward the western terminus of the Lunghai Railway.

Madame Chiang was determined that as many workers as wanted to leave Hankow should be given the chance to do so — especially women workers. Their subsequent incorporation into self-sufficient industrial units in the northwest has shown that the co-operative system, when given to responsible groups of workers, certainly does work. It is not altogether a new system in China — the old guild system held many elements of co-operation. Chinese people like to band themselves into substitute family groupings for carrying out measures to improve their livelihood, and the co-operative constitution carefully worked out by the best co-operative experts available gave them a way.

Their gratitude at being able to stand upon their own feet and to be again masters of their environment after their move from accustomed quarters was pathetic, and yet very inspiring. Their businesses succeeded. One canvas co-operative, for instance, had a profit of $13,000 to divide after the first year. Loans began to be paid back. The system began to get on a sound footing.

In the front-line areas, of course, the units had to be small and easily moved — guerrilla industry, almost. There co-operative principles succeeded easily, and it became evident that they were exactly fitted for such circumstances.

In the rear, co-operative industry has been less mobile, but still flexible and scattered, so as to come unscathed through bombing or other calamities. Of its ability to stand, the willingness of many banks to entrust loans is good evidence. It may be safely estimated that even in difficult times the majority of the societies are making a margin of profit for division among the workers.

Statistics showing the growth and present extent of Chinese Industrial Co-operative activity are given below.

GROWTH OF CHINESE INDUSTRIAL CO-OPERATIVES
DURING 1939

The earliest regional headquarters to be set up, of the five now in existence, was that in the northwest. The growth of work in that region in 1939, especially in productive capacity, shows the soundness of the structure.

Table I

Work of Chinese Industrial Co operatives in Northwest Region

1939 Month	No. of Societies	No. of Members	Value of Month's Production
January	65	1,050	$ 280,000
February	83	1,250	380,000
March	139	2,080	480,000
April	213	2,750	570,000
May	252	3,250	560,000
June	304	3,760	570,000
July	335	3,970	660,000
August	354	4,270	670,000
September	355	4,310	810,000
October	356	4,330	920,000
November	366	4,370	1,100,000
December	371	4,430	1,150,000

Joint supply and marketing agencies belonging to the Co-operative Federations have given strength to the societies wherever they have been started. The way in which the joint agency in one northwest center grew in 1939 is shown in Table II.

[264]

Table II

Growth of Joint Agency at . . .

1939 Month	Bought for Co-operatives	Sold for Co-operatives	Total Trade
January		$ 3,500	$ 3,500
February		4,300	4,300
March	$ 29,800	14,500	44,300
April	11,300	11,300	22,600
May	23,300	13,700	37,000
June	8,300	14,300	22,600
July	7,900	6,100	14,000
August	74,400	68,300	142,700
September	73,000	42,000	115,000
October	52,000	168,000	220,000
November	153,000	282,000	435,000
December	47,900	322,700	370,600
Totals	$480,900	$950,700	$1,431,600

Work in the southeast and Szechuan-Sikang provincial regions began early in 1939. Its growth is shown in Table III. Production figures for such scattered areas are not complete in detail, but it may be estimated that by December the total monthly production in each region was $1,000,000. Production in Chungking alone had reached $291,000 monthly, while Chengtu showed $240,000.

[265]

Table III

Growth of Work in Southeast and Szechuan-Sikang Provincial Regions

1939 Month	Southeast number of societies	Southeast number of members	Szechuan-Sikang number of societies	Szechuan-Sikang number of members
January	3	80	1	19
February	11	152	9	96
March	20	280	75	1,150
April	57	699	249	3,603
May	102	1,341	271	3,865
June	135	1,770	285	4,004
July	158	1,978	300	4,242
August	192	2,272	303	4,287
September	249	3,014	304	4,296
October	271	3,287	464	5,815
November	287	3,574	441	5,450
December	296	3,667	442	5,548

Work in the southwest began later, and that in Yunnan Province is still small.

In all China, by December 31, 1939, there were 1,284 societies with 15,625 members, owning their own share capital of $412,276, and using loans of $2,607,302 to produce goods worth $3,000,000 per month.

TYPES OF INDUSTRY

A list of products is given below. This is not complete, but includes the more important products. In all there are over 60 types of societies making 114 kinds of goods.

Table IV

List of More Important Products

Textiles	Metals	Chemical
Cotton yarn	Founding	Soap
Cotton fabrics	Iron smelting	Candles
Woolen yarn	Machine work	Tooth powder
Tweeds	Motorcar parts	Matches
Army blankets	Printing machinery	Ink
Medical cotton	Printing type	Dyes
Gauze	Agricultural implements	Educational supplies
Socks	Munitions	Medicine (Chinese)
Towels	Engines	Medicine (Western)
Canvas (for stretchers)	Watch repair	Alcohol (transport
Bedding	Motor repair	and medical)
Hemp yarn	Small arms repair	Leather tanning and
Linen	Coppersmith	working
Burlap	Tinsmith	Paper
Silk thread	Ropemaking machines	Dry cells
Silk fabrics		Pens
Oiled silk		Lubricating oil
		Vaseline

Foodstuffs	*Clothes*	*Woodwork*
Oil-pressing	Tailoring	Furniture
Puffed rice	Shoes	Baskets
Preserved foods	Sandals	Toys
Flour	Hats	Boats
Rice-milling	Knitted goods	Carts
Biscuits	Furs	Textile machines
Tea-baking		
Sugar refining	*Mining*	*Pottery, etc.*
Bean curd	Coal	Earthenware
	Iron	Porcelain
	Gold	Glass
		Bricks
		Tiles

Notes on some of the most significant new production and its extent are given below.

Machine shops: By May, 1940, there were in various parts of the country 15 machine shop co-operatives, mainly engaged in making spinning wheels, looms, lathes, and other machinery needed in small-scale industry. There are on an average 50 or more mechanics working in each.

Cotton Spinning and Weaving: All over the country can spinners have been introduced, and men and women taught to use them, and almost every depot has co-operatives engaged in weaving, supplying some of the immense amount of cloth sorely needed in China.

Wool Spinning and Weaving: Wool used to be exported

raw to Shanghai and Tientsin from the highlands of north-west China and Tibet. Now the wool is being spun by tens of thousands of women trained by the Chinese Industrial Co-operatives, and woven at eight centers in Szechuan Province and the northwest. With it 400,000 military blankets were woven and delivered to the army during the winter of 1939-1940. Chinese Industrial Co-operatives are now teaching women to spin fine yarn, and a beginning has been made in the production of tweed.

Tailoring: Everywhere there are tailoring co-operatives, and by co-ordination and standardization under Chinese Industrial Co-operative advice they are able to undertake big orders. During the first half of 1940 orders for clothing for soldiers to the value of $1,200,000 have been executed.

Medical Supplies: At 12 centers are co-operatives making cotton or ramie lint, and gauze for bandages.

Porcelain and Glass: Two hundred workers from derelict Chin Teh Chen in Kiangsi Province have been rehabilitated in Kwangtung Province where they are producing fine porcelain. In Szechuan Province, too, new porcelain industry has been set up to make fine china to replace the Kiangsi Province porcelain. In Kwangtung Province there is much glass made by the Chinese Industrial Co-operatives.

Paper: Paper is being made in 10 centers, and plans are under way for production of finer quality.

Printing: In 25 centers refugee printers have been set to work, either on lead-type or lithographic printing, or, usually, both.

Chemical Industries: These include distillation of alcohol. A plant in the northwest produces 500 gallons per day. More alcohol plants are planned to provide alcohol for fuel and medical uses.

In most depots there are also societies making soap and candles.

Mining: In five districts refugees wash for gold; in five, coal is mined, and in five, iron is mined and smelted. New techniques are being introduced — an improvement on the old, but yet making use of local resources.

Such notes could be multiplied many times without exhausting the variety and extent of Chinese Industrial Co-operative activity.

ESTIMATES FOR THE EXTENT OF CHINESE
INDUSTRIAL CO-OPERATIVE WORK
ON MAY 31, 1939

The wide dispersion of the work and the difficulty of communication make it impossible to give exact up-to-date figures, but the following estimates are based on reliable sources:

Table V

Region	North-west	South-east	Szechuan	South-west	Yunnan	Total
No. of societies	450	450	480	190	80	1,650
No. of members	6,000	5,400	6,000	2,300	1,000	20,700
No. of auxiliary workers	32,000*	2,000	12,000*	1,000		47,000
No. of people sustained						250,000
Capital (in million dollars Chinese National Currency)	2¼	2	2	½	¼	7
Production (monthly value in million dollars Chinese National Currency)	1½	1	1	½		4

TYPICAL EXAMPLES OF CHINESE INDUSTRIAL CO-OPERATIVE WORK

Tables VI, VII, and VIII give the statistics at the time of inspection of three typical depots, not the longest in operation, and representative in size.

* Includes women spinning wool for blanket weaving

[271]

Table VI

Month	No. of socie-ties	No. of mem-bers	Sub-scribed capital	Paid up share capital	Out-standing loans	Re-paid loans	Month's produc-tion value
1939							
November	35	505	$3,302	$1,323	$27,500	$ 175	$30,089
December	39	559	4,550	2,496	33,000	875	47,491
1940							
January	44	615	8,436	4,343	32,363	1,875	50,189
February	45	622	8,716	4,413	37,789	3,987	29,540*
March	45	648	9,542	4,532	38,408	5,377	

* New Year Holiday occurred in February.

Table VII

Statistics for December 31, 1939:

Product	Ramie	Cotton	Sewing	Printing	Miscel-laneous	Total
No. of societies	29	17	3	1	4	55
No. of members (men)	268	160	29	16	56	529
No. of members (women)	26	82	—	—	—	108
No. of apprentices	30	35	4	3	—	72
No. of auxiliary workers	80	33	2	5	8	128
Subscribed share capital	$2,648	6,100	492	400	368	10,308

Loan from Chinese Industrial Co-operatives	$4,911	8,886	—	2,342	500	16,639
Loan from bank	$27,405	37,158	7,720	—	10,208	82,491
Monthly production	$14,736	29,039	594	2,294	1,383	48,046

Production for first four months of 1940:

January	$19,426	33,559	655	?	809	54,449
February	13,772	22,586	643	?	706	37,707
March	34,802	64,863	773	?	2,158	102,596
April	37,022	63,970	1,011	2,623	1,655	106,281

Table VIII

Month 1939	No. of societies	No. of members	Subscribed share capital	Paid up share capital	Outstanding loans	Repaid loans	Monthly production
March	10	91	$ 1,810	$ 831			
April	19	202	3,475	1,873	$ 17,925		$ 11,422
May	20	208	4,975	3,374	60,645		21,200
June	22	227	8,775	3,799	76,585		25,372
July	49	443	10,985	4,349	102,765		69,807
August	49	446	10,985	4,349	119,435	$ 150	91,196
September	51	471	11,135	4,383	118,485	12,300	112,785
October	51	485	11,135	4,383	118,636	12,300	124,640
November	51	493	11,485	4,399	237,138	12,300	152,851
December	51	500	11,925	4,587	233,930	22,305	223,398

In this depot $153,000 had been repaid by April, 1940

OTHER ASPECTS OF CHINESE
INDUSTRIAL CO-OPERATIVE WORK

Research: There are three research centers — chemical in the northwest, textile in Chengtu, and another chemical in the southeast. In addition there is a good deal of minor research being done in every part of the country by enthusiastic technicians who have ideas of improving machines and processes.

Social Work: In every depot there is a program for education of the workers. Subjects taught include principles of co-operation, common sense of industry, reading and writing, arithmetic, hygiene. Selected workers are often given further classes in business management, accounting, industrial co-operation, democratic methods. In most depots there are also schemes for medical care of co-operative workers, and in some centers for recreation, games, libraries. In the northwest a contribution from Madame Chiang enabled a women's department to be started which pays special attention to the education of workers' children in nursery and primary schools, and to the development of initiative and leadership among the women co-operative members.

Evacuation from Threatened Points: The Chinese Industrial Co-operatives came into being just before the fall of Hankow, when Madame Chiang expedited the removal of what industry could be removed from that city.

CHINESE INDUSTRIAL CO-OPERATIVES

There have been many epics in the removal of machinery from threatened cities. Several plants were removed from Changsha by the Chinese Industrial Co-operatives, while in Foochow, Swatow, and Canton city, a good deal was done by Chinese Industrial Co-operative organizers to get small industry back to the country. This has been at some cost, for war is no respecter of persons.

The depot master at Wenchow was killed when on Chinese Industrial Co-operative business. A group of workers in Swatow at the time of evacuation were not heard of again.

The recent threat to Ningpo caused the Chinese Industrial Co-operatives to get busy in that area and to move south to safe districts over $150,000 worth of small machinery, which can be used to make other machines in south Chekiang Province. Before the fall of Nanchang, in Kiangsi Province, Chinese Industrial Co-operative organizers had dug up and bought machines from small machine shops which would have otherwise been lost.

The Anhwei, Chekiang, Fukien, south Kiangsi and Kwangtung provincial machine-shop co-operatives have all been brought from territory now occupied by the Japanese. Workers have been fed, and transport expenses paid mostly with special funds collected by friends abroad, through national committees, or through the International Committee in Hong Kong.

[275]

Women's Work: Work among the women from the Northwest Headquarters has been excellent. They have provided for medical treatment for refugees and for their technical training prior to their incorporation into co-operatives. Overseas relief funds have been used for this purpose.

Work on refugee villages has been done in the Southwest Headquarters, while in the Southeast Headquarters many co-operatives have been formed from soldiers' dependents, and money has been advanced to them, without interest charge, to enable them to support themselves.

The cry from the Chinese peasant always is that he wants to go and defend his country, but who will look after his family? That need is being met in some way in these outlying districts.

Crippled Soldiers: The first group of these men to be incorporated into the Chinese Industrial Co-operatives was made up of those who had been trained at an orthopedic hospital in Shanghai for industry. They are now in Kiangsi Province, and form the spearhead of a group of co-operatives, 55 in all, in one hsien (county). They have their own marketing and supply agency, and have succeeded so well that over 200 in this one little place have married and settled down.

Other crippled soldiers' centers for work have now been started in Fukien, Hunan, Kweichow and south Shensi provinces. The men are naturally slow at first, but they are desperately keen, and as they go on they become very proficient.

Transport: The possibility of organizing transport on the co-operative basis has been successfully explored. There is now motor, cart, camel and man-power transport operating on a co-operative basis, usually in conjunction with a marketing and supply agency.

One transport co-operative owns 150 carts which now travel over the Tsingling Mountains all the way from the end of the Lunghai Railway to Chengtu, in Szechuan Province.

Technical: In the technical realm, it has been the aim to improve local processes so that they come nearer to modern industrial ideals; to develop better means of spinning cotton and woolen yarn — not to be satisfied with manual power, but to use rivers and streams for direct water power, with improved water wheels; to make engines that run on charcoal; to improve and utilize old methods of dyeing; to encourage better methods of producing paper, glass, porcelain, and other consumer goods.

A new kind of engineer is being brought into being. One who will think more of people as the masters of their industry, who will encourage them to put their creative selves into their work.

On the accountant side, another new type is being developed. One who will tramp over country paths from one co-operative to another in all weathers, bringing to the societies simple and adequate systems of cost accounting, auditing and explaining.

"Indusco" — as the movement has been called — touches some very fundamental issues in Chinese life in a way that would have well pleased Dr. Sun Yat-sen.

It is the principle of people's livelihood in practice, bringing together the ideals of service, comradeship, and livelihood.

It has struck a popular trend in China, and it is by tapping such sources of strength that the Chinese people will, in the end, surmount all their difficulties and gain the right to unhampered progress, as a free people.

STAFF

The leading men in the movement are Christian Chinese, most of whom have been trained in America. Many of them were friends or pupils of that veteran missionary, Joseph Baillie, who, by his unremitting effort, made it possible for Chinese students to have years of practical work in American factories after their graduation from engineering courses.

The general and the associate-general secretaries, the chief and the assistant chief engineers, the head of the field section, and one of the regional heads, are all Baillie engineers.

Another region is headed by a returned student from

Aberdeen University who studied co-operation in Denmark, and before the war was a leading figure in co-operative work in Hopei; another, by a Canadian-born and Canadian-trained Chinese engineer who was once a secretary of the student Christian movement in his college days in Toronto.

Then in the depots, of which there are over 60, are many depot masters who were once pupils of the veteran British co-operator, Professor J. B. Tayler, of Yenching University, who now works with his students as adviser. Other advisers are Drs. Lewis Smythe and Charles Riggs, American co-operative and technical specialists, who give the movement much of their time and thought.

CONCLUSION

There is not a Chinese Industrial Co-operative depot that does not have plans for improvement and expansion of work — business, organization, technique, accounting. As fast as funds become available for capital, promotion, education, and training, the work can be pushed forward with energy as one of the forces in China making for national integrity and better living for the Chinese people.

There are scores of examples. At Chikiang (Szechuan Province) the other day, I came across a silk-weaving and silk-spinning co-operative out in the country. It was a co-operative of old-timers — people who had once worked at silk spinning, from the wild cocoons that are available locally. Then the demand dropped — and died. Then the war came. Prices went up. Old people in the villages suffered. They thought of their old trade and got together, borrowing a little capital from us.

They are paying back their loan, and producing a good heavy silk at a quite reasonable wartime price, using their very old methods. They have a nice place in the country — a converted temple, overlooking a fine stretch of river — and are really very happy. It's an ill wind that blows nobody good! I was rather touched. They were so pathetically grateful. And so proud of the stuff they made with their own hands.

Many of the co-operative members have known great hardship. Many of them have trekked many thousands of miles in their effort to find some place in which they could ply the trade for which they were fitted.

In the heart of Kansu Province there is a solid Shansi Province man called Tsao. He was brought up as a weaver, and worked in the Shansi Cotton Mills in Taiyuan, the capital of the province. As a refugee, he traveled to Sian, the capital of Shensi Province, where he found employment in a cotton mill. That was bombed and put out of action. So he went further west, looking for work. He collected other men from Shansi when he found that he could form a co-operative, and they all applied for admission to the Chinese Industrial Co-operatives. His fellow members were all people he had known all his life. "We should sweat when our brothers give their blood for us. To give sweat is easier than to give blood," he said.

There is a chairman of a bakery and foodstuffs co-operative in Kiangsi Province who could not be persuaded to leave his premises during the heavy raids that shattered the flimsy shops in his street, and filled the city with horror. "I must remain here," he said, "until I can see all the goods we have manufactured, all the raw material we possess and all our tools moved to a place that is properly safe, and where we can carry on our work without danger to our members. I am responsible for this co-operative being started, and without the co-operative my life is not worth living."

When the war started, thousands of Chinese schools and universities had to be evacuated, and the student bodies naturally scattered. A certain middle school student from Hopei Province fled southward to the Yangtze River, and came on a river steamer to the city of Wanhsien, in Szechuan Province.

He entered a soapmaker's establishment; learned something of the trade; carried on his own experiments, using local materials. His school friends joined him, and they wondered how they might put their ideas into action, for they were sure that they could make out together. They were the first to come to the recently established branch of the Chinese Industrial Co-operatives in their locality, and ask for help in setting up a productive unit. As a patriotic contribution they have sold 3,000 pieces of soap at cost price of the material giving their own labor free.

I think of a group of refugee women from Changsha, Hunan Province, who came together as weavers. Their menfolk were away as soldiers, and they had no home. They found a Buddhist nunnery, the abbess of which welcomed them, so that with their capital they bought loom and yarn, and found working room free. The nuns said their prayers daily to the accompaniment of clacking looms. The members worked and kept the place beautifully clean. They bade me farewell after my inspection by coming out under the flowering peach tree at the entrance, and singing, "Arise" — the war song of the guerrillas — while from the interior came the subdued chant of "O-mi-to-foh," and the hollow note of wood striking wood, as the nuns continued their prayers.

I think of a meeting of Cantonese fitters and mechanics, refugees from Canton city, sitting at an organization meeting in a little town in the north of Kwangtung Province. They listened, at first suspiciously, as the organizer told of the new way to organize and work, wondering what was the "catch." Then, as understanding came, they were keenly eager to co-operate. The words tumbled out of their mouths, as they described how machines could be bought, and how they could be brought in; how buildings could be erected, and how orders could be secured. The "way out" had become apparent.

CHINESE INDUSTRIAL CO-OPERATIVES

I saw peasants in a guerrilla area, desperately eager to make tools for their economic defense, and intense in their anxiety, when they had machines and technicians, to fulfill the trust that had been placed in them. "Show us still better ways," they demanded. "We must make things better — and more of them. We must know more!" No decadence here; but an earnestness that was almost frightening, so greatly did one realize the tremendous responsibility one takes in promising livelihood.

But this is the sort of thing one sees all over the country — refugees from Anhwei Province making mosquito nets in Wanhsien, away up the Yangtze River, in Szechuan Province; crippled soldiers out in the country from the same depot, etc.

One feels that everything is worth while when one sees jobs standing up on their own, and people prospering with some mastery of their environment.

The Chinese Industrial Co-operatives provide a new link to bind China together. Like a medical service, it is needed everywhere. The engineer and the doctor are always welcome. So Chinese Industrial Co-operatives have been invited from all corners to come and establish work from the Tibetan highlands; from distant Kokonor; from Ninghsia; from Suiyuan, and the Inner Mongolian regions down through the areas held by the Chinese guerrilla forces through north and central China; from famine districts in south Hopei Province, where the dykes have been cut, and the country flooded by the Japanese in order to starve the Chinese people into submission; from the tribal areas of the Miaos and Yaos in Kwangsi and Yunnan provinces; from among the Hakka women of east Kwangtung Province — and so the chain extends, bringing the doctrine of self-help and creative work.

It is not so much what the Chinese Industrial Co-operatives have done, but more what the Chinese Industrial Co-operatives can yet do in winning this struggle for us, and helping to win the peace that follows it.

A prosperous, stable China will make for a more prosperous and stable America. It is good business for every American to realize this, and to support as well as he can a gallant effort at reconstruction that is not only helping the Chinese people, but also his own, and the peoples of the world as well.

Part III

TOWARD A NEW CHINA

XXI

NEW LIFE

PRIOR to the Japanese aggression and our war of resistance the New Life Movement had been creating an outstanding place for itself as a leaven of reform in the domestic and national life of China. When the war of resistance developed, New Life automatically and naturally wove itself into the network of national defense. By the very nature of its organization it was able to assist materially in the mobilization and enlightenment of the people to meet the new trials which confronted them.

New Life was launched at Nanchang in 1934. It was designed, on the basis of a revival of certain virtues of ancient China, to provide the people in the province of Kiangsi with something spiritual and practical to guide them at a time when they needed help to recover from a long period of warfare. It is estimated that they had lost a million lives; had suffered the destruction of the homes of more than a million people; had sustained property losses valued at a total of a billion and a half dollars. The survivors emerged benumbed, impoverished, and reduced to beggary.

Something more than mere military protection was necessary to restore to mental and physical fitness the people in such a state of mind and health. Four of the cardinal virtues of old China were recalled as a possible source of reviviscence, and it was determined to essay a practical application of them to present-day conditions. They were "Li," "I," "Lien" and "Chih," the four principles which, in ancient China, governed personal behavior and relations; assured justice for all classes; inspired integrity in official and business life; demanded respect for the rights of others.

They were adopted because of our belief that these principles could be successfully employed to satisfy both psychological and physical needs. Practical application of them manifested itself in the teaching of hygiene; the care of homes and children; the cleanliness of environment; the betterment of means of livelihood; the promotion of communal help; the worth-whileness and advantages of co-operation. Their ultimate aim was the awakening of the people to a full sense of their individual and collective rights, duties, and responsibilities as citizens; and the off-setting of the inertia caused by hundreds of years of Manchu misrule which, by excluding the masses from participation in State affairs and administration, killed national consciousness and produced an apathy calamitous to national progress and well-being.

The nation at large only became aware of the real significance of New Life after demonstrations of its usefulness in Kiangsi conclusively proved that the interests and well-being of the people constituted the mainspring of national reform. Not only did the Province of Kiangsi welcome the progress and prosperity that New Life envisaged and seemed capable of ensuring, but as soon as its work became known and appreciated by the people of other provinces, the whole nation began to adopt its principles and procedure.

New organizations had to be created to give impetus to a spiritual revival in the devastated areas and to help the unfortunate millions to rebuild their homes and recover a footing for themselves. This initial step having been taken, social centers and schools, co-operative societies, and rural reconstruction agencies soon sprang to life, and began to march together in bettering the lot of the struggling people. Each co-operative began its existence as a preparatory society. When it matured, after a year of apprenticeship, it became a full-fledged co-operative; and in due course there grew up credit co-operatives, utility co-operatives, supply co-operatives, marketing co-operatives, and others with mixed functions. Then there developed unions of co-operatives for the improvement of the enterprises and interests of all.

The need for scientific agriculture soon saw the inauguration of an agricultural institution to experiment with grain, horticulture and animal husbandry. Farmers were taught how to suppress insect pests, select seeds, grow new and better crops, and co-operate with the welfare centers established by the National Economic Council and rural normal schools. Experimental stations were established throughout the province, and soon secured the services of a group of hard-working agricultural specialists, many of whom were trained in America.

A provincial health department was created which quickly gained the confidence of the people by educational efforts in the form of exhibits, campaigns, lectures and publications, as well as through practical service rendered at the clinics and hospitals.

Educational facilities were organized with specially trained teachers to inculcate in the minds of the students a sense of the responsibility of citizenship; to teach them some form of profitable vocation; and to train them in the art of self-defense. Free education was provided for children through the "pao" (a group of families) school system, and every child of school age in the province was given a simple education.

The people were encouraged to interest themselves in local administration. They quickly understood that they had a right to expose any irregularities in public affairs; and magistrates, or functionaries with the old-time ideas of official immunity in the enjoyment of dishonestly acquired wealth, soon learned to their cost that the people, in the name of New Life, could expose evildoers with full confidence that wrongs would be righted; that punishment would be meted out to fit the crime.

Then rural welfare centers began to function under the aegis of New Life. Kiangsi Province was divided into ten of them, at each of which agriculture, health, education, co-operatives, home industries and work for women and children were developed. In addition local leaders were trained, age-old customs improved, disputes arbitrated, etc. — all being integral parts of welfare work. In this connection both the national, provincial, and local governments co-operated. A comprehensive and complete economic program was worked out to deal with the whole life of the community at a moderate cost which is borne by the combined co-operative bodies.

Of outstanding interest in connection with this aspect of rural reconstruction is the Kiangsi Christian Rural Service Union. It began its work at Lichwan, in a beautiful valley which suffered terribly from the ravages of war, and where the people are much more conservative and superstitious than the average villagers in the interior. Rice fields extend throughout the valley. The near-by hills are largely barren; but the high mountains which rise in the distance are covered with pine and bamboo. These give rise to one of the great industries of the region, papermaking; and in addition to rice and paper, tobacco ranks as one of the chief exports.

At this village of Lichwan a group of young Christians were brought together to give practical application of Christian principles to rural reconstruction — Christian in purpose and in personnel. These workers included college graduates of unusual ability who could command high salaries elsewhere. But they went to Lichwan for service sake, and received a pittance of $30 (Chinese money) per month with food, though a number drew additional allowances from the missionary institutions they represented. They did splendid work for a reformed people under the New Life system by carrying out a program at each center which included four main departments — agriculture, health, co-operative, and education.

It may not be inappropriate to mention that this practical endeavor sprang from a challenge that I issued to the missionary body at a conference at Kuling some years ago when I pointed out that there was an outstanding need for practical evidence of the worth of Christianity to the Chinese people.

The work that New Life was doing in Kiangsi Province was quickly bruited throughout China by newspapers, periodicals, and speakers. The movement spread in all directions with amazing results. By the time the Japanese began their aggression in 1937, New Life had already been firmly established everywhere, and at the beginning of our war of resistance its services were immediately enlisted. Its organizations were pressed into service by the Generalissimo when he emphatically reasserted to the nation its basic principles as applicable to the patriotic defense of the country.

"Propriety (Li) safeguards us from cowardly behavior in time of danger," he said. "Loyalty (I) makes us dare death for a cause. Integrity (Lien) gives us clarity of judgment between right and wrong. Honor (Ch'ih) impels us to erase the disgrace that today hovers over the fair face of our native land.

"Cultivate these high qualities in your daily living," urged the Generalissimo. "Show your indomitable courage, and carry on the task for which your comrades in the trenches are fighting and dying." With that exordium New Life was launched into action.

By the summer of 1937, just before the Lukouchiao Incident, more than 300 senior secretaries of the New Life Movement, representing important city and provincial branches, assembled at Lushan (Kuling) to undergo a course of rigid training, and to draw up a program to be carried out systematically on a nationwide scale. Out of China's 2,000 odd hsien (counties) more than 1,400 had formed local New Life organizations. At that time there were 400,000 volunteer workers under the New Life Service Corps.

Since the beginning of the war many organizations have, of course, participated in the work of resistance and reconstruction. But New Life has had to help them all, and has consequently been able to exert a beneficial influence through ever-widening channels. It so happened that it became necessary to enlist experienced personnel in order to carry out the work efficiently. The only source of supply was the New Life Movement; and when trained men were drawn from that source they automatically infused into the organizations a new spirit of service, self-sacrifice, co-operation, and efficiency. Perhaps the introduction of this spirit into other spheres of activity is one of the most important contributions that have been made by New Life to the war of resistance.

A shining example of efficiency is the work done by the War Area Service Corps. It was organized by the Military Council when resistance began, and it was staffed by men trained by New Life. The director of this corps is concurrently the General-Secretary of New Life, Major-General J. L. Huang, and the most important offices are headed by New Life secretaries. In 1939, with 168 workers, the corps established 31 stations covering important military and strategic points and rendered services to 1,445,460 men in uniform. Out of this number 58,601 were given first-aid dressings; 60,799 fed with congee (rice gruel); 725,853 served with tea; 29,305 provided with sleeping accommodation; 13,148 letters were written for the disabled, and other forms of service, such as entertainments, etc., were given to 557,754 wounded.

Another service which reflects the New Life spirit is the Wounded Soldiers' League. Its chief duty is the distribution of the "Generalissimo's Cash Awards to the Wounded." The Generalissimo, out of deep sympathy and consideration for those of his men who were wounded during their heroic fight against Japanese aggression, issued an order on September 25, 1937, to distribute awards to all wounded officers and men. There were many difficulties, aggravated by inadequate communication with the various fronts in remote war areas; by the constant shifting of wounded to the rear, and by the unsettled conditions in the mobile field hospitals. New Life workers, however, through painstaking efforts, devised an efficient system modeled on the scheme Mr. Henry Ford uses in his factories, and this enabled awards to be distributed to the wounded within the shortest time, thus avoiding duplications, and ensuring double checks on accuracy. A distribution in a hospital of 500 patients which formerly took one full day's labor to complete, is now done in two hours. During the past three years, a total of $6,180,173.00 was distributed to several hundred thousand men; and all records have been kept up to date. Altogether 3,875 distributions have been made in various hospitals, some of which are located behind the enemy lines.

A visit to the filing room of headquarters, where colored statistical charts are hung everywhere, is impressive and worthy of commendation. One can pick out any man from among the hundreds of thousands on the wounded list, and get particulars about him. Within twenty seconds the secretary in charge can produce from the master file, a card showing full details: where and when he was wounded, where and when he received his award, and even an anatomical chart showing the wound. The fact that the High Command is sufficiently interested in the health and welfare of the soldiers has had a tremendous effect upon the fighting morale of the whole army.

A third kind of service sponsored by New Life is the "Friends of the Wounded." Its very name caught the imagination and heart of Chinese patriots. A campaign held in Chungking in commemoration of the sixth anniversary of New Life, met with surprising results. Figuring on the basis of 100,000 wounded in various army hospitals, the movement aimed at soliciting 100,000 "Friends." The goal of the campaign was to provide a "Friend" for each wounded soldier. To become a "Friend," one paid a friendship fee of $1.00 (Chinese), or more, and pledged service to the wounded. By the end of the month, the campaign had brought in no less than 654,741 "Friends," with a total of $1,332,505.74 in cash, which was 554 per cent over the top. Names of more friends and more funds are still coming in.

The efforts of the "Friends of the Wounded" are concentrated upon (a) D. B. S. Work (delousing, bathing, and scabies treatment); (b) Special nutrition to those needing special diet; (c) Laundry, and mending of clothing and bedding; and (d) Supply and distribution of comfort kits and relief articles contributed by friends everywhere. Something like 69 branches of "Friends of the

Wounded" are already in operation in various provinces. According to our plan, 80 more branches are to be formed in the near future. So far, three classes of short-course training for such workers have been held at New Life Headquarters.

Recently a challenge was put before students in the West China Union University, Chengtu, on the campus of which five Christian colleges are housed: Who would give up one year of study to serve as secretaries in charge of "Friends of the Wounded"? Sixty-five college men and women offered their services; 34 of them are, after a short period of training, now in active service.

The slogan "Have the Warphans serve the Wounded," has become the order of the day. As an experiment, the first two classes were composed of some 70 war orphans collected from the orphanages directed by myself, and from Dr. H. H. Kung's Child Welfare Institutions. These children are now rendering excellent service.

A fourth kind of service which is managed by New Life personnel, but which does not bear the name of New Life, is the Aviation and Transportation Hostels. At the outbreak of hostilities our young aviators suffered unnecessary physical fatigue and nerve strain because the remote air fields offered no adequate temporary accommodation. New Life immediately took the matter in hand, and within a short space of time had 46 hostels erected in strategic centers to administer to the comfort of our flying personnel. In any of these centers, at any time of the day or night, our airmen may procure a good meal, a bath, a comfortable room — and, last but not least, a warm welcome from a friendly New Life secretary. The Generalissimo, seeing the excellent influence of these hostels upon the health and morale of the air force, has ordered similar establishments to be opened for the staffs of the organizations responsible for the transportation of materials necessary for national resistance. There are now 18 of these located on the various highways over which supplies are hauled.

Then there are other activities which do bear the name of New Life:

(1) There is the New Life publicity van. It is equipped with radio, movie apparatus, visual educational equipment, pictorial stands, loud-speakers, health clinic supplies, and several recreational features. It is a showboat on land. It is a traveling Chautauqua on wheels; welcomed everywhere it goes. In seven months this New Life van covered five provinces, a total distance of 12,546 kilometers. It has shown visual educational pictures 156 times. It has given in all 296 short talks and lectures; inoculated 4,300 persons against cholera; organized 52 short first-aid classes, reaching a total of 31,100 persons. Altogether no less than three-quarters of a million people were contacted one way or another. It has had in operation four

publicity trucks, 12 hand-pushed field service carts, and a regular hot-dog wagon to serve our airmen.

(2) Last year, a campaign in the form of "Offering Gold to the State" was launched by New Life in Chungking in connection with its fifth anniversary. In the short period of 15 days, a sum of $2,602,684.32 was raised by voluntary contributions to enrich the war chest — a feat that has broken the record of any campaign of a similar nature. The Women's Team alone raised over $600,000.00 — surpassing even the Bankers' Team.

(3) After the inhuman and insensate bombing of Chungking last year, the streets of the business quarter presented an unforgettable scene of mutilated corpses, carnage, and charred ruins. No food was available in the city. New Life took the lead in organizing free congee and tea kitchens for the thousands of destitute refugees. In eight days, 62,685 persons were served. In conjunction with the Women's Advisory Council, New Life has undertaken an even more lasting form of relief. In Nanchuen (80 kilometers southeast of Chungking) it has built a "New Village" for those who were bombed out of their homes. Thus it set a pace for other organizations to follow.

An emergency medical unit is also operated by New Life. In many cases the Japanese warplanes, after bombing open towns, put out of action — with calculated cruelty — mission hospitals and Red Cross units, depriving the people of even the most elementary first aid. In such cases the New Life emergency first-aid unit hops on a plane, a truck, a mule cart, a sampan, or whatever other means of transportation may be at hand, and plunges into rescue work until some more permanent form of medical attention becomes available.

(4) Continuance of national resistance against aggression entails greater need for economy and self-sacrifice on the part of the whole country. Even before the hostilities began New Life laid emphasis upon rational living. Since the war began, this principle has become not only desirable but necessary. The need of it inspired New Life to celebrate its fifth anniversary last year by sponsoring exhibitions in all the main cities to show the people the most practical ways of utlizing local products. Houses furnished with only native goods were exhibited. Bamboos were used as water pipes, and bed mattresses were made of palm bark — far cooler and almost as resilient as the foreign "Beauty Rest" mattresses, and costing a fraction of the price of the latter. In every phase of life people were encouraged to take advantage of the materials at hand.

New Life started a cafeteria system. It meets a particular need arising from the war. Many people having been driven away from or bombed out of their homes found the problem of obtaining nourishing food almost insoluble. They had to put up with what our national humor classifies as "guerrilla eating," that is eating anything, anywhere. Now the New Life cafeterias help to solve the

problem in a way novel to China. The fact that the cus-
tomer serves himself enables him to get a nourishing meal
for 65 cents — a no mean accomplishment in these days
of soaring prices. High officials consider it to be quite the
thing to invite friends to these cafeterias. Everyone saves
time and money — two forms of economy which are becoming increasingly popular as New China girds her loins
and tightens her belt. To save time in China is surely a
change pregnant with great possibilities since the accepted
legend is that time is of no account in Old Cathay. The
endeavor to have good food available at reasonable prices
has led to the invention of a new article of food — "Vita-
cake." It is becoming very popular, especially as "air-raid
rations." It provides something portable and nutritive to
eat during the long hours in dugouts. It is made of half
wheat flour, and half soya-bean milk residue. Formerly
the latter was used only for the feeding of chickens.

Not only do the people now save money and time in
eating, but they also save themselves worry by singing.
Community singing in China is another sign of modernization for which the war has been responsible. It was
New Life that foresaw the possibilities of such a thing.
As a stimulant to patriotism mass singing was started in
the officers' training camps which the Generalissimo instituted several years before the Lukouchiao Incident. The
voices of men singing in unison greeted the sunrise and
bid farewell to the sunset each day. They sang so well that

the officers took the practice back to their troops. The schools and colleges attracted by the harmony started singing; every organization whose purpose was to help win the war followed suit, and the people listening soon became infected by the vibrant voices of the children and the youth as they imitated the soldiers.

"Mass marriages" were also started by New Life. Couples who wish to abandon single blessedness without incurring the high cost of the elaborate ceremony hitherto dictated by considerations of "face" can now get married in a group ceremony for the nominal sum of $20 (Chinese currency) for each couple instead of expending hundreds or thousands of dollars and, in some cases, involving themselves in ruinous, lifelong debt. Mass marriage takes place in groups ranging from 10 to 100 at a time. They have all the ceremony and dignity befitting such an occasion — a large hall, music, attendants, bridesmaids, candles, decorations. The ceremonies are presided over by the highest local dignitary, or city father, who also bestows upon the happy couples his official blessings. Order and impressiveness mark the occasion. There is no irreverence; no facetiousness; and, so far as can be ascertained, the wedded ones seem to live "happy ever afterwards."

The promotion of good health and the cultivation of good physique have always been a foremost concern of New Life. New Life arranges and sponsors athletic meets of all sorts. In the midst of the continual bombing at

Chungking during the Dragon Boat Festival, it made the bulk of the populace interested in dragon boat races and swimming events. While bombs were dropping and exploding the people were in their dugouts. As soon as the "all clear" sounded (and sometimes before) spectators in thousands rushed to the banks of both the Kialing and Yangtze rivers, where the dragon boats were to race. Bombs and death and ruin were forgotten, while lusty people battled for supremacy in and on the river waters.

This spirit to meet with courage each new threat of the Japanese military is a source of power which no display of ruthless force could crush.

The Japanese would like to annihilate New Life, of course, for they fear its influence. Recently an American missionary traveling from America in a China Clipper, asked a Japanese fellow passenger, an official returning from Washington, why Japan had chosen this time to invade China. "If Chiang Kai-shek should succeed in his New Life Movement," the Japanese retorted, "do you think there would be any chance left for Japan in China?"

While the war of resistance saw the men's section of New Life responding centrifugally to war's demands by diffusing its experience, influence, and energies along several separate channels, the women's section reacted quite in a contrary manner. It concentrated women's efforts and centralized them. Instead of supplying trained personnel to other organizations it absorbed certain of the existing

[303]

organizations themselves and made them departments, but without interfering with their policies, or, indeed, their finances or personnel. In short, it brought all women's endeavors within its ambit, thus promoting efficiency and economy. How that has contributed to China's three years of resistance is told in a general way in the chapter on "Women's Work" in this book.

Not the least important accomplishment of New Life, however, is the development of its close relationship for the public weal with the foreign missionaries—one of New Life's most striking successes. In 1934, when the Generalissimo and I began our travels in northwest China, it was at Sian that we first assembled all denominations of the foreign missionary body to explain New Life to them, and to devise means of co-operation to ameliorate the condition of the people. The missionaries were elated. A scheme of co-operative effort was promptly arranged and their genuine response was productive of good for their institutions and for New Life, while the people reaped benefits from both. Later on co-operative committees were set up with the co-operation of the missionaries at Lanchow, Suiyuan, Kaifeng, Taiyuanfu and other cities.

The good work of the New Life Movement was quickly appreciated by the people. There are many who had lifelong experience of paying taxes without participation in any kind of State affairs; who knew every trick and artifice of the oppressor, and were, therefore, quick to distinguish between the good officials and the bad. They were quick, too, to promote and protect their personal interests. So they eagerly embraced New Life and more than willingly co-operated with it in every possible way for their material and spiritual benefit, for the exercising of their rights and the discharging of their responsibilities as citizens and for assuring their due place in the national scheme of reconstruction. In fine, for the political unity of the country and the inculcation of patriotism of a kind hitherto believed nonexistent. New Life is entitled to full honors.

XXII

WOMEN'S WORK

No ACCOUNT of China's reconstruction program, however sketchily written, would be complete without mention of the significant role Chinese women have played since they began to take an active part in the defense of their country against Japanese aggression.

Even before this war began, the Chinese woman was beginning to emerge as an important social and economic factor in the molding of national consciousness. She was coming into her own for two main reasons.

First, because new ideas in China — generally more revolutionary in their initial stages than is the case in Western countries — are, whenever found practical, adopted with a swiftness as startling as it is effective, despite the apparent conservativeness of the Chinese mind.

Second, because the Chinese woman has learned from the restrictions and seclusion forced upon her by environment and custom to adapt her talents to ever-changing social conditions with a flexibility and ease born of natural aptitude and necessity.

The war, however, has undoubtedly hastened her emergence and emancipation. It has fired her patriotism and given her scope for activities which were dreamt of but

[306]

hitherto unrealized; it has given her opportunities to do her part as a member of society on an equal footing with her menfolk; it has given her the initiative to assume responsibilities hitherto discharged by men with long experience; and, finally, it has given her means of self-expression as a creative force in helping to defeat the ravagers of her fatherland.

In every government organization there are women workers. They have shown astonishing aptitude for public service. Ten women are members of the People's Political Council, which is composed of leaders in every walk of life, and representing every shade of political opinion. In 21 provinces 317 women's organizations are participating in war work. These are found even in the remote provinces of Sikong, Chahar, Chinghai, and Suiyuan — real frontier regions. The Women's War Relief Association has 35 branches in China, and is international in scope, for it has nine branches in other parts of the world where Chinese women are congregated. In the newspaper world women are no less active and keenly alive to the march of events. Three years ago there were only two publications in China exclusively published for women by women: *Woman's Life,* and *Woman's Voice.* Today, there are over 50 magazines published for women — weekly, biweekly and monthly.

It would be an exaggeration to say that all the women of China have been mobilized. To accomplish this would take considerable time and an enormous, specially trained, personnel. Considering how little and inadequate were the facilities available for this work, and how large a proportion of our masses are illiterate, it is surprising to see that so much has been achieved.

At the beginning of the war there were only a few women's organizations which were national in scope. Soon after hostilities began they sprang up in every part of the country with the rapidity of sprouting bamboo. To prevent duplication of work due to lack of co-ordination and correlation, a Women's Conference was held at Kuling, in May, 1938. Fifty leading women, representing every line of endeavor and profession, and selected from all parts of the country, decided to utilize the Women's Advisory Council of the New Life Movement as the head and front of women's participation in war work. Ever since then that council has been in direct touch with all women's organizations in China.

Apart from the work directed by the various departments of the council, the women of China are carrying on activities in other fields. Far in the rear they toil and spin; they have co-operatives to reclaim waste land (in Chekiang and Shensi Provinces in particular). Close to the front they cheer, comfort, and inspire the soldiers with songs, amateur theatricals, and tales of ancient and modern deeds of heroism. Many of the illiterate women group themselves together, washing and mending clothes, working in the field hospitals, and acting as stretcher-bearers to carry the wounded to base hospitals.

I once read somewhere that there are three things which no man can escape: birth, death, and a determined woman. The women of China have an inflexible determination. The Japanese are already paying for their folly in having, at the outset of their invasion, overlooked the sturdy resistance of Chinese women. When, in several of the provinces, the Japanese military molested the women, the older women of the village — the mothers and mothers-in-law — used axes and meat choppers upon the next contingent of Japanese troops to arrive. These amazons surprised the enemy in the dead of night, and caused many a Japanese head to roll upon the ground.

Women, young and old, have organized themselves almost down to the last baby in many areas adjacent to the Japanese-occupied territories. They are always on the lookout for spies and traitors (fifth columnists, as they are now euphemistically called in Europe), and the children are taught to report anybody who looks suspicious. Many a traitor has been trapped, thanks to the alertness of the country women. One day a group of women were washing clothes by the bank of a stream. Three Chinese strangers approached. One stopped to ask the way to a village occupied by the Japanese. One woman delayed him by giving him confusing directions, while another proffered him pretended help. "Oh, you would never find the place from her description of it," she said. "Come on, my home lies that way, I will show you!" Slowly she walked along with the men, while the other woman secured their arrest by informing the local authorities.

There are women guerrillas, who, while their guerrilla husbands are away on expeditions, guard their villages, and help to disrupt communications by cutting the roads just behind the enemy lines to stop the Japanese advance. On the other hand, in Hopei, Shantung, Kwangsi, Chinghai and Kansu provinces, women have helped to build highways. As one news agency has pointed out, the 240-mile Kansu-Szechuan highway will stand as an immortal monument to the women of Kansu when it is finished. Thousands are now working on it. They also helped to build the Kansu-Sinkiang highway, working solely with primitive tools — spades, hammers, axes, and even vegetable choppers.

Turning to another sphere of activities, we find that women who have shown their capacity to engage in village political and administrative affairs have been elected village chiefs. Others, yielding to the patriotic urge, have divorced their husbands on account of the latter's affiliation with Japanese puppets, while daughters of puppets have publicly denounced and disowned their fathers for working with the Japanese. There is, for instance, a Miss Sung Pei-lan, one of the women who had been acting as a guide for troops marching through difficult mountains.

One day she discovered that during her absence a large group of Japanese soldiers had taken refuge in her home. She immediately assembled all the members of her family in the outskirts of the village, and, with the help of the guerrillas, deliberately set fire to her ancestral home. Not a single Japanese escaped from the cordon thrown around it.

Courage and determination to resist the enemy exist not only in Free China, but also in the occupied territories. In a Shanghai Chinese factory seized by the Japanese, a puppet manager installed by the enemy raised the flag of the Rising Sun over the factory buildings. The workers were all women. They hooted the flag; threw mud and stones at it; tried to pull it down. They were overpowered by the Japanese military; they went on strike and would not resume work until the despised enemy flag was removed. When Japanese soldiers made free use of the premises of another factory and molested some of the women, all the workers not only fell upon the ruffians to protect the victims, but went on strike until the Japanese authorities were compelled to forbid entrance by their soldiers.

Miss Nyi Ving-yoh, the seventeen-year-old daughter of a former president of the Shanghai Bankers' Association, ran away from home in Shanghai to join in the defense of her country. The pathetic letter she wrote to her mother describing her feelings upon seeing her compatriots murdered and her country marauded, will remain as a moving testimony to the invincible spirit of China's womanhood. Thousands of young women, many of whom are now amongst our best workers, had also run away from their comfortable homes in occupied areas to offer their services to the State.

Two widowed Mongolian Princesses — Princess Chi Chun-fang, of the Western Banner, the first woman Chassack in Mongol history, and Princess Pah Yun-ying, of the Eastern Banner — are other noteworthy examples of the stern metal of which China's womanhood is forged. Both distinguished and accomplished horsewomen and accurate marksmen, they braved the fire of Japanese troops in breaking through the cordon to reach Free China. Before making this final dash to liberty they had led several hundreds of their troops still remaining loyal to them in guerrilla skirmishes against the enemy. Princess Chi brought out her old mother and her little three-year-old son; while Princess Pah was accompanied by her eleven-year-old son. The sight of these two slender, almost fragile-looking young women, and the story of their resolve to be loyal to the cause for which their husbands had lived and died, impressed me as being typical of the inflexible purpose and unity of China's womanhood.

One could relate many more accounts and stories illustrating the patriotic devotion to their country's cause of women in every stratum of Chinese society, but space permits only a bare outline of women's organized work in every part of the country, under the Women's Advisory

[312]

Council. There is a standing committee composed of leading women, including Mesdames H. H. Kung, Ho Ying-
chin, Chen Cheng, Feng Yu-hsiang, Ma Chao-chun,
Chang Chi-chung, Dr. Wu Yi-fang, Dr. Tseng Pao-
seng and myself, with Mrs. William C. Wang as the general secretary. The council carries on its work through the
following departments: (1) Co-ordinating; (2) Training; (3) War Area Service; (4) Rural Service; (5) Livelihood; (6) Cultural; (7) War Relief; (8) Refugee Children; and (9) Production, and is now concentrating its
energies upon Szechuan Province as a base for national
reconstruction. We hope to complete our work in two
years — a vast undertaking, seeing that the province has
an area larger than present-day Germany, and a population of 52,000,000. Szechuan has more hsien (districts)
than any province. There are 134 of them, and we have
work proceeding in 34. In another two years we shall have
mobilized the female population of every hsien in Szechuan for active participation in the war of resistance, and
the equally important tasks of rehabilitation and reconstruction which lie ahead.

Eight other provinces have provincial work corps under the direction of the standing committee, with a similar
set up of departments. The wife of the provincial chairman is responsible directly to the standing committee for
the women's work of her province. Madame Wu Ting-
chan, wife of the Chairman of Kweichow Province, a typi-

cal old-fashioned lady and mother of the most conservative type, is a notable example.

Kweichow itself was the poorest province in all China, for until three years ago it grew practically little else besides opium. But that was before the war. Now no opium is grown, and the province is fast developing its natural resources. Madame Wu daily attends office on the dot, and woe to any who lags behind! Under her eagle eye the Kweichow Work Corps runs with dispatch — a sight delightful to behold. To all movements sponsored by the advisory council, Kweichow responds with a celerity second to none.

Madame Chu Shao-liang, of Kansu, and Madame Ma Pu-fang of Chinghai Province, are also noteworthy examples of women of the "old school" who have cast aside their reserve and have, since the war, been tirelessly spurring on the women in their native provinces to participate in war work. A few days ago Madame Chu remitted to the advisory council another $150,000 for relief projects.

Wherever these women, wives of provincial chairmen, are — at the front or in the rear — whatever type they are — young college graduates or conservative "tai-tais" — they all take a deep and serious interest in discharging their responsibilities. They realize that they must keep pace with the quickstep of time; that the day is past when a woman could rely on her husband's position to justify her existence; that the day has dawned for her to exercise her right to think and act as an individual interested in the future destiny of her country. That, to my mind, is all to the good, and bodes well for the future.

Reverting to the work of the standing committee, I would like to give a brief account of its various departments.

(1) *Co-ordinating Department*

By means of investigation, correspondence, and personal interviews, the Co-ordinating Department acts as the liaison for all the women's organizations in the country. At the beginning it emphasized the importance of work with the students and the families of recruits.

The department also keeps all the women's organizations au courant with national movements of particular interest to women. For example, when we had the "Offer Gold to the State Movement," the "Thrift Movement," and various other movements not covered by the other departments of the Women's Advisory Council, the Co-ordinating Department made it its business to keep women's organizations throughout the country informed, and gave them advice and directions so that they may contribute toward the success of these movements. Recently the department inaugurated discussion groups to stimulate interest in the People's National Congress to be convened in November of this year for the adoption of a National Constitution.

[315]

(2) *Training Department*

We found that the greatest difficulty at the beginning was the lack of trained personnel. Young and enthusiastic students were ready to sacrifice all for their country, but they lacked practical experience and knowledge of how best to utilize their talents.

The Training Department was, therefore, set up, and has since been systematically training workers. Over 1,000 of them, mostly young high school graduates, are now doing field work, having been trained for the War Area Service and the Rural Service Departments. As experience proved that the workers could perform their tasks more efficiently when in groups under older and more experienced women, they were divided into teams of 20 with an older girl as counselor for each team. She is usually a college graduate who has gone through the same course of training

Primarily the girls are taught how to approach the inhabitants of rural regions; how to give instruction in character building; how to improve the standard of living of the people; how to safeguard the interests of the people; how to promote wholehearted and unselfish devotion to the winning of the war.

The work of this department has been so satisfactory that we decided to establish a college offering a short course on staff work for older workers, who, in turn, can train junior workers in their native provinces. This spring 150 women of college grade, drafted from every province, were given a short, intensive course of three months, and have just been graduated. In this way women's training as a whole could be made to spread throughout the provinces, it being obviously impossible for this department to train junior workers for the whole country.

Almost all these graduates had already held positions of responsibility and trust, but it was felt that if they could join us and become familiar with the methods so successfully employed by the Women's Advisory Council, they could increase the effectiveness of their work.

Two very important results of the work of the last graduated class soon became apparent. Women from every part of the country were familiarized with the spirit and training of the New Life Movement, and were given opportunities to know conditions in other parts of the country by close association with their fellow students.

(3) *War Area Service Department*

The War Area Service Department began work in the vicinity of Hankow. After the Central Government had withdrawn from that city, the department carried on its work for a year in Hunan Province. It operated in places right behind the front lines where communications were difficult and customs were conservative. It trained farmers and encouraged them to enlist in the army; it trained the local women in their homes, and it trained local staff members so that the work could be continued after our workers withdrew.

The members of this department also work in the field and base hospitals. They write letters for the wounded; they cheer them with songs and theatricals; they nurse them, and, in every way, do their best to uphold their morale. They are not only zealously doing first aid in the hospitals, but are teaching the convalescents as well. Many a soldier has thus been taught the elements of the three R's. Among the trophies sent to the advisory council from our workers are specimens of writings and drawings done by the wounded with the left hand, the right hand having been mutilated. Heart-rending stories have been told of the eagerness with which the recruits and the wounded imbibe knowledge; how their otherwise monotonous days were enlivened and cheered by learning to read and write. Ink slabs being scarce, the porous back of a coarse rice bowl has done duty as a slab upon which to rub the ink.

In recent months, the everyday interest of our soldiers in the outcome of the European conflict shows that they clearly recognize that the war here and the war in Europe are one and the same.

The most significant achievement, perhaps, of the department has been the bettering of the relations between the army and the people. In the old days soldiers were

[318]

anathema to the people, so it was natural that at the beginning of the war of resistance the people should be suspicious of the army, and the army resentful of the attitude of the people. Now, after three years, the people and the army are one. The necessity to defend our country produced a patriotism which caused an infusion of new blood into the army and so weeded out the old-style undesirables among the soldiers. At least part of the credit for the valuable co-operation and better relationship which have developed between army and people must be given to these young women workers who were their liaison.

The girls exert themselves with much zeal in the interests of the soldiers. They teach the people to welcome the troops and speed them on their way to the front; and, in time, they drive home to the people and the local authorities the realization that these men are not mercenaries but patriots who are prepared to sacrifice their lives in defending their country.

The appearance of these young girls in regions where ancient customs prevail naturally produced at times hidden, if not open, opposition from the inhabitants. The old people looked askance at them, but the young ones regarded them with wide-open eyes, and had a great desire to join them. It is a tribute to the tact of the girls that they have eventually won over all opposition, and are able to train the local girls to take over the work themselves.

The girls delve into every stratum of society for helpers

to win the war. As they muster all women who can work, so they reform the "singsong girls." In a surprising number of cases they have caused these unfortunates to give up their mode of life for a better one. Even those who do not reform are anxious to show their patriotism by detecting and reporting spies, and they do excellent work in helping to frustrate traitorous activities.

An interesting development is that our girls in time come to be regarded by the villagers as teachers, and in conformity with the time-honored traditions of China, they are respected by their aged "pupils," and acquire a surprising influence over the country people despite the great disparity in ages. How well the girls and their helpers did their work is shown by statistics. Within one year they worked in 15 hsien; rescued 300 orphans; cared for 41,640 people; trained 11,498 women, 15,938 recruits, 5,858 children, 12,814 wounded, and 17,570 refugees.

A few months ago these workers returned to Chungking for a month's refresher course, and they are now active once more behind the lines, this time on the Ichang front.

This is what they have done since their return to the field. They helped to carry 87,345 wounded soldiers from the wharf to the hospital; changed 53,285 dressings for the wounded in the hospitals; wrote 59,100 letters; trained 5,408 soldiers for promotion; held conferences and discussions 390 times; trained 2,041 women and 1,469 children.

(4) *Rural Service Department*

The work of the Rural Service Department is very similar to that of the War Area Service Department, except that instead of working directly behind the front lines the members work among the rural population in the rear.

The task of this department is to develop a true sense of patriotism among the people; to raise their cultural standard with the cooperation of the Cultural Department, and to improve their standard of living with the cooperation of the Production Department.

This department particularly emphasizes with good results one of the three principles of Dr. Sun Yat-sen, namely, the principle of the People's Livelihood. On a recent inspection trip taken with my sisters, Madame Sun Yat-sen remarked that good health and cleanliness were noticeable among the people in the different hsien covered by the work of the department.

As this department has only been functioning a few months, it is not possible to get the exact figures of the number of people who have come under its salutary influence. That noteworthy work has been done can be seen from the spontaneous letters of appreciation that have come from the local gentry and authorities in the districts concerned. They succeed largely because they are influenced by an earnest desire to serve the people. Their method of approach is through house-to-house visits; holding meetings; conducting classes for men, women and children, particularly the latter two; giving amateur theatricals on subjects calculated to stimulate patriotism; issuing war posters depicting the significance of what is happening to the whole country in this critical period.

The advisory council makes it a practice to get in touch with the magistrates of different hsien to impress upon them that our girls are there not to interfere with their administration but to help the people to become better citizens; that official co-operation and assistance are necessary for the attainment of our objective. Almost without exception the magistrates give their full co-operation, with the result that our workers have done much to help the development of a better understanding between the local authorities and the masses.

The people as a whole are friendly; they welcome the easy and kindly manners of their young visitors. Sometimes they embarrass the girls with hospitality which they can ill afford. A favorite country dish for guests of honor is poached eggs in wine sauce. Oftentimes the hostesses would insist on their visitors partaking of this refreshment while they themselves carefully abstained from doing likewise. An egg is an expensive luxury not to be lightly indulged in.

When the workers feel, after several months of instruction, that the local girls have been sufficiently trained, they depart to seek new fields to conquer. Usually, however, they leave two or three members of the team behind to help the local girls so that the work will not lag behind.

Usually the scene of parting is very touching. The girls tell me that invariably the villagers, with tears in their eyes, walk 10 to 20 li to bid them godspeed, and show genuine reluctance at losing their friends. Testimony of these feelings is given by the number of banners from the villagers which now adorn the walls of the Women's Advisory Council office.

Proof of the good effects of the work was shown on a recent tour of inspection. In one of the hsien we visited, some 20,000 people were gathered to hear my sisters and myself speak. Considering how much noise there is in every Chinese gathering, from a funeral to a wedding, the order and quietness were startling. The audience paid such close attention to what we were saying that one could have heard the drop of a pin. An air-raid alarm sounded during the meeting; but there was no panic. Our girls calmly told the people how they were to march to the hills and scatter themselves; and quietly they did so. It was amazing to see how a few youngsters could direct the dispersal of so huge a crowd with such efficiency and dispatch. A new thing in old China!

I have on my desk a report from one of these hsien. It shows that within six months this one team of girls, with

[323]

the help of the local women they had trained, had influenced the lives of over 300,000 people. One of the teams worked with the hardened inmates of a prison. The prisoners jeered at them and paid them no attention at first, but by sheer persistency and kindness the obdurate ones were finally won over. When I passed through that district the girls proudly showed me wall posters made by the prison inmates denouncing the ruthlessness of the Japanese militarists, and urging their fellow countrymen to help continue resistance against the enemy.

Various and abundant as their work is, the girls find time for more. After bombing raids they are in the forefront of the relief workers. In many ways they are more efficient than the police, simply because the people among whom they live have confidence in them.

Their spirit is magnificent. On one of my inspection tours I noticed that they did not return to their quarters for luncheon. They said that to go for lunch was too much of a waste of time. When asked what they ate at midday, they replied that they bought and ate raw turnips, or whatever the farmers had in the field.

I invited one of the teams to my temporary quarters for a two days' conference. As it was Mid-Autumn Festival, I gave each of them a package of sweets and cakes. When I noticed that they did not eat the confection, I inquired if they disliked them.

"Oh, no," they replied, "but we decided that, if you

do not mind, we will keep these and take them back to one of our women's classes, for they have been so friendly and we want to reciprocate their good will."

These girls get only $30.00 (Chinese currency) each month as an allowance. They do not receive salaries. Their uniforms are provided; all else is paid by themselves. Yet they manage to save $1.00 each to contribute to the poorest in the districts — those who are unable to buy salt to flavor their food. I once explained to the girls the limited amount of our funds; but I insisted that I wanted to keep them in good health. "If your allowance is not enough," I said, "I shall try to increase the amount, but it would mean that we would not be able to train more workers." "Which do you prefer," I asked, "the present allowance, so that we can train more workers, or an increase of your allowance?"

"Train more workers!" the girls shouted. "Never mind about us," they added, "we are young; we can stand hardships. The important thing is more workers to help mobilize the women throughout the country. Victory will then come sooner." A similar spirit pervaded every team I visited.

Recognizing the worth of our work, the Szechuan Provincial Government recently promised to bear the expenses necessary for maintaining a small staff to help the country people in each hsien. This is testimony indeed of the success of our young workers.

(5) *Livelihood Department*

The Livelihood Department was instrumental in helping to evacuate 30,000 women from Hankow, transport them to the rear, and assist in finding them new employment before the removed factories had been re-erected. Ever since then the Livelihood Department has taken a particular interest in factory workers.

Today, at the request of several factory owners, this department does the work of what, in foreign countries, would be considered the social department of large factories. At present, it has an experimental center for training workers to specialize in methods to improve the standards of living of women all over the country.

Another important line of its work is the maintenance of an information office where women may ascertain the whereabouts of their menfolk in the army, and also obtain information concerning positions open to them.

(6) *Cultural Department*

The Cultural Department provides all material needed by the War Area Service and the Rural Service Departments, the Provincial Work Corps, and all other women's organizations. It promotes mass education for women, and now continues classes in West China that were started in Hankow. It publishes newssheets, weeklies, monthlies — recording anything of interest relating to the work being done by the various organizations and departments.

It gets out primary readers for mass education, particularly those used by women, and it edits a weekly page for the *Central Daily News*. Incidentally, it was to inaugurate this page that the first article of my "Resurgam" was originally written; the others subsequently followed on successive Sundays.

(7) *War Relief Department*

At the time of the Kuling Conference the Women's War Relief Association and the Refugee Children's Association had already been formed. Since these two organizations were already functioning it was decided to allow them to remain nominally as they were and not to amalgamate them. To make them more efficient, however, they were correlated with those departments bearing the same name under the advisory council. The secretaries-general of the two above-mentioned associations were ex-officio heads of these two departments respectively. A great deal of overhead expense was thus saved and duplication of work avoided.

The War Relief Department has raised $50,000,000 in Chinese money, surgical equipment, and medical supplies since the beginning of the war. The Winter Garment Drive, begun last October, realized $10,000,000. Over 500,000 winter padded coats and jackets, and 500,000 pairs of shoes, were distributed among front-line troops within the last nine months. The department interests itself in helping the wounded soldiers, bombed civilians, and families of the recruits. It has trained, and is maintaining, several hundred girl workers who are now doing yeoman service in the hospitals for the wounded.

The department operates several factories and workshops turning out garments for the wounded soldiers. These workers are mostly members of the families of recruits. From time to time it sends out responsible women to the front to bring messages of encouragement as well as comfort kits to the troops and distributes medical supplies impartially to the different army corps. It co-operates closely with other organizations doing similar work. Whenever we find organizations such as "The Friends of the Wounded," the Orthopedic Hospital of the Army Medical Corps, or the national field units of the Chinese Red Cross, or various military hospitals in need of special funds to carry out necessary projects, the department, after careful investigation, donates substantial contributions. We insist, however, that every cent spent must be scrutinized with the utmost care, since the money was contributed to us by donors, which makes us trustees of this fund.

In this connection too much emphasis cannot be placed upon the commendable spirit of patriotism of our overseas compatriots whose generous and abiding loyalty to China's cause has increased the funds received by our department. Our overseas compatriots often write and tell

[328]

us that they feel that in contributing to our department they are, in a measure, doing their duty, while we in China are contributing our share by devoting our time and energy to alleviate the sufferings of the defenders of the country and the war orphans and refugees. What I have just said regarding the spirit of the overseas Chinese toward the Relief Department applies as well to the Refugee Children's Department.

After Japanese bombings, which now take place daily in Chungking, not only the members of the Relief Department, but also other members of the advisory council, go to the bombed areas to succor and comfort the victims.

(8) Refugee Children's Department

There are at present 16 branches under this department. It has under its care 25,000 war orphans gathered from various fronts, and maintains 49 homes and two receiving stations.

Not all of these children may technically be called orphans, as many of them had been voluntarily given up by their mothers who were unable to care for them when the enemy invaded their districts. If this department had not taken care of them they would have died of starvation.

Wherever possible the department has undertaken to transport other children to the rear and return them to their families. This task has not been an easy one, due to the indiscriminate bombing and machine-gunning of refugee boats, trains, and even pedestrians, by the inhumane invaders. Several batches of our children have thus been killed in cold blood.

During the first year the department attended only to collecting children and to preserving their health. Conditions were such that just to keep them healthy was all that could be done. During the second year, however, great strides were made in the care and education of the children. At the Superintendents' Conference recently held in Chungking, after careful consideration and discussion of the problems involved, a comprehensive program was drawn up regarding the upbringing of these children as useful citizens.

The beginning was beset with many difficulties, and there were many problems to be mastered. One, peculiar to China, was the babel of tongues — different provinces having different dialects, habits, customs, and styles of food. Fortunately for adults, there is one written language. Unfortunately for us and for the children, the latter, in the majority of cases, could neither read nor write. But they all proved to be adaptable, and possessors of imitative faculties which quickly enabled them to escape from the consequences of initial lack of understanding.

The bump of mischief was well developed in most of them; some were recalcitrant because of the strangeness of their new environment and the absence of the faces with which they were previously familiar; some were just

[330]

naturally "boys" full of devilment, and some of the girls
were naturally "angels," who smiled away all the ruffles
and helped the teachers develop an order that is now seldom marred by any unpleasantness. Patience and perseverance on the part of the teachers, and acute sensitiveness
and intelligence on the part of the children worked won-
ders.

Vocational training had an immediate appeal. Manual
activity provided an outlet for exuberant spirits, and served
as a substitute for the perhaps more exhilarating mischief
that idle hands will always find to do. Toys are fashioned;
wood is worked; weaving is done; shoes (sandals) are
made; animal husbandry is learned; crops are raised; gar-
dens are cultivated.

The children apply themselves to their lessons with intelligent zeal, and the well trained go out to the nearby
villages to impart their knowledge to their elders. That
seems to stimulate them, and through it they imbibe the
sense of communal service and co-operation which we
wish to see developed in them as part of their character
equipment as good citizens. Further expansion of that idea
comes to the children through the opportunities provided
for them to govern themselves. They already have a u-
nique understanding of their duties and their responsibilities toward their fellows, and react encouragingly to the
new education that is being given to them. Out of the
flotsam of the war is being fashioned new men and women

to help practically with the burdens of the new China.

Wherever possible the help of Christian missions, and other social organizations interested in the welfare of children, has been invoked. On the board of the department we have two American women and one Canadian woman whose assistance has been invaluable. The Salvation Army is now starting a home for 1,000 of the older boys to be trained in agricultural and industrial pursuits. In all the homes except those of kindergarten age, some form of manual handicraft is being taught.

Impartial inspectors are sent to the various homes so that we can be kept in close touch with every aspect of the lives and education of these children. Six teams of doctors and nurses make periodical rounds among the homes. The salaries of these medical officers have been donated by sympathetic friends in occupied areas.

(9) *Production Department*

The Production Department devotes itself mainly to the improvement of sericulture, the production of cloth, and the promotion of handmade embroidery. All these enterprises employ the co-operative system, and are known as the "New Life Co-operatives."

At present, there are eleven hsien in which work in sericulture is carried on. Szechuan was originally a silk producing center. Chengtu silk was famous in olden times, in the Imperial days of the Manchu regime. In recent years, due to diseased cocoons, the quality of silk deteriorated to such an extent that foreign exporters were no longer willing to take the risks of uneven weaves. The Production Department, therefore, decided to introduce modern methods of sericulture. Last year, in spite of the skepticism of the local people, the crops produced by the improved methods were 70 per cent better than those of the previous year. They would have been 100 per cent better had the directions given them been strictly carried out. This year, however, the farmers are paying more attention to the directions, and the crop should therefore be far superior to that of last year. The silk co-operatives under this department number over 12,000 families.

In cotton production this department maintains an experimental station at Sungchi, an out-of-the-way district hitherto little known to the outside world. Before it started, the economic level, low as it was in recent years, had taken an even more serious tumble, so that half of the stores were closed. Now, two years later, the place presents an entirely different atmosphere and appearance. The people are all cleanly and well dressed; the old stores reopened; new stores, carrying a line of goods bordering on luxuries, have opened, and their stocks alone show how the standard of living has gone up. We have in that district over 1,500 co-operative members engaged in producing cotton.

[333]

As elsewhere, wherever there is "New Life" work, education for the masses goes on apace. A three months' course of training in spinning and weaving is the order of the day. During the first month the pupils get their board and lodging free. During the second month they are able to bear half of the expenses. At the end of the third month they can support other members of their families. When they are graduated they return home, and six months later they generally have made enough money not only to support themselves and their families, but to pay for the wheel, or the looms, bought on the co-operative plan.

The Production Department has also trained several hundred women as staff workers in handmade embroidery. These women are now being sent out to various districts to train the local women to produce embroidered articles mostly from ramie (sometimes called grass linen, or China grass) which finds a ready market both at home and abroad.

In this connection it may be of interest to mention that Madame H. H. Kung has been particularly interested in the improvement of ramie fiber. For the past eighteen months she has subsidized a woman scientist, Dr. Feng, educated in America and Germany, who has perfected a new formula for the degumming and softening of ramie. This process not only renders the fiber as soft as silk and as warm as wool, but it also enables 95 per cent of its durability to be retained, as against 20 per cent in the case of the present native processes.

Madame Kung, who is a member of the standing committee of the advisory council, has offered this process to the New Life Movement. It should prove of immense value in supplying a popular need, and developing a new staple product, since Szechuan is not a cotton-producing province, and, as the war continues, it will become increasingly difficult to obtain cotton for the production of cloth.

The above are the main experimental centers of the Production Department, but wherever there are teams of our workers we have some form of production going on. In each district the type of work is decided by the raw materials produced. In one district where the clay makes good porcelain, we are specializing in the making of artistic dishes and bowls at low cost.

Szechuan is one of the most richly endowed provinces in all China; rich in agriculture, in raw materials, and in minerals. And yet, surprisingly enough, the amount of poverty and the large percentage of the population who are almost destitute is unbelievable. This is partly due to the incessant civil wars that marked the first 20 years of the Republic, and partly to the universal smoking of opium. Now that the Central Government has banned the cultivation of the poppy from which opium is extracted, and is introducing modern methods of developing natural resources, the day will not be far distant when Szechuan will again become the richest province in China, and its people one of the best nourished.

Besides the Provincial New Life Work Corps there are also many other work corps under the direction of the Women's Advisory Council. In every government organization there is such a corps. The wife of the head of each department is responsible for organizing the women under her, just as is done in the case of the Provincial Work Corps. The lines of work undertaken by each corps are similar to those pertaining to the different departments of the standing committee. The funds for carrying on the work come, however, from the members themselves.

At present, there are 37 government work corps. Each corps has numerous subcorps. As in the case of the War Ministry Corps, where over 25,000 women are participating, there are 50 odd subcorps located in all parts of the country and under its immediate direction.

Wives of Cabinet Ministers, and heads of other government organizations, are all made responsible for mobilizing the wives of the staffs serving under their husbands.

Women of leisure are thus finding new channels for exercising their faculties. As one of them told me the other day: "Those of my friends who first laughed at me when I protested that I had no time for frivolities, are now so busy working for the wounded, the war orphans, and the refugees, that they, too, have no time for the gossip and the scandal of the mah-jongg table." Truly enough, the clack of the mah-jongg tiles and the wagging of idle tongues have been drowned by the click of needles and thimbles!

In carrying out our program a number of our workers have been killed and wounded while on duty. The risks of a ruthless war come to us all. Some met death when Japanese bombs fell in their midst; others were drowned when their sampan overturned as the enemy bombers machine-gunned them from overhead. At the time of writing, our office in Chungking has been attacked repeatedly, bombs landing in the compound. So long as our buildings stand, we will remain in our present quarters, our staff being serene in the sense of security which comes from the steady performance of patriotic duties.

The fact that Chinese women are rising to unusual heights of self-sacrifice is, however, nothing new. Here is a story from the Warring Period in Chinese history (fifth to third century B. C.) which shows that the capacity to forget self in face of greater issues is inherent, and is as true today as it was in the past.

The Chi kingdom sent an army to attack the Lu kingdom. On the Lu border a general of the Chi forces, at a distance, observed a woman carrying one child and leading another. As the Chi army pressed closer, the woman put down the child she was carrying, picked up the one she was leading, and resumed her journey. The abandoned child began to cry, but the woman paid no attention to it.

The General approached the crying child and asked, "Who is that woman?"

"My mother."

Hurriedly the astonished General approached the woman and asked why she acted as she did.

"The child in my arms is my brother's. The one whom I have deserted is my own. The Chi army is advancing apace, and as I have not the strength to care for two, I was obliged to abandon my son."

"Which is dearer to you — your son, or your brother's son?" he inquired.

"Of course, my own son. But to save my own child is selfishness; to rescue my brother's is duty. Although my son suffers, it is but right."

The Chi General thereupon withdrew his army from the Lu border.

Returning to his lord, he reported: "Lu is unconquerable. Even a woman of the common people places duty before self. How much more should one expect of its scholars and officials? Hence I withdrew my army."

"How great is the strength of a sense of duty. Although only a woman, yet upon her depended the destiny of the country," the recorder of the Annals commented.

And today China is as unconquerable as was the Kingdom of Lu in the past.

XXIII

CHINESE THOUGHT ON DEMOCRATIC POLICY

My EXPOSURE of national weakness in the opening chapters of this book was frank and sincere. It was purposeful. It was designed to spur my countrymen to make a virtue of necessity, to take prompt advantage of the detergent effects of the destruction of life and property that had for so long been visited upon us, and to institute radical reforms, moral as well as physical.

There is nothing like a great conflagration to clear the way for large-scale city improvement, and there is perhaps nothing like a war such as we have been waging in self-defense to prepare the way for a far-reaching remolding of our national character in particular and our national life in general. So much that was good in China had already been swept involuntarily into the crucible of war that I felt our own volition might well be exercised to cause much that is evil and unnecessary to follow suit.

Before I had written those chapters the fires of war had already begun to burn into our soul — and blazon upon the sky for all who have eyes to see — some startling revelations and unexpected changes. The political disunity that had so disfigured the first two decades of our national endeavor to inaugurate a democratic system of government, in place of the old oligarchic misrule of the Manchus, disappeared in a flash before Japanese aggression. But more important than anything and everything else that is subject to metamorphosis under the impact of war, the physical and moral cowardice which was supposed to be born and bred in our bones and blood faded as if by magic. Instead of ancient China falling prostrate and groveling before the Japanese invaders, its ill-armed people, unsupported by other nations, stood on their feet in stalwart defiance, and were mowed down in their millions by the most ferocious and inhumane type of warfare that had ever been let loose upon human beings.

The Japanese invented, and applied, in defiance of all humane reasoning, instincts, or decency, the "total" warfare that is now known and accepted by "civilization" as a "blitzkrieg." But the Chinese people, contrary to all expectation and belief, have shown the world how to face and endure it. They have now been standing up, single-handed, to studied cruelties and a veritable unhalting hurricane of high explosives, delivered by all manner of modern devices, for three long years. Truly a miracle, if ever a miracle has, in contemporary times, been chronicled. And if one miracle is possible, why not another?

This thought has led me to make an attempt to stimulate my compatriots to reform by laying bare certain evils

[340]

which became inherent solely because they were of benefit to the old-time official class, and have been tolerated up to this period because no one cared publicly to condemn them. Some of my American friends have written to me expressing admiration for my "courageous attitude" in openly criticizing my fellow countrymen. Such compliments I do not deserve; rather they should go to those of our people who have accepted the criticisms in the spirit in which they were written, and who will realize, as the war proceeds, that times have really changed and will readjust themselves to the new conditions which are certain to come into being when the war is over. The influence of the young blood which will then have been purified by the process of war that calls forth all those powers of endurance, of philosophy, of adaptability, possessed by our people will surely make itself felt in one way or another throughout the length and breadth of the country.

What I do not like to see is that foreign readers should gain the impression that I hold our people solely responsible for all that is wrong with China, or imply that what is right with China is due solely to foreign influence. Far from it.

Occidental science, technique, and learning of all kinds, have conferred great benefits upon China. We have still much more to draw from the founts of foreign knowledge, and I have always urged my countrymen to lose no opportunity to drink of them, fully and satisfyingly. They probably would not agree, after these three tragic years of unrestrained desolation of their land, that much that is good or wise could be learned from the equivocal evolution, as they have witnessed it, of foreign policy. In fact, some rather strong views upon that subject are being entertained, and, since I have been free in pillorying the pet "peccadillos" of our people for foreign edification, they consider it as incumbent upon me to express their feelings and reactions with regard, at least, to the value of foreign promises and performances in the field of international politics, especially as they affect China.

Illuminating volumes could be written upon Sino-foreign impacts and intercourse in general, but not just now. Suffice it to say that Democratic statesmen have fallen far short of that lofty ideal of honorable recognition and fulfillment of obligations that has been set up before our people as the precept to which responsible nations should always strive to adhere.

All around us we have witnessed how the mighty have fallen from grace! Expediency in action, casuistry in argument, have replaced the splendid forthrightness of the great men of other times. Treaties, agreements, and understandings have gone with the wind of self-interest, and, so far as we of China are concerned, we have been virtually abandoned, and even victimized, by those in high authority whom we have been taught we could regard with unshaken confidence as our friends. To our people it is unutterably sad that for three weary, heart-breaking years of heroic resistance we have been left without help to combat a savage aggressor in a war which is not ours alone but which is that of all democracies.

Human nature being what it is, I feel prone to wonder how those American friends of mine who applauded my outspoken condemnation of the faults of my countrymen will view, say, an exposure of the critical attitude of the Chinese mind toward the manner in which the governments of the great democracies met their obligations toward China. I am moved to comply with the wishes of my compatriots to give expression to their views — and this for several reasons. One reason is that it might help to clear away any possible misapprehension or misunderstanding on their part in case the rehabilitation and the remodeling of our country should have to be undertaken with the assistance of western learning and experience. Another reason is that China is compelled to expose how she has been refused assistance in her battle of the democracies against aggression, and how, instead, she has been victimized by the material help that the democracies have given to Japan during the whole course of her first three years of aggression. However, whatever my friends may think, *Il n'y a que la vérité qui blessé* — only truth hurts.

It is painful to have to say that my countrymen, rightly or wrongly, have been forced, by their terrible experiences, to a conclusion derogatory to the democracies. The people of China are convinced that the responsibility for the outbreak of the appalling warfare now cleaving Europe and shocking the whole world is directly due to failure of the democracies to appraise correctly the character and intentions of Japan.

It is the opinion of the Chinese people, too, that the negative attitude of the democracies toward Japanese aggression in China constituted in itself a violation of treaties and international undertakings which was as reprehensible and as disastrous to international honor, good conduct, and respectability, as the positive abrogations and acts of violence of which Japan was guilty when she invaded Manchuria in September, 1931, and China proper in July, 1937.

Japan's easy conquest of Manchuria by unscrupulous means was but an example of how an aggressor could safely kick irksome principles into limbo and survive unscathed to enjoy not only the possession of the "conquered" territory, but also the continued political, economic and social good will and friendship of those democratic nations which were originally the most vociferous in their denunciation of the aggression. Japan had tested international reactions to undeclared warfare, to the wholesale abrogation of treaties, and she found them empty of danger — either immediate or remote.

What other encouragement did the militarists of Japan

[344]

require to set about tackling China? None. When her plans were perfected for further outrage she expanded the "Manchurian Incident" into the "North China Incident," and that, in turn, into the "China Incident." Soon it promises to assume the stature of an "Asia Incident." War has not been declared, but the democracies have virtually conceded to Japan all the rights of a belligerent, while they refuse to give any assistance of a military nature to China.

When Japan invaded Manchuria we refrained from resisting because the League of Nations undertook to adjust matters. They lost the region for us. There was a difference, however, when the Japanese repeated the invasion of China. We abandoned faith in international undertakings, and we fought. For three years now Japan has been gouging with ferocious intensity at the very vitals of our country. She set the example for the wholesale slaughter and destruction now running riot in Europe — an example that might never have materialized had the democracies only possessed the wisdom to see the truth of the old Chinese saying, "Punish one to warn a hundred," and fulfilled their obligations to China by restraining Japan. The penalization of Japan would have nipped aggression in the bud. The pity of it is that up to now there has been no actual punishment, nor has there been any rebuke for her impertinences, her trespasses upon the rights of the democracies, or her bellicose bluffing.

Without any appreciable aid from the democracies, which professed to be horrified at the unceasing atrocious inhumanities which were being perpetrated by Japan, the people of China have suffered untold hardships such as no other race on earth has ever been called upon to suffer or to endure. We have survived the ordeal; and, contrary to all preconceived ideas entertained by foreigners claiming expert knowledge of China, we have succeeded in inflicting punishment in full measure upon the Japanese, and in bogging down their colossal military machine in our vast hinterland.

For those three years, however, the Chinese people saw the professed defenders of international law and order failing to come to the aid of our outraged and victimized country in any practical, material way, or even to support our cause openly. We know the explanation, the excuse — that no one was ready to fight. Nor were we: but we fought. Think what would have been the situation in the world today had we refrained from defending ourselves, had we surrendered.

Those nations who were expected to employ every means in their power to defend right against might have made it abundantly clear to the Chinese people that they would not openly help to defend anything — in Asia. They could not be induced to resist injustice, or even to oppose the perpetration of inhumanities which were supposed to be impossible under these codes of modern civilization hitherto believed to be paramount in the protection of human life.

On the contrary they seemed to be striving to avoid difficulties, and evade obligations, by obeying the dictates of Japan. The American Government ordered airplanes, bought by China before the opening of hostilities, to be removed from an American steamer then at a port on the west coast of the United States; the Australian Government refused to permit even the parts of a private passenger airplane to be assembled in Sydney and flown to China. But both countries eagerly supplied war materials to Japan for the furtherance of aggression. The British and French Governments were meticulous in preserving "neutrality" in every possible way, as well as in avoiding actions of any kind calculated to give umbrage to Japan. The British Government refused to allow British military or air experts to aid China; the American Government threatened its technical instructors working with the Chinese Air Force with loss of citizenship. A similar fate was to befall any American who volunteered to fight in the air for China. Yet, quite a contrary policy was pursued with regard to the war in Spain.

All this our people had before their eyes while they saw their homes being blown to pieces by bombardments from air, land, and sea; and their fellow beings slaughtered, robbed, reduced to beggary, or made victims of opium and narcotics.

[347]

The shirking of responsibility by the democracies, their unwillingness to offend in any way the susceptibilities of marauding and murderous Japan, and their cautious inaction in the defense of even their own citizens, interests, and property, naturally increased Japan's appetite for conquest at all costs.

The continued willingness of the democracies to regard Japan as an equal, to shake the bloodstained hands of her ambassadors, to court her trade emissaries, and covet her money, while lodging futile and empty "face-saving" protests which did not save anyone's "face," presented an astonishing spectacle for the Chinese people; and encouraged the Japanese to laugh up their sleeves while they flouted the protests. It was no wonder to our people that Japan refused any longer to respect, or fear, the supposed sincerity, courage, or retaliatory power of the democracies.

At this writing France has capitulated to Japan's pressure, and the route of supplies through Indo-China was closed with the suddenness of a pinpricked balloon; Great Britain has vainly attempted to appease by the "temporary" closing of the Burma route. And America? America, after three years, has only now placed a controlling hand upon the sale to Japan of scrap iron and petroleum, but even that has been done with the cautious explanation that this measure has been adopted merely for the sake of self-defense, and was not necessarily aimed specially at Japan. This has led the Chinese people to think that

America could not in any wise explain away her attitude of the past three years, for it must be remembered that while impartial, justice-loving Americans did try to do all they could to point out the significance of China's struggle, and aid China in relief work, others in America amassed profits by selling to Japan the necessities of war which enabled her to continue her destruction of Chinese life and property. 80 per cent of Japan's war supplies came from America — and 95 per cent of the aviation gasoline which was used by Japan in her ruthless and indiscriminate bombing was American.

China has thus been compelled to fight a war, not of her own making, with a power credited with transcendent military skill and equipment, and one which has been aided and abetted unstintingly by the markets of democracies. These markets have been virtually closed to us, for no help has been given us to avail ourselves of them. China has been fighting not only in her own defense, but, as it has turned out, in defense of international decency, justice, and righteousness as well. She has been the champion of the principles for which other democracies are now at war, but mention of what China has been able to do for the cause is seldom if ever alluded to — an amazing situation.

In engaging in a long and costly war with Japan, instead of compromising as she might have done, China has served the democracies in a remarkable and unprecedented way. If contemporary judgment does not accord her credit for that, then history surely will. But this reflection is cold comfort. Everyday the toll of our mutilated men, women, and children; the destruction of the means of livelihood of our surviving population, and the ruin of our institutions of learning and culture, mount ever higher.

If China has done nothing else, she has at least crippled the might of Japan so that Japan cannot fulfill the program long ago revealed in the notorious Tanaka Memorial for securing the hegemony of Asia, and the domination of the whole Pacific, if not of the whole world. With an army, an air force, and a navy intact and with no shackling millstone round her neck such as a tenacious and resisting China, she would have been able with consummate ease to have destroyed British, French and American power in Asia. She may still be able to do so if she is given continuous help against us.

Our people feel that America, instead of giving assistance to Japan, should recognize the debt she owes to China. Our stalwart resistance, courage, and singleness of purpose, during the past three years have kept occupied in China about 3,000,000 men of the Japanese Army including those killed and wounded, thus giving America time to catch her breath and strengthen her defenses. China's resistance has been a serious handicap to Japan in numerous ways and should be acknowledged by all the democracies without stint or reserve.

That it is not acknowledged at all is causing our people to feel more and more that if China's rights and contributions continue to be ignored China will be forced to pursue but one policy in the future: to conduct herself so that the democratic governments may know that if China could get along without them in the terrible turmoil of war she could, with equal chances of triumph over difficulties, get along without them in the less parlous times of peace.

This would be a regrettable attitude for China to be constrained to adopt, since it has always been felt by thoughtful and intelligent Chinese that the destiny of their country lies indubitably with the democracies. I have personally expressed that conviction and sentiment time and again; in fact, upon every occasion when reassertion of principles seemed to be necessary.

It should be pointed out, however, that the trend of thought of our people toward a revision of their ideas of the value of democratic association is not the product of momentary fancy, nor has it been molded in any way by the startling and unexpected events in Europe.

Whatever change of thought may take place will be born of the realization of democratic unwillingness and inadequacy in defending proclaimed principles; plus the studied refusal to treat Japan as an aggressor; plus the apparently considered refusal to credit China with her unprecedented contribution to democratic stability and defense; plus the absence of free and fair acknowledgment of her help, of her great and grievous sacrifices, and of her sufferings in fighting aggression and thus upholding democratic principles.

It remains further to be said that the list of avoidable delinquencies of the democracies which I have briefly mentioned above cannot in any way be ascribed to that spurious wisdom which often comes after the maturity of an event. Space does not allow me to quote the many warnings I have uttered during the past three years with regard to the serious consequences of the indifference of the democracies to happenings in China. That these Cassandran prophecies have come true is no more gratifying to us in China than they must be to the democracies who have sown the wind and are now reaping the remorseless whirlwind.

Comparisons are invariably odious, but sometimes circumstances compel the making of them. This is one of the times. Intellectual honesty constrains me to point out that throughout the first three years of resistance Soviet Russia extended credits to China for the actual purchase of war materials and other necessities, several times larger in amount than the credits given by either Great Britain or America. Both these countries, indeed, circumscribed their advances with conditions which prevented even one cent of the money being used for badly needed munitions, equipment, or war material of any kind. Furthermore, at the meetings of the League of Nations, it was Russia who took an uncompromising stand in support of China's appeal that active measures should be adopted to brand Japan as the aggressor. Russia acted similarly during the Brussels Conference. On both occasions Britain, France, and other member nations compromised their consciences. When Japan protested through her Ambassador in Moscow that the aid extended to China by Russia was a breach of neutrality, Russia did not wilt, or surrender, or compromise, but continued to send supplies of arms to China.

It will doubtless be said that Russia has been aiding China for selfish interests. In reply to this I may point out that Russian help has been unconditional; that China has never asked any nation to fight for her; but has repeatedly pointed out to the democracies that by not doing justice to China they would endanger their own prestige and interests in the Far East. And, I may add, if democracy is to survive the policy of "One for one and all for none," statesmanlike foresight should see that it is replaced by that of mutual help and coexistence as exemplified in the policy of "One for all and all for one."

What has happened, however — and, more important, what has not happened — is another great lesson to the Chinese people; another bitter lesson that they will never forget; another painful lesson that will be taken to heart by every Chinese child of school age. They will remember never to believe in international promises or professions — no matter how well-intentioned they may appear to be; no matter how many imposing-looking seals may adorn the documents. The people of China had faith that the foundation of democratic nations was based upon just and humane principles. They believed that a great principle could not be divided — that one could not approbate and reprobate. But in this our people feel they have been betrayed.

To be sure, this new wisdom of theirs has been dearly paid for; it will have to be paid for over and over again in more loss of blood and life. But, then I suppose they will have to learn the lesson of life that where there are no pains, there can be no real gains.

As I write, there comes another slap in China's face. Hong Kong is stopping the shipment of tea. This move means, of course, that our foreign exchange will be considerably reduced. But one might well ask: of what use would foreign exchange be to us since our lifelines of communication have been cut? Truly a vicious circle.

One thing we have been taught is that China must aim, in her future national development, at attaining self-reliance. She will have to devise means so that for all time she will not need to depend upon others. I have been trying to emphasize this idea in the training of my students, so that they might have competency and be capable of facing life without fear. If the war should end tomorrow a firm foundation on this score can be erected, not necessarily by me, but by anyone who is not afraid of hard work.

Whatever these years have not done, they have made me, for one, realize to the full the value of self-reliance. Life at best is an ephemeral phenomenon. It permits of no stability; no constancy; no permanence. We have been taught that international relations in particular are of the flimsy texture of cobwebs; just as evanescent, but not nearly so systematically conceived. While some will not blame other nations because they think and act in terms of immediate and selfish interests rather than hollow ideologies, it is distressing to see the principles of democracy, and all that they stood for in the progress of civilization, gradually disappear like a mulberry leaf being absorbed by a silk worm.

What the future holds no one can tell, of course, since international entities seem to be imitating globules of quick silver on a shaking table in their seemingly uncontrolled collapses, their circumfusions, and their coalescences.

If, unhappily for the democracies as well as for China, we were defeated in the end, at least the world ought to know that we were beaten not because of lack of courage — either moral or physical — but because, by the concerted action of the democracies, China was strangled to death by an economic noose fashioned by Japan out of

British appeasement, American profiteering, and French fear.

With the innate qualities of recuperation and reviviscence which characterize our people, and which are daily become more evident, the spirit of China is unconquerable. Whatever happens, we will prove our valor and our honor. An old-fashioned word — honor; yet a word of sterling worth. It has suffered an eclipse, or a partial eclipse, in international relationship for some years, but we hope to see it emerge again shining like a lustrous beacon guiding to a safe haven those peoples who might unfortunately be tossing helplessly upon an ocean of trouble not of their own making.

To all the citizens of the democracies who have given their time, their substance, and their sympathy to succor and encourage the millions of stricken ones in our country, goes out the abiding gratitude of all the Chinese people.

Set in Linotype Estienne
Format by A. W. Rushmore
Composed and printed by The Golden Eagle Press
Published by HARPER & BROTHERS
New York and London

DATE DUE

MAR 2 '65		
AP 30 '66		
FEB 4 '68		
FEB 18 '68		
MAR 2 '68		
MAR 6 '73		
E H		